Infusing IB Philosophy and Pedagogy into Chinese Language Teaching

Dr Ian Hill

Dr Mark S K Shum

First Published 2015

by John Catt Educational Ltd,
12 Deben Mill Business Centre, Old Maltings Approach,
Melton, Woodbridge IP12 1BL
Tel: +44 (0) 1394 389850   Fax: +44 (0) 1394 386893
Email: enquiries@johncatt.com
Website: www.johncatt.com

ISBN: 978 1 909717 65 7

Set and designed by Theoria Design Limited
www.theoriadesign.com

CONTENTS

Part three: innovative pedagogy in IB Chinese teaching

About the Editors

Ian Hill

Dr Ian Hill joined the International Baccalaureate (IB) Organization in Geneva in 1993 as regional director for Africa, Europe and the Middle East, and became deputy director general from 2000 until his retirement in 2012. Prior to joining the IB he was head of a bilingual IB Diploma school in France and from 1986 to 1989 was senior private secretary/advisor to the Minister for Education in Tasmania and represented Australian government ministers of education on the IB Council of Foundation in Geneva.

In Australia he was teacher, deputy head and curriculum developer in the government school system, and university lecturer in education. He has published widely on international education and in 2005 co-authored with Jay Mathews, of the *Washington Post*, Supertest: how the International Baccalaureate can strengthen our schools. In 2010 his International Baccalaureate: pioneering in education (*International Schools Journal Compendium* vol 4) – a history of the IB – was published.

He has been Visiting Scholar at the University of Hong Kong in 2014 and again in 2015 in the Faculty of Education; the major focus of his work was how to infuse IB philosophy and pedagogy into Chinese language teaching.

Mark Shiu-kee Shum

Dr Mark Shiu-kee Shum was the Founding Head of Division of Chinese Language and Literature (2009-2015) and is an Associate Professor in the Faculty of Education at The University of Hong Kong. He is the Deputy Director of The Centre for Advancement of Chinese Language Education and Research. He developed the MEd (Teaching Chinese as a Second Language) Programme which received unconditional recognition from the IB that the graduates of the course can obtain an IB Certificate of Teaching and Learning.

His research interests are Chinese language education, systemic functional linguistics and its application to teaching, text analysis, teaching of Chinese writing, assessment of composition and teaching Chinese as a second language. His major publications include Functions of Language and the Teaching of Chinese; Teaching Writing in Chinese Speaking Areas; Infusing IB Philosophy and Pedagogy in Chinese Language Teaching; Subject-specific Genres of Liberal Studies and the Skills of Expression; Appliable Linguistics Across Chinese Speaking Areas: Language (in) Education in China, Hong Kong and Singapore, *etc.*

About the contributors

Chun Lai

Dr Chun Lai is an Associate Professor in the Faculty of Education, University of Hong Kong. Her research interests include technology-enhanced language teaching and learning, second language pedagogy, and teacher development for international education.

She has published widely on topics including self-directed use of technology for language learning outside the classroom, task-based language teaching, and teacher development in cross-cultural teaching contexts.

Cho-yam Lam

Cho Yam Lam is currently pursuing her PhD in the University of Hong Kong. She began her international school teaching career after she obtained her PGCE in LOTE in Australia. Her experience in IBDP started when her school was a candidate school for authorisation in 1999.

Since then she has worked in three IB schools as head of Chinese, and taught IBDP Language A2, Language B and TOK. She was attracted to the IB philosophy and its educational aims, especially in terms of creating critical thinkers that embrace a worldview and care for others. With this in mind, she started to embark on her study about the integration of TOK in the second language IBDP classroom in Hong Kong.

Tung-fei Lam

Tung-Fei Lam was a lecturer in the Faculty of Education at the University of Hong Kong and has taken up a co-principal position in the Yew Chung International School (Hong Kong) since August 2015. He graduated from the University of Hong Kong with a BA degree in Chinese Language and Literature, and received Master's degrees from the University of Melbourne and the City University of Hong Kong.

He also holds an EdD degree in the field of teaching material in Chinese as second language from the University of Hong Kong, and continues to work on research areas of teaching material development, curriculum design, teaching and assessing Chinese in international contexts. He taught the IGCSE, IB MYP and IB DP programmes, and has led school-based curriculum development at different international schools in China and Hong Kong over the past ten years.

Kwok-ling Lau

Kwok Ling Lau is currently a lecturer in TCSL and a PhD candidate in the Faculty of Education at the University of Hong Kong. She received her Masters of Education (Educational Studies) at the University of Sheffield and a Bachelor of Education from National Taiwan Normal University in 2001 and 1996 respectively. She was also a teacher of Chinese at King George V School in Hong Kong.

She is a member of the Modern Language Association and a member of the American Council on the Teaching of Foreign Languages. Her PhD research examines the enabling factors in the promotion of International Mindedness in the International Baccalaureate Diploma Programme (IBDP), Chinese B course.

Elizabeth Ka-yee Loh

Elizabeth Ka-Yee Loh is an Assistant Professor at the Faculty of Education, University of Hong Kong. She is the principal investigator of a number of projects, including 'mChinese – The Application of Apps to Assist Non-Chinese Speaking Students to Learn Chinese Characters (2015-2017)' (HK$0.54M, Quality Education Fund, Hong Kong SAR Government) and 'Tradition and Innovation: Supporting the Learning and Teaching of Chinese Language for Non-Chinese Speaking Students in Secondary Schools (2013-2015)' (HK$8.2M, Education Development Fund, University-School Support Programmes, Hong Kong SAR Government).

She is part of the research team awarded the Richard M Wolf Memorial Award (The International Association for the Evaluation of Educational Achievement, 2007), the Faculty of Education Research Output Prize 2007-08 and the Faculty of Education Knowledge Exchange Award 2014 (the University of Hong Kong). The major focus of her current research is teaching and learning Chinese as a second language, and she has published more than 42 refereed journal articles and book chapters as well as three academic books.

Martin Ting-fung Mak

Martin T F Mak is the head of foreign language Chinese in an IB international school in Hong Kong. He is an experienced teacher of Chinese, and he has taught Chinese to both non-native and native speakers. He is also an IB examiner for Theory of Knowledge. Interested in second language acquisition theories, he finished his Master of Philosophy in Research in Second Language Education at the University of Cambridge in the United Kingdom.

His dissertation focuses on materials development and materials adaptation for students learning Chinese as a foreign language. After his MPhil he has not stopped improving his teaching and he proactively shares his teaching experience with his peers and novice teachers.

Malcolm Pritchard

Dr Malcolm Pritchard is the Head of School at the Independent Schools Foundation Academy, a K-12 Chinese-English, bilingual immersion IB World School in Hong Kong. Previously he led Kormilda College, a culturally diverse IB school in Northern Australia; he also founded Caulfield Grammar School's experiential immersion program in Nanjing, China.

At Melbourne Grammar School, Dr Pritchard taught Chinese and served as the head of languages. He holds a Bachelor of Arts in Asian history. His Master's dissertation examined information technology related Chinese text processing issues.

The theoretical underpinnings of experiential learning formed the focus of Dr Pritchard's doctoral research at the University of Melbourne. He currently serves on the IB Asia Pacific Regional Council, he is the chairman of the Association of Chinese and Mongolian International Baccalaureate Schools, and is a member of the board of governors for the Ming De Experimental School in Shenzhen, China.

Dan Shi

Dan Shi is currently a post-doctoral Fellow in the Faculty of Education at The University of Hong Kong. She is working with functional linguistics, multimodality, discourse analysis, and sociological theory of education in her research. Her research interest also includes learning style and scaffolding within L2 contexts, and exploring learners' engagements with texts.

Loretta Chung-wing Tam

Loretta Chung-Wing Tam is a post-doctoral Fellow at the Centre for Advancement of Chinese Language Education and Research (CACLER), Faculty of Education, University of Hong Kong. She completed her Chinese as a Second Language teacher training at the International Chinese Language Program, National Taiwan University, and subsequently earned an M.App.Ling. in language program management from Macquarie University and a PhD in anthropology from the Chinese University of Hong Kong.

Her research interests include language maintenance and revitalisation, ethnicity and nationalism, curriculum development and evaluation, as well as intercultural pedagogy.

Ben-nan Zhang

Dr Ben-nan Zhang is an Associate Professor in the Faculty of Education, University of Hong Kong. He is the course coordinator of MEd (Teaching Chinese as a Second Language) Programme which received unconditional recognition from the IB that the graduates of the course can obtain an IB Certificate of Teaching and Learning. He is also the Honorary Director of the Hong Kong Putonghua Education and Assessment Centre in the Faculty. His experience covers a wide range of teaching Chinese as a second language, Chinese literature, and Chinese teacher education.

His research interests are as wide as his teaching areas, but mainly focus on applied linguistics, covering areas of bilingual studies, Chinese linguistics, Chinese language teaching and learning, social linguistics, and psychology of learning. His research has emphasised two domains in the past few years: Chinese language and culture, and the psychology of language learning.

Chapter 1

Introduction

Ian Hill and Mark Shiu-kee Shum

Preamble

We believe this book makes an important contribution to language teaching in general, to IB language teaching, and more precisely to the teaching of Chinese both in IB and non-IB classrooms. The IB constantly sifts through the latest thinking in pedagogy for all its programmes. For that reason readers who are up to date with the cutting edge of language teaching method, particularly for Chinese, will find reassurance and confirmation of their approach in this book whether they are IB teachers or not. Those who feel they are not aware of the most up-to-date thinking in language teaching, again particularly for Chinese, will find ample advice in the chapters that follow.

This publication is also a significant milestone in the advancement of IB philosophy and pedagogy because it brings an Asian/Chinese perspective to that discourse. The aim of IB programmes is to develop international mindedness (IM) in students. The IB has been aware for many years that the roots of its programmes have been in the Western tradition, and that its flagship philosophical document, the IB Learner Profile (IBLP), has had some criticism, not unjustified, that it represents values and characteristics that relate more to the West than to other cultures.

We know for example that critical thinking skills, one of the fundamental IB pedagogical planks and an important methodological component of IM, is not necessarily well received in some regions of the world. However the concepts of IM were already in the minds of Confucius, Mencius, Lao-Tzu and others many centuries before the term itself appeared in the West in 1951 with the creation of the Conference of Internationally Minded Schools (Hill 2010 p20-22). This was an association under the auspices of UNESCO which brought together heads of schools interested in discussing international education.

The dawning of the IB

The IB was created during the 1960s as a programme for the growing number of international schools dotted around the world catering for the children of internationally-mobile families working for the UN, embassies, and multinational companies. The initiative came from the staff of the International School of Geneva (founded in 1924) as a result of visits to a number of international schools in Asia, Africa and Europe carried out by Bob Leach, head of history, during the 1961-62 northern hemisphere school year. Leach's travel was funded by the International Schools Association (ISA), founded in 1951, which was closely linked to his school in Geneva. Leach found that:

the national programmes they used were unsuited to the international experience of their students, since they normally provided a national perspective only;

recognition of national programmes was problematic when they returned to their home country or moved on to other countries;

these schools felt somewhat isolated and urged the ISA to provide more assistance with administration advice and curriculum development;

the schools were unanimous about the need for a common school leaving qualification with international acceptability.

The head of Leach's school, Desmond Cole-Baker, urged his staff to forget about their current national programmes, to take a clean sheet of paper, and to imagine which knowledge, skills and attitudes young people would need to be citizens of the world. Thus, the IB 'project' began with a first draft of a contemporary history course by the end of 1962, and other subjects quickly followed.

Schools in other countries also joined the initiative, among them Atlantic College in Wales and the United Nations International School in New York. Curriculum development meetings took place and a structure was created which was eventually registered in Geneva in 1968 as the International Baccalaureate Office (later changed to Organisation). A number of influential educators from different nations were attracted to the project which they saw as an ideal vehicle for education reform in their own countries.

The IB was created for practical, visionary, and pedagogical reasons. Practically there was a need for an educational passport to university entrance world-wide; students needed an international perspective, not just the view of their home or host nation; and pedagogically the education reformers wanted to diminish rote learning and memorisation and replace it with critical thinking skills and a holistic education that looked at affective as well as cognitive development.

Although the IB started as the Diploma Programme for international schools, it was not long before national systems of education, both private and public (state), started offering it. The USA remains today the country with the largest number where more than 90% of the schools are state funded without tuition fees.

Let us now move to the present and see to what extent the current description of an IB education has remained faithful to those early pioneering ideas.

IB philosophy and pedagogy

The visionary (philosophical) and pedagogical underpinnings of the IB have not changed since the 1960s, but have been developed further by practitioners and scholars over time. IB provides international education programmes; these are programmes which seek to develop international-mindedness (IM) – the key term which we associate with the IB vision since ten years or so. IM includes intercultural understanding, learning languages, consideration of global issues, knowledge about the interdependence of nations, solidarity, human rights, sustainable development, respect for others, compassion for those less fortunate, and appreciating multiple perspectives. Other terms are used, such as preparing students for global citizenship; for IB, this presupposes a strong association with one's own culture in order to have a reference point for understanding and showing empathy towards others.

Intercultural understanding is a key element of IM. It is enhanced by a thorough knowledge of one's own culture. The ingredients of intercultural understanding have been nicely captured in the following statement by a former director general of the IB:

> ... we require all students to relate first to their own national identity – their own language, literature, history and cultural heritage, no matter where in the world this may be. Beyond that we ask that they identify with the corresponding traditions of others. It is not expected that they adopt alien points of view, merely that they are exposed to them and encouraged to respond intelligently. The end result, we hope, is a more compassionate population, a welcome manifestation of national diversity within an international framework of tolerant respect. Ideally, at the end of the IB experience, students should know themselves better than when they started while acknowledging that others can be right in being different.
>
> IB 1988 Report of the Director General,
> Roger Peel, to the Council of Foundation

Today, the IB has distanced itself from the notion of 'tolerance' because it is considered to portray, even unconsciously, a certain cultural superiority which could be construed as: 'my culture is the right one, but I'm prepared to tolerate yours'. Otherwise Peel's statement above is totally in tune with the current IB vision.

The IB has been a recognised non-government organisation (NGO) of UNESCO since 1970. It is not surprising, therefore, that the IB's educational philosophy is aligned with that of UNESCO which defines international education as an education for peace, human rights and democracy (UNESCO 1974). This was reaffirmed by declaration at the International Conference on Education (ICE), Geneva, 1994. The aims of international education identified by this declaration (UNESCO 1996 p9), were to develop:

a sense of universal values for a culture of peace;

the ability to value freedom and the civic responsibility that goes with it;

intercultural understanding which encourages the convergence of ideas and solutions to strengthen peace;

skills of non-violent conflict resolution;

skills for making informed choices;

respect for cultural heritage and protection of the environment;

feelings of solidarity and equity at the national and international levels.

The over-arching idea of IM incorporates all of the above.

The following key concepts underlie IB teaching methodology: critical thinking, child-centred pedagogy, constructivism, life-long learning, interdisciplinarity, and holistic education. Critical reflection and inquiry is the key that unlocks other aspects of the pedagogical approach and it was expressed very well by Bob Leach when he described the methods to be used to deliver the new IB contemporary history syllabus.

Leach told his students not to expect reassurance for holding conventional or closed opinions; he said they should be prepared to challenge accepted views, to dissect and weigh the issues 'in whatever universal scales the teacher may find immediately useful'. Students needed to be prepared to retreat from entrenched positions and to appreciate and analyse multiple perspectives (Leach 1969: 208-9).

This pedagogy was applied to all IB diploma subjects and later to the MYP and PYP. Today approaches to learning and teaching, together with differentiated learning, are essential components of all IB programmes. This is the means by which education is focused on the child, on the needs of the individual.

Constructing their own meaning from what is already familiar enables students to 'own' their learning, and therefore to be more likely to remember and use what was accomplished. Constructivism has links with creativity which in turn has links with interdisciplinarity. By looking for the connections between subject disciplines, students open their minds to constructing solutions to problems that may come from seemingly unassociated subject areas, either individually or combined.

Holistic education refers here to aspects such as students undertaking community service – giving time to the less privileged in order to grow as individuals and take on responsible citizenship at the local, national and international levels. It also includes helping students affectively as they grow to make sense of the world and their own place in it. Life-long learning is a skill and an attitude which can be developed. Students must realise that education does not stop at grade 12, or after university or other qualifications – it is a never-ending process of critical inquiry, inspired by an insatiable curiosity to know more.

However, IB programmes are not simply the antithesis of traditional teaching methods of memorization, didactic teaching, and translation (for language learning). There is a balance between depth and breadth of learning, didactic and constructivist approaches, interdisciplinarity and the integrity of the subject disciplines, and the cognitive and affective domains of learning. It is the judicious juggling act which contributes to a good international education: knowing when a student needs more of one than another, but never excluding any of the approaches. It's all about getting the right balance.

The IB Learner Profile is cited in a number of chapters and it represents the characteristics of IM as perceived by the IB. It is a combination of educational philosophy and educational practice. IM becomes particularly prominent in chapter 2 which appropriately challenges its Western bias, and in chapter 5. The latter chapter provides an interesting description of IM and furnishes another layer of analysis by attributing its components to one or more of knowledge, skills and attitudes – the fundamentals of any curriculum.

Aspects of IM recur throughout the book as the authors seek to show how this IB concept can be infused into second language Chinese education.

Structure and content of this book

The initiative for the book comes from Mark Shiu-kee Shum, Head, Division of Chinese Language & Literature in the Faculty of Education, University of Hong Kong (HKU) and Ian Hill, the former deputy director general, International Baccalaureate Organisation (IBO).

Established in 1911, HKU is a world-class institution of higher learning with a strong research bent. Geographically situated in a top-ranked world city that is often also regarded as a gateway to China, the Faculty of Education at HKU has sought to position itself as a premier hub of Teaching Chinese as a Second Language (TCSL) in the Asia-Pacific region. In tandem with both the rise of international education and the increasing popularity of Chinese language learning around the world, researchers at HKU have carved out research areas that address the design and evolution of pedagogical approaches and methods suitable for today's hyper-connected, globalised society.

These research areas include cross-cultural or intercultural methods of language pedagogy, as well as the global trends and development of Chinese teaching and learning. Much of this work stems from a belief that educational and pedagogical research should anticipate and prepare for the needs of tomorrow's world, while addressing and improving upon the issues of today's world.

In this respect, HKU maintains a close relationship of collegial collaboration with the IB. As the only IB-accredited professional development programme for Teaching Chinese as a Second Language (TCSL) worldwide, the Master of Education (MEd) programme in TCSL at HKU integrates IB theories and practice with its curriculum, catering for the unique needs of pre-service or in-service teachers of TCSL in IB World Schools. Most of the contributions to this book come from HKU staff members and from experienced education practitioners who serve in IB schools which have forged strong partnerships with HKU.

The book is divided into three sections. The first, 'IB philosophy teaching and learning' discusses the IBLP from a Chinese perspective, provides feedback from MEd student teachers of Chinese (all native speakers) enrolled at the University of Hong Kong, and concludes with a chapter on the immersion method of experiential learning of Chinese by the Australian Head of a well-known independent IB school in Hong Kong, Malcolm Pritchard.

In chapter 2, by Mark Shiu-kee Shum, Ben-nan Zhang and Chun Lai, the reader is given a fascinating glimpse of the IBLP seen from the inner recesses of Chinese minds, and how Chinese teachers would implement the IBLP in their classrooms. This is a rare analysis of the IBLP from a non-Western perspective by non-Western educators; it points up important lessons in intercultural understanding for us all.

Take for example the notion of 'caring'. In the Confucian tradition it relates first to filial piety, obligation, respect and love between family members which includes the young respecting their elders and vice versa. This extends to all others outside the family, treating them with kindness, empathy and compassion. When this occurs 'the kingdom may be made to go round on your palm' says Mencius. What a beautiful image: being able to cradle family, friends, the nation together in a harmonious whole within the palm of one's hand – a part of the body that conjures up warmth, protection or compassion when the palm of a hand is placed on the shoulder or head of a child or adult.

Chapter 3 is a response to the research question: how did MEd students grow professionally out of the university-school partnership in Hong Kong? Mark Shiu-kee Shum *et al* treat the reader to case study vignettes of three pre-service MEd students on teaching practice in IB schools. They undertake a school attachment phase to observe good teaching practice and then plan and take lessons under the guidance of an experienced mentor teacher.

The excellent relationship between the university and the IB schools contributes in no small way to the overall success of the teaching practicum, an essential aspect of the MEd course. Teaching is an intense, quite personal activity because it relies on the establishment of a positive classroom climate that depends very much on how the teacher interacts with the students.

Moreover, in international schools the teacher is working in a cross-cultural environment which increases the need to be sensitive to different cultural behaviours. It is not surprising, then, that student teachers need, not only pedagogical advice, but also emotional and social support. The importance of school context, mentor attitude and behaviour, and student teacher initiative is portrayed through the varied experiences of the three MEd students described individually as 'an active participant, a discouraged mentee, and a proactive learner.'

Malcolm Pritchard's chapter provides a very helpful overview of current pedagogy for language learning and situates this in a theoretical framework for experiential learning. Memorisation of vocabulary, syntax and written characters is an important first step of scaffolding before the learner can proceed to a constructivist approach by creating utterances which lead to increasing fluency. Autonoetic memory of authentic learning 'adventures' evokes not only the cognitive linguistic aspects but the emotions associated with them.

Emotional energy is a strong motivator for recall. Pritchard can speak authoritatively on this subject since he is a scholar of the Chinese language and received many groups of Australian students for residential experiential learning at a school campus in China.

The second section covers the implementation of IB philosophy in the classroom and includes the development of support materials. Kwok-ling Lau's chapter opens this section with a case study of how IM is integrated into a Chinese language classroom. She proposes a 'definition' of IM in terms of knowledge, skills and attitudes (or values), and uses this framework to identify IM practices in the classroom.

Her chapter then selects a number of IM components for analysis of classroom practice and makes the point that some IM components can pertain to more than one of the categories used to classify them: knowledge, skills or attitudes. For example, intercultural understanding requires *knowledge* about other cultures, the *skill* of critical thinking to find similarities and differences, and also an *attitude* which is open to the acceptance of other cultures. The teacher comments are instructive and illuminate cultural perspectives.

Cho-yam Lam's chapter outlines the main pedagogical objectives of the Theory of Knowledge (TOK) course, focusing on the development of interdisciplinary and critical thinking skills. Her paper goes on to discuss how teachers integrate TOK into their Chinese B lessons, and identifies factors which may facilitate or impair the application of critical thinking by students in those classes.

The author notes that students need to be able to discern useful and reliable information, particularly on the internet, as opposed to information which is bereft of authoritative confirmation. Today, knowledge acquisition is not the main aim of education as it once was; knowledge is easily obtainable from the internet – it can be literally plucked from the air. Today students need the skills to filter the massive over-supply of information, to make the connections between the various disciplines of knowledge, and to develop a discerning eye which will protect them when confronted with the powerful rhetoric of politics and publicity world-wide. The author makes a plea for giving attention to the skill of critical reading as well as critical thinking. This chapter is a good critical appraisal of the new TOK guide and how it translates into practice; it points up ways to assist the enactment of TOK in the classroom.

In chapter 7, Tung-Fei Lam looks closely at the theory and practice of developing materials to support IM in the Chinese classroom. With reference to major scholars of language acquisition, this study shows how support material adaptation takes place differently depending on how teachers view the purpose of language teaching. The reader is introduced to learning language and learning *through* language and how this can lead to concepts of basic and deep understanding. The former is interpreted as learning about the host country culture only, while the latter refers to a wider appreciation of cultural differences across several countries.

Teacher decisions concerning support material are directly influenced by which of these orientations they adopt. Language learning can be a powerful tool to unlocking the treasures of intercultural understanding, but, as the author reminds us appropriately, mastery of another language does not of itself guarantee an appreciation of other cultures. It requires the will to adopt a positive disposition towards others so that the language learner is openly curious and empathetic, rather than xenophobic towards behaviour and language which may be quite different from his/her own.

The third and final section introduces the reader to some innovative approaches to teaching Chinese. Chun Lai's chapter on the use of IT to facilitate Chinese language learning is packed with practical advice on effective web-based resources to support IB pedagogy in teaching Chinese. She discusses how IT can assist the development of IM: rich cross-cultural experiences grow out of global networking. The internet contains visual and audio stimuli to assist intercultural understanding when linguistic skills lag behind, preventing students from expressing what they would like to say.

The author also wisely cautions that immersion in web-based intercultural communities is not itself a sufficient condition for intercultural understanding to occur and outlines a three-stage model to assist students. IT also helps to address the lack of sufficient instructional time by providing independent rote learning and drills, leaving more class time for (IB) progressive pedagogies such as inquiry based learning, collaborative learning, a student-centred approach, interdisciplinarity, constructivism, and web-based exposure to intercultural understanding.

Chinese is a language where the mastery level can be less, for an equivalent effort, in comparison with languages using, for example, a Roman script or Arabic alphabet. So teaching methods which can render the task more enjoyable and efficient are always welcome. In chapter 9, Elizabeth Ka-Yee Loh *et al* address an effective method for teaching and learning Chinese characters. The method proposed improves recognition and retention. It is thus more motivating for Chinese language learners. It involves the Integrative Perceptual Approach for teaching Chinese characters based on Variation Theory. Importantly, when successfully accomplished, this approach increases students' literacy level and elevates their orthographic sensitivity to enable them to see patterns and connections thus facilitating the recognition and construction of written Chinese.

Students are able to progress and attain higher performance levels more rapidly. The chapter includes a blow-by-blow account of a sample teaching plan supported with photos which teachers can transpose easily to their own classrooms. The sample design is also an incentive for teachers to create their own, based on this approach.

The final chapter provides practising teachers with an effective method for teaching good reading and writing of Chinese to non-Chinese speakers. Anchored in a theoretical framework of the Halliday school of linguistics, this case study uses poverty issues in China (related very much to IB global issues such as social injustice and hardship) as the content to be treated by teachers and students in the classroom. The authors use genre based literacy pedagogy, in this case explanation genre, and develop the 'reading to learn, learning to write' method as a genre-based tool.

The Halliday school sees linguistics as supporting the social function of language, enabling people to communicate appropriately in societal contexts. The authors use classroom discourse analysis and systemic functional linguistics to analyse student utterances and writing. Through rigorous, detailed pre and post testing and the identification of three learner levels – high, medium, and low achievers – the research shows significant improvement in students' ability to use Chinese.

Concluding comments

The geographical location of the research in this book is mainly Hong Kong and the subject focus is the teaching of Chinese. The first IB schools and programmes to be authorized in Hong Kong and China are:

Hong Kong – first IB schools
1988 French International School – DP
2004 Chinese International School – MYP
2004 Kingston International School – PYP
There were 54 IB schools in Hong Kong in April 2015.

Mainland China – first IB schools
1991 International School of Beijing – DP
1995 Beijing No 55 High School - MYP
2000 Nanjing International School – PYP
There were 89 IB schools in April 2015.

Taken collectively, the chapters of this book all participate in, and generate discussion about, one of the most relevant issues concerning the development of the IB and international education: how educators can navigate the challenges that arise in the face of teaching culturally-rich non-Western heritage languages, like Chinese, in the context of the internationally-minded (or as some argue, Western-biased) IB classroom without erasing or disavowing the values and roots of any of the linguistic source cultures.

In conversation with one another, the chapters raise and offer different perspectives on some key issues relating to the theorisation, design and implementation of Chinese education in the IB classroom. These are issues that cannot be ignored or conveniently glossed over, but which need to be addressed directly with sensitivity and openness, in order for the IB to stay relevant at the forefront of international education in today's globalised world. The following are three of these key issues or questions that we wish to ask our readers to consider:

East Meets West: How should IB Chinese teachers teach the subject matter of Chinese Language, inseparable from, and inextricably influenced by, the values and viewpoints of the richly textured culture(s) from which it originates, while at the same time ensuring that their teaching is informed and guided by the values of IB philosophy? How do educators engage in negotiation between Chinese and Western culture, making room for and carrying the best of both worlds into IB education, while fully respecting the integrity and wholeness of both?

Intangible Values vs Tangible Results: How does the teacher strike a balance between pushing students to strive for tangible academic success in terms of examination and assessment performance, and guiding students in appreciating and understanding the intangible values and attitudes that weave the fabric of intercultural human understanding?

Infusing the Theory of Knowledge into Language Education: How might educators foreground the Theory of Knowledge (TOK), hitherto often treated as a stand-alone subject, by integrating it with the teaching of Chinese or other languages, and by incorporating TOK's ways of thinking and seeing into Chinese language teaching, or the teaching of other subjects?

This book is an important addition to elucidating and developing the concept of IM from an Asian perspective and through the teaching of an Asian language. As such it represents a landmark in the discourse on the appropriateness of IB philosophy and pedagogy to cultures other than Western. The internet, ease of travel, mixed marriages, and business partnerships across cultures have reduced the differences, but East and West still find their roots in ancient, almost opposing, traditions.

Chinese philosophers such as Confucius had an important effect on many Asian countries; he stressed the importance of responsibility towards working in harmony with each other, spirituality, ecology and respect for nature, cooperation, and adhering to group norms. On the other hand the West inherited contrary traits from the ancient Greeks which we might describe today as: debate and competition, materialism, lack of respect for nature, and critical thinking. The reader will realise that these characteristics are in the absolute; in reality, they are tempered and not as pronounced for some individuals. However, the fact that Eastern cultures were originally energised by collective agency and Western cultures by individual agency still explains much of the behaviour in those parts of the world today.

We hope readers enjoy the book and that you will not hesitate to make us aware of any comments you may have.

References

Hill, I (2010) *The International Schools Journal Compendium vol 4: International Baccalaureate: pioneering in education.* Peridot Press (UK).

IB (International Baccalaureate) 1988 Report of the Director General to the Council of Foundation. IB archives, Geneva.

Leach, R 1969 *International schools and their role in the field of international education.* Pergamon Press, New York.

UNESCO 1974 *Recommendation on education for international understanding.* UNESCO General Conference, Paris.

UNESCO 1996 Declaration and integrated framework of action on education for peace, human rights and democracy. International Conference of Education, Geneva.

Part one:

IB philosophy, teaching and learning

Chapter 2

When IB Learner Profile meets Eastern Confucian tradition: From the perspective of Chinese Language teachers

Mark Shiu-kee Shum, Ben-nan Zhang & Chun Lai

Abstract

The International Baccalaureate (IB) curriculum has a philosophical core of international mindedness and has an IB Learner Profile (IBLP) as its focal curriculum ideology (Hill, 2007). The IBLP is expected to guide school operations and classroom practices (Cambridge, 2010; IBO, 2008) and become a seamless part of the curriculum (Gigliotti-Labay, 2010). However, recently more and more scholars are pointing out that the philosophical basis of the IBLP is that of a Western liberal humanistic tradition of values (Wells, 2010; Walker, 2010). These scholars are questioning the extent to which the values espoused in the IBLP represent the attributes in different cultures throughout the world.

The Western philosophical bias of the IBLP may be challenged in terms of its receptivity and local relevance when IB programmes are implemented in cultures that have a strong Eastern Confucian tradition. How would teachers in cultures with a strong Eastern Confucian tradition respond to an IBLP? This chapter examines Chinese language teachers' reactions to the IBLP in Chinese language teaching.

In particular, it focuses on the interplay between Chinese traditional values and IB philosophical principles in Chinese language classrooms, and the teaching strategies that are frequently used by Chinese teachers to deal with the cultural differentiation and integration between the IBLP and traditional Chinese educational values. This study intends to illuminate how Chinese language teachers utilize the *intercultural understanding* of IB and fuse western and eastern values in their daily practices to enrich and localize the IBLP.

Key words: IBLP, international mindedness, Western humanity, traditional Chinese culture, IB Chinese teacher, teaching strategy, culture integration.

Introduction

The International Baccalaureate (IB) is a system of international education which states in its mission the goal of developing 'inquiring, knowledgeable and caring' (IBO, 2013) students who would 'create a better and more peaceful world through intercultural understanding and respect' (IBO 2013). Intercultural understanding is a core value for the IB, and is a process of developing, identifying and reflecting on one's unique perspective, as well as seeking to distinguish, learn about and reflect on the perspectives of others (IBO, 2013).

To facilitate this process of 'understanding the world's rich cultural heritage' (IBO, 2013), IB programmes foster students' exploration of 'human commonality, diversity and interconnection' (IBO, 2013), as well as their learning of 'how to appreciate critically many beliefs, values, experiences and ways of knowing' (IBO, 2013). The IB curriculum is engendered by, and centred on, a philosophical core of international mindedness.

The IB Learner Profile (IBLP) goes further by setting out the IB's focal curriculum ideology (Hill, 2007; IBO, 2008), translating the IB mission statement into a set of learning outcomes presented as ten attributes, valued by IB World Schools, that IB learners are expected to embody or develop. According to the Learner Profile, IB learners endeavour to become 'inquirers', 'thinkers', 'communicators', 'risk-takers' who are 'knowledgeable', 'principled', 'open-minded', 'caring', 'balanced' and 'reflective' (IBO, 2013).

The learner profile provides a long-term vision of education. It is a set of ideals that can inspire, motivate and focus the work of schools and teachers, uniting them in a common purpose. The IB asserts that such attributes 'can help individuals and groups become responsible members of local, national and global communities' (IBO, 2013). The IB programmes aim to develop *internationally minded people* who, recognising their common humanity and shared guardianship of the planet, help to create a better and more peaceful world (IB 2013). The Learner Profile is expected to guide school operations and classroom practices (Cambridge, 2010; IBO, 2008), forming a seamless part of the curriculum (Gigliotti-Labay, 2010).

The IB mission statement and IBLP have won wide praise from IB World Schools and academics (*eg* Hill, 2007, Gigliotti-Labay, 2010). In a literature review commissioned by the Academic Division of the International Baccalaureate, Kate Bullock (2011) makes the broad claim that the Learner Profile has been received with virtually 'universal acceptance among educators in IB World Schools'.

Despite Bullock's (2011) opinion that the IBLP is clearly a good thing and few would deny its value in nurturing the aims of the IB, researchers have identified possible insufficiencies in the ability of the Learner Profile to fully capture the unadulterated meanings of key IB principles like 'international mindedness'. In particular, scholars are pointing out that the philosophical basis of the Learner Profile is largely inherited from a Western liberal humanistic tradition of values (Wells, 2010; Walker, 2010).

Arguing that the philosophical basis of the Learner Profile is inclined towards a 'Western bias' rather than being truly internationally and interculturally agreeable, relevant, and applicable, scholars are questioning the extent to which the attributes espoused in the Learner Profile adequately represent or relate to the values of different, and especially non-Western, cultures around the world. Given its Western bias, the Learner Profile and its philosophical underpinnings can be challenged in terms of the receptivity with which it is met, along with its local relevance, when IB programmes are adopted and implemented in cultures that bear the legacies of non-Western traditions of thought, such as those of a rich Eastern Confucian tradition. (Wells, 2010; Walker, 2010)

Some IB researchers try to summarize the main differences between traditional Western liberal humanistic values and traditional Eastern educational values by comparing the two cultures. Hill (2015: in press), for example, lists six cultural differences between the two sets of value systems, proposing a dichotomy of key cultural differences between the West and the East, which serves as a framework with which to begin thinking about Western culture in juxtaposition with Eastern culture:

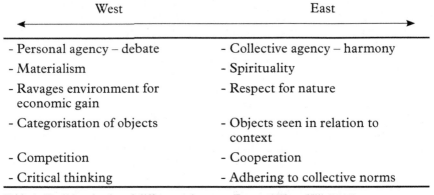

West	East
- Personal agency – debate	- Collective agency – harmony
- Materialism	- Spirituality
- Ravages environment for economic gain	- Respect for nature
- Categorisation of objects	- Objects seen in relation to context
- Competition	- Cooperation
- Critical thinking	- Adhering to collective norms

Table 1: Traditional cultural differences between East and West. Hill (2015)

Another example is Walker (2010) who summarised the works of Nussbaum (1997), Nisbett (2003) and Hofstede (2001, 2005), and identifying four major cultural areas in which there is 'strong evidence to suggest that Eastern attitudes differ markedly from those of the West' (Walker, 2010).

To begin with, Walker (2010) asserts that Eastern values express a 'concern for the group rather than the individual' (Walker, 2010), recognizing that, on the face of it at least, the IBLP appears to have placed emphasis on attributes that signal individual development and achievement much more than on qualities that promote an individual's participation and contribution to a group or community.

Walker (2010) points out that of the ten attributes described in the IBLP, only one – 'caring' – ostensibly necessitates the involvement of another person. By contrast, the main task of parents and other socialising agents in traditional Chinese culture is more focused on teaching children the standards and norms they ought to know and adhere to, as well as their place, along with its attendant roles, in a hierarchical society, training them in the 'responsible behaviours and skills' required to 'maintain group harmony and interpersonal cooperation', ends that are beyond and bigger than the well-being and desires of the self (Wang *et al.*, 2008).

Moreover, Walker (2010) points out that Eastern values emphasize a 'respect for authority'. The learner profile has nothing to say about student–teacher relationships, while Confucian tradition regards students respecting their teachers as the key to a successful education. (Walker, 2010)

Furthermore, Walker asserts that Eastern values afford a holistic view of the world (Walker, 2010). There is much evidence that those from Eastern cultures 'see the whole picture' when confronted with an issue. When something goes wrong they are more likely to examine the context of the problem than blame the individuals involved and they seem better able to live with complex shades-of-grey conclusions than their black-or-white Western counterparts (Walker, 2010).

Finally, Walker (2010) argues that Eastern values are based on an 'aversion to risk'. Of the IBLP's ten attributes 'Risk-takers' is the most distinctive one. Comparatively, in Western societies, parents prefer children to be a higher level risk taker, who engages in systematic processing of information only when uncertainty needs to be resolved; and Eastern societies encourage children to take an action only when a careful preparation and enough information are ready. Uncertainty-oriented action is not much encouraged by Chinese traditional education (Wang *et al* 2008).

The IBLP and Confucian values

Inspired in part by Hill's (2015) dichotomised framework of Western and Chinese values which offers a paradigm with which to examine these values by means of contrast, this paper seeks to draw a parallel framework, so as to examine the ten attributes of the IBLP by means of comparison with that which may appear to be corresponding or similar attributes or values extolled and promulgated in the Confucian tradition of thought.

Inquirers

The IBLP describes the ideal IB learner as someone who strives to be an inquirer, an attribute that hearkens back to the Renaissance, which catalysed the arrival of the age of scientific inquiry, or even further back to Socratic dialectics and the ancient Grecian spirit of rational inquiry. Contrary to a general observation of Eastern Asian students being more reserved in the classroom than their Western counterparts, the spirit and practice of inquiry is evidently recognised as a crucial part of learning in the Confucian tradition of thought.

For example, *The Great Learning* (Confucius, tran. by Legge J., 1971, p.358) attributes the furtherance of knowledge and understanding to the process of knowledge inquiry, stating, 'Wishing to be sincere in their thoughts, they first extended to the utmost their knowledge. Such extension of knowledge lay in the investigation of things.'

「欲诚其意者，先致其知，致知在格物。」《礼记·大学》

Moreover, the teachings of Mencius also differ from the oft-criticised practice of rote-learning in Asian societies, pointing out the importance of questioning ideas and information with a critical frame of mind, asserting that: 'If one believed everything in the *Book of History*, it would have been better for the *Book* not to have existed at all.' (Mencius, tran. by Lau D.C., 2003, p.311) 「尽信书，则不如无书。」《孟子·尽心下》

The spirit of inquiry is also fundamentally engineered in the Chinese language itself, as the second character in the Chinese phrase for 'learning', '學問', literally means 'to ask' or 'to question', inextricably entwining the spirit of inquiry with the act of learning.

Knowledgeable

In close relation to the attribute of being an inquirer, IB learners are expected to become knowledgeable. This stems from the humanist tradition of using the cognitive faculty of reason to acquire, understand and assess that which is factual, so that one gains knowledge that could be used for the betterment of humanity. Likewise, the Confucian tradition of thought places a strong emphasis on knowledge, though it often highlights the importance of ethics, morality and propriety in qualifying, balancing or tempering the emphasis on the pursuit of cognitive knowledge.

This leads to a happy effect of learning and propriety combined. In *Lunyu* (1971), for instance, it is stated that 'The superior man, extensively studying all learning, and keeping himself under the restraint of the rules of propriety, may thus likewise not overstep what is right.' (Confucius, tran. by Legge J., 1971, p.193) 「博学于文约之以礼，亦可弗畔矣夫。」《论语·雍也》

Thinkers

IB learners are also envisioned to be thinkers, a quality which builds on, informs, and qualifies the aforementioned attributes. This is in line with Western humanist thought, which places heavy emphasis on critical thinking, rational thought and empiricism. Confucian thought, on the other hand, may not traditionally foreground the importance of empiricism, but it does emphasise the importance of thought, asserting that learning, reading and thought are complementary and intricately interwoven parts of the same process. As stated in *Lunyu*, 'Learning without thought is labour lost; thought without learning is perilous.' (Confucius, tran. by Legge J., 1971, p.150) 「学而不思则罔，思而不学则殆。」《论语·为政第二》

Furthermore, Confucius required his disciples to possess, on top of a thirst for learning, an ability to think critically about new knowledge, inferring or deducing one idea from another. In *Lunyu*, for example, the Master says, 'I do not open up the truth to one who is not eager to get knowledge, nor help out any one who is not anxious to explain himself. When I have presented one corner of a subject to any one, and he cannot from it learn the other three, I do not repeat my lesson.' (Confucius, tran. by Legge J., 1971, p.197) 「不愤不启，不悱不发，举一隅不以三隅反，则不复也。」《论语·述而》

Communicators

Reminiscent of the intellectually rigorous discussions held in Parisian salons in the 17th century, IB learners are portrayed as communicators who express their opinions while collaborating with others and listening to other people's ideas and viewpoints. Confucian thought, meanwhile, goes further by highlighting the importance of peace and harmony in the meeting of minds. In *Lunyu*, the Master said, 'The superior man is affable, but not adulatory...' (Confucius, tran. by Legge J., 1971, p.273) 「君子和而不同。」《论语·子路》

This points out that people can have different standpoints and ideas, but still be able to stand together with one another, allowing for the accommodation and coexistence of people and opinions that are divergent from one's own. Moreover, the Master said, 'The superior man is dignified, but does not wrangle. He is sociable, but not a partisan.' (Confucius, tran. by Legge J., 1971, p.300) 「君子矜而不争，群而不党。」《论语·卫灵公》

This adds a moral quality to being a communicator, reminding one that in seeking to collaborate with others, one should not engage in acts that divide or exclude.

Principled

IB learners are expected to be principled. Likewise, Mencius said, 'Only when there are things a man will not do is he capable of doing great things.' (Mencius, tran. by Lau D.C., 2003, p.175)

「人有不为也，而后可以有为。」《孟子·离娄下》

The IBLP emphasised concepts like 'integrity', 'honesty', 'fairness', 'justice', 'dignity' and 'rights', principles which are in the foreground of the United Nations Declaration of Human Rights, guide the rule of law, and, through the actions of able, principled individuals and groups, give hope to underprivileged peoples around the world.

The teachings of Mencius point to the same direction, albeit at times on a more personal, individual level: 'He cannot be led into excesses when wealthy and honoured or deflected from his purpose when poor and obscure, nor can he be made to bow before superior force.' (Mencius, tran. by Lau D.C., 2003, p.127)

「富贵不能淫，贫贱不能移，威武不能屈。」《孟子·滕文公下》

Open-minded

While holding to one's principles, the IBLP encourages learners to seek to understand and be open-minded towards diverse perspectives, very much like Confucian teachings, which portray a similar concept lyrically and metaphorically, asserting that 'The Ocean is so vast because it never rejects any water. The mountain is so tall because it never repels any rock and earth.' [Chapter 'The Situation', Guanzi] 「海不辞水，故能成其大。山不辞土，故能成其高」《管子·形势解》

Caring

IB learners are described as capable of being empathetic, compassionate and respectful, personal ideals that are also highly valued and taught in the Confucian tradition of thought. Confucian thought, however, locates respect and care first and foremost in the family and especially in parent-child relationships, advocating the concept of filial piety, which, although closely related to general respect and empathy, encapsulates elements of natural responsibility, obligation, sacrifice and love – elements that are absent in the general Western notion of being caring.

To illustrate this, Mencius teaches one to 'Treat the aged of your own family in a manner befitting their venerable age and extend this treatment to the aged of other families; treat your own young in a manner befitting their tender age and extend this to the young of other families, and you can roll the Empire on your palm.' (Mencius, tran. by Lau D.C., 2003, p.19)

「老吾老以及人之老，幼吾幼以及人之幼。天下可运于掌。」《孟子·梁惠王上》

Likewise, the Doctrine of the Mean points out that 'Benevolence is the characteristic element of humanity, and the great exercise of it is in loving relatives.' Confucius, tran. by Legge J., 1971, p.405)

「仁者，人也，亲亲为大。」《中庸》

Risk-takers

At first sight, being a risk-taker appears to contradict the more conservative Confucian tradition of values, and does not appear to even be in line with Western humanism, but the IBLP qualifies the term by clarifying that the meaning of risk-taking here is to take decisive, informed action, rising to the occasion in the face of uncertainty, challenges and change – constant qualities of the modern world. The IBLP emphasizes that such 'risks' are not of the foolhardy and reckless variety. In this sense, Confucian thought seems to agree. In *Lunyu*, the Master said, 'The wise are free from perplexities; the virtuous from anxiety; and the bold from fear.' (Confucius, tran. by Legge J., 1971, p.225) [Book IX: Tsze Han Confucian Analects]

「知者不惑，仁者不忧，勇者不惧。」《论语·子罕》

Balanced

Reminiscent of the Grecian maxim of 'nothing overmuch', IB learners are expected to balance different aspects of their lives 'to achieve well-being for ourselves and others'. Confucian thought prizes the concept of balance as well, and goes further to include the notions of harmony and equilibrium. In the Doctrine of the Mean, it is said, 'While there are no stirrings of pleasure, anger, sorrow, or joy, the mind may be said to be in the state of Equilibrium. When those feelings have been stirred, and they act in their due degree, there ensues what may be called the state of Harmony. This Equilibrium is the great root from which grow all the human actings in the world, and this Harmony is the universal path which they all should pursue.' (Confucius, tran. by Legge J., 1971, p.384)

「喜怒哀乐之未发，谓之中；发而皆中节，谓之和。中也者，天下之大本也；和也者，天下之达道也。」《中庸》

On the level of the individual, the notion of balance invokes Renaissance humanism, which advocates that humans should seek to develop all of their faculties to the fullest extent, an ideal that was manifest in the concept of the Renaissance man, a concept that was embodied by polymaths like Leonardo da Vinci. This sense of balance in the development of the person is highly agreeable with Confucian teaching for, according to the Rites of Zhou, the mastery of six diverse skills formed a rite of passage for young aristocrats in ancient China, during the Zhou Dynasty (1122-256 BC). Only when the six skills, or arts, namely 'Rituals, Music, Archery, Charioteer, Books and Numbers' were mastered could a person be considered accomplished. 'The goal was to train a corps of leaders to help the king govern the nation. Men who excelled in these six arts were thought to have reached the state of perfection, an ideal gentleman.' (The Rites of Zhou, Siku quanshu, 1997)

「而养国子以道，乃教之六艺。」《周礼·地官·保氏》

Reflective

The final attribute listed in the IBLP is that of reflectiveness, a fitting close to the set of ten attributes, as regular reflection would help to ensure that such a set of values does not remain static, but are thoughtfully applied in daily life. Again, this attribute strikes a chord with Confucian thought, which qualifies the attribute by including the notion of action as a result of reflection, keeping the practice of reflection from being 'overmuch' by requiring that one does not hesitate or stall when it is time to act. 'Chî Wan thought thrice, and then acted.' (Confucius, tran. by Legge J., 1971, p.180) [Book V: Kung-Yê Ch'ang]

「季文子三思而后行。」《论语·公冶长》

Nonetheless, Mencius expounds on the value of inward reflection, asserting, 'If others do not respond to your love with love, look into your own benevolence; if others do not respond to your attempts to govern them with order, look into your own wisdom; if others do not return your courtesy, look into your own respect. (Mencius, tran. by Lau D. C., 2003, p.153)

「爱人不亲，反其仁；治人不治，反其智；礼人不答，反其敬。」《孟子·离娄》

In Lunyu, the philosopher Tsang describes a pragmatic routine of reflection, stating, 'I daily examine myself on three points: whether, in transacting business for others, I may have been not faithful; whether, in intercourse with friends, I may have been not sincere; whether I may have not mastered and practiced the instructions of my teacher.' (Confucius, tran. by Legge J., 1971, p.139) 「曾子曰：吾日三省吾身：为人谋而不忠乎？与朋友交而不信乎？传不习乎？」《论语·学而》

A general parallel that might be drawn between the IBLP and the values of Confucian thought would be that the attributes in the Learner Profile should not be interpreted in isolation, but should be considered as parts to an infinitely textured whole, just as Confucian values need to be understood in relation to other values, and more importantly, in relation to each unique context in which a value or attribute is being called into question.

This comparison shows that large areas of commonality can be found between Western and Eastern cultures, but it is important not to conflate commonality with sameness, for true intercultural understanding lies in the appreciation of nuanced meanings, differences in emphases and priorities, as well as unarticulated concerns.

The evolving Confucian-based society

Taking the iconic IB attribute, 'risk-taker', as an example, Wang *et al* (2008) found that the number of uncertainty-oriented students (risk-taker) is increasing in China in urban primary schools. Chinese parents may realise that, in order to function adequately in a larger society and to adjust to the changing demands of contemporary society, children need to learn independent and assertive skills. The academic activities in Chinese schools ought not be too passive or focus too much on acquiring existing knowledge, but should instead be active, creative and self-directed, focusing on questioning, problem-solving and critical thinking (Li, 2003; Stevenson *et al*, 1990). It may not be surprising that uncertainty-oriented (risk-taking) students are more likely than others to benefit from school activities and display competence in learning, and consequently perform well in academic work (Sorrentino & Roney, 2000).

The literature review reveals that Eastern and Western cultures differ but do not necessary conflict, and can even mutually support and complement each other. The Confucian tradition of thought can inform and enrich the IBLP.

> The world is changing, and there is evidence that we are entering a 'post-international environment': borders are weakening, multiple citizenships are more commonplace, migration has reached record levels, and we have encountered the 'death of distance'. We are increasingly living next to, working alongside, sharing our leisure with, choosing our partners from people with different cultural backgrounds.
>
> (Walker 2010: 69)

In modern Eastern societies, the Confucian traditional values have been undergoing change. More and more Western values are accepted and practiced by young and educated Eastern people. As Walker (2010) infers, analysing differences between cultures and integrating their similarities works to form 'a sense of shared humanity'. Ian Hill (2014) points out that intercultural understanding is not a one-way street. It requires interaction between different cultures.

According to Zhou (1996), 'If and when the East and West could learn and benefit from each other, integrating each other's cultural strengths – for example, the individual initiative with the collective team spirit, competitiveness with cooperativeness, the technological capacities with the moral qualities – then desirable universal values will gradually develop and a global ethic will be formed, which will be a fundamental renewal of cultures and a great contribution of education to humanity.'

Although the world is getting smaller today, and the distance between West and East is reduced by information technology development and political or economic issues, the value differences between West and East listed above are easily observed and evidenced by us today. Language and culture are intricately intertwined. Anytime you teach a language you will also teach the culture of that language. Brown (1994: 25) points out: 'Whenever you teach a language, you also teach a complex system of cultural customs, values, and ways of thinking, feeling, and acting'.

Because of this, the differences between West and East affect language teaching and learning, especially in East Asian countries or regions such as China, Japan, Korea, Taiwan, Singapore, and Hong Kong, where there is a strong Eastern Confucian tradition. Taking Hong Kong as an example, there are 53 IB World Schools in Hong Kong offering one or more of the three IB programmes (IBO, 02 March 2015). All of them offer Chinese as a language subject. Hong Kong is a multicultural region, where the Eastern culture or traditional Confucian philosophy is a significant component of school educational value systems.

Research problem and methodology

The issue is: how do IB Chinese language teachers in Hong Kong deal with the cultural differences between West and East in their classroom?

The possible disjuncture between the IBLP and the cultural setting in which it is being implemented gives rise to the question of how teachers originating from, or teaching in, cultures with a strong Eastern Confucian tradition of thought would respond to the IBLP. This study seeks to address this question by exploring IB Chinese language teachers' perceptions and teaching strategies when the IBLP meets the Eastern Confucian tradition in their classes in Hong Kong international schools, *ie* their reception of, reactions to and interactions with the IBLP in Chinese language teaching.

To do so, five experienced IB Chinese teachers (indicated by teachers A, B, C, D and E) from different Hong Kong international schools were invited to participate in the study as interviewees in individual semi-structured interviews. All the participants were MYP and DP Chinese teachers. The face-to-face interview was recorded and, afterwards, transcribed for analysis. In addition to this, some related school documents, such as school mission statements or curriculum and teaching materials used by teachers, were also studied as references.

Taking a look at how Chinese language teachers interpret and convey, and possibly even appropriate and inform the IBLP, this study focuses on the interplay between traditional Chinese values and IB philosophical principles in Chinese language classrooms. The study aims:

- at the level of teacher perception: to examine Chinese language teachers' reactions to the IBLP in Chinese language teaching; and

- at the level of teaching strategy: to illuminate how Chinese language teachers fuse Eastern values in their daily pedagogical practices to enrich and localize the IBLP.

In this study, the term 'Confucian tradition' is loosely used to denote a non-Western value system that is predominantly manifest in East-Asian countries and regions such as China, Japan, Korea, Taiwan, Singapore, or Hong Kong. The terms 'Chinese culture' and 'Eastern culture' are at times used to denote similar concepts.

Findings and discussion

The findings can be categorized into two related levels: teacher perceptions, and teaching strategies.

Teacher perception level

There are three significant perceptions to be highlighted:

a) compatibility between the IBLP and Chinese culture;
b) differences between the IBLP and Chinese culture;
c) and comparative interpretations.

Perception (a): A level of compatibility between IBLP and Chinese culture

All the participants perceive a level of *compatibility* between Chinese traditional cultural values and most attributes in the IBLP, because the latter highlighted some 'universal humanitarian values' as its core. Teachers think, 'these core values belong to all human beings and should not be said to be Western or Eastern, or come from Chinese traditions or foreign traditions' (Teacher D). Highlighting universalism and downplaying the differences between Western and Eastern cultures, Teacher B asserted, 'We cannot say that this thing is Chinese and that one is Western. But rather, they are part of being human, the great things in humanity. The expectations for being honest, respectful and diligent are the same everywhere'. Teacher E felt that values such as mutual respect and love among people are equally highlighted in both Chinese tradition and Western culture, and stand for the ideals of human beings.

This universal perspective on the IBLP led to the perceived high degree of compatibility between the IBLP and Chinese cultural values. This universal perspective even shaped the teacher's expectations for her students: 'to become more like a global citizen. I don't want purely Eastern. Neither do I want purely Western' (Teacher B).

Taking *being caring* as an example, teachers said: 'Although the attribute of "being caring" prioritizes social stratum in some philosophical camps, the philosophy camp of Mencius encourages universal mutual care and love, similar to the Western interpretation. The co-existence of different views in Chinese culture broadens its capacity of entertaining the IBLP' (Teacher B). Taking a dynamic and relative view towards Chinese traditional values helps the participants find greater compatibility between them and the IBLP.

At the same time, the participants also viewed Chinese cultural values as a dynamic phenomenon that is constantly evolving, and advocated for a critical view towards the relevance and meaningfulness of Chinese traditional values. In Teacher B's words, 'traditions are not the dead past, but rather a flowing river. Although we still use the same terms, the interpretations are to be updated.'

They questioned the suitability of a literal interpretation of traditional values: 'Traditional values such as "filial piety" and "obedience" have changed in modern Chinese people's eyes. Whether to follow these values, in effect, depends largely on the specific situation' (Teacher E). Teachers C and D also felt that some values in Chinese traditions are no longer relevant to modern society and cannot be accepted or maintained without critical thinking. Teacher C listed 'being faithful' as an example.

She pointed out that the traditional value of being faithful to one's country is not relevant to some of her students due to their mixed cultural backgrounds and immigrant histories: 'to whom should they be faithful?' Thus, Teacher E emphasized that 'we should not take culture as a closed system, but rather take a more open-minded and accommodating view.' Furthermore, Teacher B and Teacher E highlighted that Chinese traditional culture itself is very diverse and contains different views about the same phenomenon.

Perception (b): Some differences between the IBLP and Chinese culture
The teachers point out some differences or conflicts between the notions of the IBLP and traditional Chinese cultural values. For example, in general, the IBLP relates to developing the learner's quality as an individual, rather than his/her development in group relationships. Teachers think that the IBLP is very much individually oriented whereas Chinese cultural values highlight group harmony (Teachers A & B). It is a major difference between the IBLP and Chinese culture.

Caring, one of ten attributes of the IBLP, shares the core 'universal humanitarian values' as mentioned above, but does *Caring* indicate group harmony? Not all teachers agree with that. Teacher E insists that 'Caring does not necessarily contain group awareness, and collaboration does not necessarily lead to group awareness. Group awareness refers more to being responsible to others, being responsible to the society without too much consideration of personal interests' (Teacher E). In Teacher E's opinion, it is evident that the notion of group awareness in the IBLP may not be immediately apparent to every person who reads it.

However, the IBLP states that its ten attributes, with 'others like them, can help individuals and groups become responsible members of local, national and global communities' (IBO, 2013). While the discrete attributes of the IBLP may not always place in the foreground the notion of group awareness, taken as a whole the attributes in the IBLP are meant to help and facilitate the growth of those who are expected to become capable of and inclined towards acting for the interests of the group or community at the local, national and international levels.

Moreover, Hill (2015) draws attention to the description of each IBLP attribute, arguing that the quality of being caring is outward looking and necessitates a sense of group awareness, so long as 'we accept that showing respect and compassion can only be gauged by the way we behave towards others' (Hill, 2015). Furthermore, Hill's (2015) (Western) analysis points out that most of the IBLP items are of a collective nature, with only three – 'knowledgeable, thinkers, reflective' – attributes of a solitary character, which nonetheless can be deemed indispensable qualities in the holistic development of an all-rounded learner who is to be capable of appreciating, examining, understanding, and acting in the interests of group harmony, or for the collective good. In this way, there are some differences between the IBLP and Eastern culture in terms of degree.

The participants also pointed out that some Chinese cultural values are hard to express and comprehend in English since it involves 'cross cultural and cross linguistic' reinterpretation (Teacher B).

Perception (c): Some differences depend on interpretation

Whether participants perceive Chinese cultural values and the IBLP as controversial or compatible sometimes depends on the interpretations brought to the texts of those attributes. Taking *Risk-taker* as an example, teachers think:

> You can interpret risk-taker as overcoming one's fears to accept new challenges and wading in with great perseverance. It is a mind-set. You cannot interpret it as 'I need to climb the mountain even though I cannot'. It's not that simple. I feel that it should be interpreted as an internalized attitude to overcome one's fears to reach the goal you set for yourself. Chinese culture is full of stories like that. (Teacher D)

> *Risk-taker* is controversial since a lot of times students simply venture out their answers during class without careful thinking because of this risk taking spirit (Teachers A & B).

Furthermore, the participants' (re)interpretation of Chinese culture also affected their perceptions of the compatibility between certain Chinese cultural values and IBLP. Loyalty to one's country has been listed by the majority of participants as a traditional Chinese value that is not represented by the IBLP. Some participants, like Teacher C, even questioned its relevance and meaningfulness in the modern, globalized society.

However, at the same time, the participants were highlighting the importance of reinterpreting traditional values beyond their literal meaning to make them more relevant to modern society (Teachers A, B, E). For instance, Teacher B reinterpreted what loyalty means by broadening it beyond the historical sense of being loyal to the emperor to embody it with modern meaning:

> There are things external to each individual that are greatly valued and worthy of individuals to spend their whole life to pursue. To different individuals, this thing [loyalty] is different. It could be loyalty to the emperor. It could be to environment protection. It could also refer to one's career. This is something bigger than yourself that you are willing to maintain unconditionally (Teacher B).

This reinterpretation of loyalty added an individual dimension into this traditional value and made it compatible with the values highlighted in the IBLP.

Interpretation can also be discussed at teaching strategy level as well. More details are in the sections below.

Teaching strategy level

Strategies frequently used by IB Chinese teachers to identify the differences between the IBLP and traditional Chinese culture are outlined below.

Strategy (a): Concretising

The first teaching strategy frequently used by Chinese teachers to deal with the cultural distance between West and East is *'concretising'*, which means to realize the abstract concepts of the IBLP through the help of Chinese cultural illustrations. In Chinese language class, it is an effective way for teachers to use examples of Chinese culture to make the abstract attributes of the IBLP more vivid and understandable. Teacher B said:

> The IBLP is the backbone and Chinese cultural values are the muscles and blood. Chinese cultural values help concretize the IBLP and make it comprehensible (Teacher B).

Since the IBLP contains, more or less, abstract concepts or principles, it accommodates interpretations from different cultural perspectives. For example, the Chinese cultural value of devoting oneself wholeheartedly to society without too much care for personal loss can be used to concretize the IBLP on becoming a *caring* global citizen (Teacher D). Furthermore, Chinese traditional values, such as respecting teachers and parents, can be used to embody the attribute of being principled in the IBLP (Teacher A).

Strategy (b) Interpreting

'Interpreting' as a teaching strategy means leading students to make 'new interpretations' of the IBLP or Chinese cultural values. As mentioned earlier, whether participants perceive Chinese cultural values and the IBLP as controversial or compatible sometimes depends on their interpretations of IBLP and/or Chinese cultural values. An obvious example is the interpretation of *Risk-taker*, the most controversial attribute of the IBLP:

> I told my students to learn to judge when they should be a *risk-taker* and when they should not be a risk taker. We discussed that the Risk Taker in the IBLP is not to ask us to do whatever without much consideration of the consequences. They need to be principled in judging when to be a risk taker. In some situations, they need to think carefully before taking actions (Teacher C).

In this way, a most controversial attribute, like *Risk-taker*, has been translated into a compatible value successfully. However, sometimes a difference is too obvious to be re-interpreted. In this situation, teachers will adjust their teaching approach by using different teaching strategies, namely comparing and co-accessing.

Strategy (c): Comparing

'Comparing' means to encourage students to engage in comparative and critical thinking in relation to the IBLP and Chinese cultural values. Brown (1994: 25) advises teachers to: 'Discuss cross-cultural differences with your students, emphasizing that no culture is "better" than another, but that cross-cultural understanding is an important facet of learning a language.' That is, teachers can lead their students to compare the same issues, *eg* weddings or relationships between parents and children, in different cultures.

Comparing is a very effective strategy frequently used by IB Chinese teachers in their teaching of Chinese as a second language with students coming from different cultural backgrounds. For example, Teacher D and Teacher E said they often used this strategy 'to engage students to do critical discussion around the IBLP and Chinese cultural values'.

Furthermore, teachers also tell the reasons why they often use this strategy, as the extracts from Teacher B and D shown below:

> Students live with both the IBLP and local school learner profile. The simultaneous presence of the two makes the profiles not something to regurgitate but something that elicit comparisons which accompany their whole school life (Teacher B).

> I often discuss with my students. Such discussions open room for them to choose. I think they have the right to choose (Teacher D).

Students can compare, discuss, and even have a right to choose. 'Choose' includes evaluating and critical thinking, which is helpful for students in their development though teachers avoid encouraging students to consider whether one culture is 'better' than another. Below are two examples.

Example 1: *Individual vs. Group*
The IBLP in general emphasizes individual skills and quality. Being reflective, a thinker, an inquirer, a risk-taker, caring are all individual attributes. In the Western world where individuals are at the centre, education is about fostering attributes which individuals need to possess. It is quite different from the Chinese traditional values of loyalty, filial piety, harmony and so on. Loyalty and filial piety are meaningless if we only consider individuals, to say nothing of group harmony (Teacher B).

Example 2: *Risk-taker*
Risk-taker exists both in Chinese cultural values and in the IBLP. However, they highlight different dimensions of risk-taking: the IBLP encourages students to be courageous and take challenges, whereas Chinese cultural values emphasize studying, observing and waiting to be mature enough and well prepared before venturing out to face a challenge (Teacher A).

Difference does not necessarily translate into conflict. As we mentioned earlier, teachers believe that the IBLP and traditional Chinese educational philosophies share almost the same ultimate educational aims. Based on this perception, a frequently used teaching strategy by Chinese teachers is *Co-access*.

Strategy (d): Co-access

'*Co-access*' means the co-existence of the IBLP attributes and Chinese cultural values both help students to access the same goal by their choices, as the teachers said below:

> It is a matter of entrance. You can lead students to enter through Western cultural values. You can also lead them to enter through Chinese cultural values. So, different entrances, but the same goals. Since I'm a Chinese teacher, I surely choose to take Chinese culture as the entrance point to help my students understand more (Teacher D).

Hong Kong is a very unique region in the world with both Western and Eastern cultures co-existing in the same place. In this context, most IB World Schools in Hong Kong declare their bilingual and bi-cultural school missions or visions, for instance the schools under the English Schools Foundation (ESF) and Independent Schools Foundation Academy (ISFA).

The mission of ESF, which owns a number of primary and secondary IB schools, indicates: 'ESF offers a personalized and inclusive approach to learning for students of all abilities, with programmes based mainly on the values of the International Baccalaureate [...] Chinese language and culture form a critical component of our curriculum and we are deeply committed to our origins and development in Hong Kong.' (ESF 2015)

The school vision of ISFA says it is 'deeply rooted in Chinese culture, global in understanding and experience, and excellent in all endeavours' (http://www.isf.edu.hk/en/about-us/vision-mission-and-values/, accessed on 26 February, 2015.) For its 'core values', ISFA declares: 'Grounded in Chinese culture and with a global perspective, The ISF Academy community lives and learns under the umbrella of core values that draw from the school's Chinese heritage and which are updated to be relevant to today's world.' ISFA promotes the so called 'Eight Virtues + One', which is a value system based on Chinese traditional culture with some updated revisions. (ISFA 2015).

In general, no IB international school in Hong Kong omits traditional Chinese culture as a value system parallel with IB philosophies. Pritchard (2013), in his illustration of the ISFA's fusion of Chinese traditional values with the IBLP, points out, 'the duality of the human experience, as both individual and members of communities, suggests that other social virtues might be incorporated to reflect a more complete model of the 21st century international learner'. Therefore, it is not surprising when IB Chinese teachers say:

> The traditional Confucian values have the same goals with Western humanism, but in a different way, a Chinese way (Teacher D).

In summary, the four strategies the teachers adopted can be represented by Table 2 below:

Notions	Strategies
Similarity in Difference	**a)** Concretizing: Realization of the IBLP in a more understandable way through examples from Chinese culture
	b) Interpreting: New interpretations of the IBLP or Chinese cultural values
Difference in Similarity	**c)** Comparing: Engage critical thinking between the IBLP and Chinese cultural values
	d) Co-access: The co-existence of IBLP attributes and Chinese cultural values helps students to access the same goal by different choice of the teachers

Table 2: Teaching strategies frequently used by IB Chinese teachers

As shown in Table 2, we can categorise the four most frequently used teaching strategies into two categories by their notions. Notion One includes strategies (a) and (b), because the two strategies, Concretizing and Interpreting, elucidate the similarities between the IBLP and Eastern culture, trying to explain the IBLP in a deductive way. While strategies (c) and (d) can be categories in Notion Two, since Strategies (c) and (d), in contrast, posit themselves on the difference between West and East, in an inductive way, to a certain extent.

Conclusion

In this study, we examined the IBLP from the Chinese cultural perspective, discussing how the IBLP could be potentially enriched from the Chinese cultural perspective. This discussion is based on a review of classical Chinese texts and the interviews with a group of IB Chinese language teachers on how they interpret and enact the IBLP in their daily practices. The study found that this group of Chinese language teachers perceived a certain level of compatibility as well as some differences between the IBLP and traditional Chinese culture. And such perceptions led them to engage the IBLP and Chinese traditional culture in a dialectic fashion, using both to complement each other and critically reviewing and adopting both to create a more holistic worldview.

This study reported on a few strategies these teachers adopted to successfully facilitate learner involvement by constructing a culturally integrative context in which learners effectively achieve the goals of the IB. Although researchers have been pointing out that the IBLP consists of abstract and evasive concepts that lead to possibilities of misinterpretation and misunderstanding (Lai, Shum & Zhang, 2014), the agentive actions the participants in this study took to enact the IBLP from the Chinese cultural perspective suggests that the abstractedness of IBLP could be interpreted and utilized positively to provide opportunities to accommodate diverse interpretations from different cultural perspectives, making the IBLP more culturally inclusive.

Thus, when developing teachers' understanding of IBLP, a culturally responsive approach is needed where explicit discussions of the dialectic relationship between the IBLP and traditional cultures in different regions need to be included. Teacher-initiated culturally responsive positioning strategies may also need to be highlighted to help teachers develop their enactment strategies to maximize the potentials of the IBLP in realising the core values of the IB, of which international mindedness is central.

The three teacher perceptions and four frequent teaching strategies outlined above enhanced our awareness of IB international educational philosophy and the challenge of its implication in different local cultural contexts, such as in Hong Kong where there is a strong Eastern Confucian tradition. The foundation of the IBLP is *international mindedness (IM)*. Though discussion about the definition of IM continues in a multicultural world today, scholars, like Hill (2015), believe that a contemporary model of IM should be 'inclusive of non-Western input' and therefore potentially more universally acceptable.

International education is not 'a one way street' (Hill 2014); it needs interaction between different cultural agents. From this perspective, the use of different effective teaching strategies by IB Chinese teachers in Hong Kong guides their students in thinking critically about the IBLP and traditional Chinese culture. This is not only a successful teaching method, but also contributes to 'a sense of shared humanity' (Walker 2010).

References

Brown, H. D. (1994). *Teaching by principles: an interactive approach to language pedagogy.* Englewood Cliffs, N.J.: Prentice Hall Regents.

Bullock, K. *(2011). International Baccalaureate learner profile: Literature review.* IBO.

Cambridge, J. C. (2010). The International Baccalaureate Diploma Programme and the construction of pedagogical identity: A preliminary study. *Journal of Research in International Education,* 9(3), 199-213.

ESF (English Schools Foundation) website (2015) http://www.esf.edu.hk/about-esf/our-values, accessed on 26 February, 2015.

Gigliotti-Labay, J. (2010). *Fulfilling its Mission? The Promotion of International Mindedness in IB DP Programmes.* EdD Dissertation, University of Houston, Houston, US.

Hill, I. (2007). International education as developed by the International Baccalaureate Organisation. In M. Hayden, J. Levy & J. Thompson (eds.), *The SAGE handbook of research in international education,* 25-37. London: SAGE Publications.

Hill, I. (2012). Evolution of education for international mindedness. *Journal of Research in International Education, 11*(3), 245-261.

Hill, I. (2014). *The International Baccalaureate: history, philosophy, and pedagogy.* A public lecture on 3rd March 2014 at Faculty of Education in The University of Hong Kong.

Hill, I. (2015). The History and Development of International Mindedness. In M. Hayden. J Levy, J. Thomas (eds.) *The SAGE Handbook of Research in International Education, Second Edition* London: SAGE Publications, in press.

Hofstede, G. 2001. *Culture's Consequences.* London. Sage Publications.

Hofstede, G. 2005. *Cultures and Organizations*. New York. McGraw-Hill.

ISFA (International Schools Foundation Academy) website (2015) http://www.isf.edu.hk/en/about-us/vision-mission-and-values/, accessed on 26 February, 2015.

IB, (2013). *IB Learner Profile*. IB, Geneva.

IB, (2013). *What is an IB education?* IB, Geneva.

Lai, C. Shum, M. S. K. & Zhang, B. (2014). International mindedness in an Asian context: the case of the International Baccalaureate in Hong Kong. *Educational Research* pp1-20.

Lau, D. C. (2003). *Mencius*. Hong Kong: Chinese University Press.

Legge, J. (1971). *Confucian analects: The great learning, and the doctrine of the mean.* New York: Dover Publications.

Li, N. (2003). *Approaches to learning: Literature review.* IB research paper, IB, Geneva.

Nisbett, R. (2003). *The Geography of Thought.* New York. The Free Press.

Nussbaum, M. (1997). *Cultivating Humanity.* Cambridge, MA. Harvard UP.

Pritchard, M. (2013) Together alone: Peaceful co-existence between the IB Learner Profile and the 'Eight Virtues + One'. *International School (IS) Magazine, 16*(1), 20-23.

Rickett, W. A. (1965). Kuan-Tzu: *A repository of early Chinese thought.* Hong Kong: Hong Kong University Press.

Sorrentino, R. M. & Roney, C. J. R. (2000). *The uncertain mind: Individual differences in facing the unknown.* Philadelphia, PA: Psychology Press.

Stevenson, H. W., Lee, S. Y., Chen, C., Lummis, M., Stigler, J., Fan, L., & Ge, F. (1990). Mathematics achievement of children in China and the United States. *Child development,* 1053-1066.

Siku quanshu cunmu congshu bianzuan weiyuanhui bian (Eds.). (1997). *Siku quanshu cunmu congshu. Jingbu [Collection of the Extant Emperor's Four Treasuries].* Tainan: Zhuangyan Cultural Enterprise Limited.

Walker, G. (2010). *East is East and West is West.* IB position paper. IBO.

Wang, Z, Chen, X, Sorrentino, R and Szeto, A. (2008). 'Uncertainty orientation in Chinese children: Relations with school and psychological adjustment.' *International Journal of Behavioral Development. Vol 32, number 2.* pp 137–144.

Wells, J. (2011). International education, values and attitudes: A critical analysis of the International Baccalaureate (IB) Learner Profile. *Journal of Research in International Education, 10(2),* 174-188.

Chapter 3

The professional growth of Chinese language student-teachers in teaching practicum in the IB Certificate of Teaching and Learning Programme

Mark Shiu-kee Shum, Ben-nan Zhang, Chun Lai,
Elizabeth Ka-yee Loh & Tung-fei Lam

Abstract

Surveying the mostly uncharted waters of professional development for Teaching Chinese as a Second Language (TCSL) in the IB context, this paper examines the professional growth gained by Chinese language student-teachers through their participation in an IB-oriented TP offered as part of the Master of Education (MEd) programme in TCSL at the University of Hong Kong (HKU).

With a 'Three Ws Feature' in mind, HKU established partnerships with schools in Hong Kong that would act as TP host schools, providing an immersive 'Whole School Experience' with 'Whole Mentoring Support' to complement 'Whole Preparation' in the form of modular classes at HKU. Graduates of the programme are also awarded IB Certificates in Teaching and Learning.

This study asks whether and how student-teachers participating in TP benefit from university-school partnerships in terms of professional growth. To address this question, this paper uses models to analyse and evaluate the levels of professional growth that student-teachers reach in TP; examines the relationship between their professional growth and the role of practicum schools and mentors; and explores the interplay of different factors that go into building successful TP experiences.

Two cohorts of pre-service Chinese language teachers enrolled in HKU's MEd TCSL programme were interviewed and their reflections were analysed. This paper argues that university-school partnerships play an important role in creating a favourable environment for professional growth, but that student-teachers can only benefit from facilitative and enabling environments if they exercise individual agency in their interactions with their practicum school and mentor, proactively making the best of every situation and environment, be it conducive or challenging.

Introduction

This paper explores the professional growth of Chinese language student-teachers participating in a teaching practicum (TP) as part of the Master of Education (MEd) in Teaching Chinese as a Second Language (TCSL) programme at the University of Hong Kong. Inaugurated in 2009, the programme received unconditional recognition from the International Baccalaureate (IB) Organisation in 2010. Graduates of the programme are eligible to be awarded the IB Certificate of Teaching and Learning. Between 2011 and 2014, 130 pre-service and in-service teachers graduated from the programme, and the enrolment for 2014-15 stands at around 65.

The TP is a very important component in teacher education, through which student-teachers have the opportunity to put theories into practice in real classroom situations. Universities and other tertiary educator training institutions around the world are establishing strong partnerships with schools, cooperating closely to enhance the professional growth of pre-service teachers during their TP, as well as to support the continued professional development of in-service school teaching staff.

On a mission to be the hub of IB Chinese Language teacher training in the Asia-Pacific region, the University of Hong Kong has built strong relationships with nearly all of the IB international schools in Hong Kong, securing teaching practice placements for its student-teachers. The University has plans to develop a self-funded Postgraduate Diploma in Education (PGDE) programme for IB Chinese, as well as an online IB Chinese teacher training programme for in-service teachers.

The aims of this study are to explore models for building successful TP experiences for pre-service teachers; to observe the levels of professional growth of student-teachers in the process of learning to teach; and to investigate the relationship between their growth and the schools' support. In this study, student-teachers and graduates of HKU's MEd in TCSL programme were interviewed to solicit details of their TP experience and the support they gained in the process. The reflections of the interviewees were analysed. The results reveal that in learning to teach, student-teachers have to struggle through painful stages before they attain any level of professional growth; a supportive teaching environment that partnership schools provide facilitates the process.

Literature review

According to Coolahan (2003), there are three stages of professional development for teachers. They are known as the '3 Is', referring to Initial Teacher Education (for pre-service teachers), Induction (for beginning teachers) and In-service Training (as continuing professional development). In Kagan's study, she highlighted five stages that constitute the process of professional growth for pre-service and beginning teachers. These stages are identified as an increase in metacognition, the acquisition of knowledge of pupils, a shift in attention, and the development of standard procedures with growth in problem solving skills (Kagan 1992:156).

The TP is a central aspect of quality initial teacher education that assists pre-service teachers to grow in their real school experience. Previous studies show fruitful discussions with regard to the relationship between TP and the teacher's professional growth, and key factors to make TP effective (Shum & Law, 1998; Lewin 2004; Brouwer and Korthagen 2005; Sutherland, Scanlon *et al.* 2005; Behets and Vergauwen 2006).

In Darling-Hammond's study, factors in relation to effective TP were identified and included strong relationships, common knowledge, and shared beliefs among school and university-based faculty (Darling-Hammond 2006). Cozza (2010) shared similar views and promoted a model of professional development that could transform school culture and lead to successful collaborations between pre-service teachers, in-service teachers and the university professor.

She discussed five generic factors in relation to such partnerships, stemming from which a collaboration agenda, student-learning goals, assessment strategies to evaluate each goal of a programme, and so on, should be clearly determined and shared by all stakeholders (Cozza 2010:240). However, Kagan (1992) argued that most pre-service programmes generally failed to address the needs of pre-service teachers who were expected to accomplish the tasks of acquiring learners' knowledge, (re)constructing their self-image of being a teacher through using such knowledge and developing standard procedural classroom routines for instruction.

In relation to the factors contributing to effective and successful TP, a number of recent studies revealed the challenges that might hinder pre-service teachers' growth, *ie* the expectations of different participants in school-university partnerships (Hodkinson & Hodkinson 1999; McCullick 2001; Edwards & Mutton 2007; Chambers & Armour 2012), the transition from theory to practice (Gram & Karlsen 2004; Brouwer & Korthagen 2005; Neville, Sherman *et al* 2005; Sutherland, Scanlon *et al* 2005), and the quality of teacher mentors (Lewin 2004).

With regard to the expectations of participants in school-university partnerships, Hodkinsons' study was concerned with the innate tension of pre-service teachers who struggle with their dual roles as student and as teacher (Hodkinson & Hodkinson 1999), whereas McCullick's study was concerned with divergent expectations between schools and university regarding their respective roles in teaching pre-service teachers (McCullick 2001). Chambers & Armour (2012) further pointed out that there was also a perceived lack of parity between schools and university, especially in the process of TP grading.

With regard to the transition from theory to practice, Neville and his colleagues (2005) regarded TP as a limited and disconnected component of university coursework, and Garm & Karlsen (2004) identified the struggle of putting theory into practice in TP periods as a major theme of related literature. Brouwer & Korthagen (2005) concluded with three crucial features of TP to integrate theory and practice, *ie* adopting a cyclical model to schedule university study and TP, supporting pre-service teacher's individual learning and facilitating intensive cooperation between university teachers and school mentors. With regard to the quality of school mentors, Lewin (2004) perceived TP as a place to demonstrate best practice through the support of well-trained mentors.

Informed by the studies cited above, we share the view that TP is a central aspect of initial teacher education, that IB philosophy and pedagogy support best teaching practices, and that the school-university partnership is vital for the success of the TP. The key questions here are how to build networks to share knowledge and how pre-service teachers can leverage on the support they are given in their TP, in the framework of Kagan's professional growth model.

This paper argues that the key ingredients to a fruitful TP experience include the combined efforts of the course lecturers and TP supervisors at the university, the principals and mentor teachers of practicum schools, and perhaps most importantly, the student-teacher. The university researchers, lecturers and TP supervisors play the role of building up and maintaining a network of professional educators, experts in their field who are able, through events and conferences organised by the university, to share and exchange the knowledge distilled from years of practical experience on the training, learning and development of pre- and in-service teachers.

Schools play the role of facilitating the TP experience, not only by providing physical resources such as AV equipment and office space, but more importantly, by generating a welcome atmosphere that is conducive to the student-teacher's process of encounter, reflection, exploration and development. TP mentors, working with the student-teachers under the structure of partnership schools, offer invaluable professional support, encouragement and guidance.

Three Ws feature

In designing the MEd (TCSL) programme at HKU, the question that had to be addressed was: How do we structure our programme and university-school partnership? In seeking to approach the question from a number of angles, a three-pronged holistic method was designed and named the Three Ws Feature, involving the processes of Whole Preparation, Whole School Experience, and Whole Mentoring Support.

Whole Preparation

Whole Preparation refers to the structure of the programme, which seeks to educate student-teachers in the different theories and applicable methods of pedagogy, and also to integrate IB philosophy into Chinese language teaching. The programme consists of ten compulsory and elective modules: four core modules pertaining to pedagogy, curriculum, assessment, and TP; two modules on research methods; one IB-designated compulsory elective, 'Integrating IB Philosophy in Chinese language teaching'; and a dissertation (three modules) or a project (one module) with two additional elective modules of the student's choice.

The four core modules offered in 2014-2015 are Teaching Chinese in International Contexts, School-based Curriculum Design, Chinese (L2) Assessment and Reporting, and Research and Teaching Practice in the Second Language Classroom. The two modules on research methods consist of two parts, namely General Research Methods and Research Skill-based Workshops.

Teaching Chinese in International Contexts equips student-teachers with knowledge of the philosophies and latest developments in international education, especially that of the IB, but also comprehensively covering other international or foreign education programmes such as the International

General Certificate of Secondary Education (IGCSE), the General Certificate of Secondary Education (GCSE), the General Certificate of Education (GCE), AP (Advanced Placement), *etc.* In collaboration with the IB, students are granted access to the IB Online Curriculum Centre (OCC) upon commencement of the programme, providing them with the most up-to-date IB-approved teaching and learning resources.

Whole School Experience

To integrate the knowledge acquired at the University with real school teaching experience, students of the MEd in TCSL programme are required to complete a core module, Research and Teaching Practice in the Second Language Classroom, which involves two stages of TP: the School Attachment Scheme (SAS) and the Main Teaching Practice (MTP). Student-teachers are hand-matched and sent to an international school in partnership with the university, preferably one offering Chinese as a subject in the IB curriculum.

The first stage, the School Attachment Scheme, is a prelude to the main part of teaching practice. The School Attachment Scheme takes place during the second academic semester, usually between January and March, and lasts for approximately eight weeks. At this stage, student-teachers go to their assigned schools for a minimum of one day per week to participate in classroom observations and other school experience activities.

The aim of this scheme is to familiarise student-teachers with day-to-day teaching practice at international schools in Hong Kong, as well as to help them begin to develop their practicum portfolio. The specific format and duration of the scheme is subject to the arrangement and needs of each participant school.

During the school attachment period, student-teachers focus on acquiring an understanding of the students in the school, the school culture and the roles and responsibilities of teachers, picking up techniques related to teaching such as classroom management strategies, lesson and activity design, and teaching pedagogies. Student-teachers are required to keep a weekly reflection journal on their experience and perception of their observations there, including what they have learnt about the students, what they have learned about being a teacher in the school, and the pedagogical knowledge and skills they have picked up during the week.

The portfolio should contain an opening essay that is written before the student-teacher starts the teaching attachment experience, delineating the student-teacher's perception of language teaching and teacher identity. The portfolio also includes a weekly journal and a paper at the end of the semester reflecting on the change or non-change of perception about language teaching and teacher identity throughout the semester, along with the things the student-teacher has learnt through the teaching attachment experience.

The second stage, the Main Teaching Practice, is the principal part of the TP. It lasts for about six to seven weeks from March to April. At this stage, student-teachers are advised to do six hours of independent or semi-independent teaching each week on average, and to continue developing their practicum portfolio.

The aim of the Main Teaching Practice is to engage student-teachers in actual teaching at international schools in Hong Kong. The length and format of each individual lesson is flexible and may vary from school to school. Aside from that, student-teachers participate in the usual full-time staff activities of the school, such as team development activities, student counseling and staff meetings. Student-teachers are also encouraged to conduct a research project with permission from the school.

During the main TP period, student-teachers focus on refining their understanding of curriculum design and skills in planning and implementing effective lessons and activities. Student-teachers are required to engage in critical evaluation and reflection of their practicum teaching activities; and to develop a TP portfolio that consists of their critical evaluation of and reflection on three lessons during the TP.

The evaluations and reflections should contain an initial teaching unit plan with more than two lesson plans and rationale for the design; evidence of reflection on the actual implementation of the lessons (*eg* records of students' responses and reactions, videotaped lessons, notes on observations and reflections); and a revised teaching unit plan, lesson plans, and the rationale for the revision.

Whole Mentoring Support

During the TP, student-teachers are attached to mentor-teachers from their practicum school who, in partnership with TP supervisors from the University, fully supervise the student-teachers' TP through a variety of methods such as classroom observations and tripartite conferences involving mentor-teachers, student-teachers and university supervisors. Mentor-teachers perform different roles to support, nurture, guide and co-learn with the student-teachers. Mentor-teachers often take on more than one mentoring role (Kwan & Lopez-Real, 2005) during different stages of the TP.

The performance of the mentoring relationship is often related to the learning attitude and personality of the student-teacher, the mentoring experience of the mentor-teacher, practicum expectations and the organisational culture of the placement school. Mentor-teachers are encouraged to adjust their mentoring role according to the stages of the student-teachers' performance, so as to suit the learning curve of student-teachers (Maynard, 1996), and to shift their mentoring roles as they become more reflective in their own approach towards working with student-teachers and university-tutors (Pollard & Tann, 1993).

Such changes in the role of mentor-teachers often result in the easing off of a supervisory, hands-on role and the strengthening of a supportive and complementary role. The mentoring relationship moves away from a one-way process (mentor-teacher to student-teacher) to a two-way interactive process (mentor-teacher *and* student-teacher) to help relationship building, and leads to the professional development of both student-teachers and mentor-teachers.

To cultivate quality mentorship relationships, the University provides teacher training in school professional development events, and also provides consultations for school programme reviews. Each year, to build strong partnerships with the mentoring schools, the University of Hong Kong invites overseas experts of international education and International Baccalaureate curriculum to hold seminars, and invites IB school principals, school administrators and mentoring teachers to attend these seminars as a form of IB teacher professional development. In the past, these international experts have included Dr Mary Hayden, Professor Jeff Thompson and Dr Ian Hill. The HKU has also held cocktail receptions for these mentoring teachers and presented them with certificates of appreciation during these events.

Research question
How do students grow professionally out of the university-school partnership?

Methodology
To answer this, two cohorts of Chinese language pre-service teachers enrolled in the MEd for TCSL teacher training programme at HKU were interviewed on their professional development experience in the programme.

Participants
The participants were 53 Chinese language teachers enrolled in a one-year full-time Master of Education programme at the University of Hong Kong. They were all ethnic Chinese with mostly K-12 educational experience in Chinese-speaking areas. The majority of the participants were fresh graduates from Bachelor's degree programmes in Chinese language and literature or Teaching Chinese as a Foreign Language from different universities in Mainland China, Hong Kong, Singapore and Taiwan.

Data collection
Each participant teacher was interviewed three times – the first time prior to the school attachment phase; the second at the end of the school attachment phase; and the third at the end of the main teaching practice phase. These semi-structured interviews focused on the participants' perceptions of language teaching, their feelings about themselves as teachers, their stories of their educational experiences and their teaching practice experiences at the TP schools, their interaction with their mentors, perceived learning and changes emanating from their teaching practice experiences, and their self-efficacy in teaching. The interviews were conducted in the participants' native language and each interview lasted for around 40 minutes.

Data analysis
The interview recordings were transcribed verbatim and the transcriptions were imported into the qualitative data analysis software, Nvivo 8, which was used to facilitate the coding and analysis of the data. The interview transcriptions were read through first so that the authors of this paper got an overall impression of the cases, paying special attention to the changes in the participants' perceptions during each of the three data collection phases.

Field notes were taken during the first reading. Each transcription was then read again carefully for detailed coding, focusing on the participants' perceptions of teaching and of themselves as teachers. The transcriptions were read through reiteratively, and bits of data that struck the researchers as interesting or important to the study were coded. Similar codes were aggregated into analytic categories. The initial coding of analytic categories was compared across interviewees to search for repeating ideas to saturate categories with repeated supporting evidence and to cross validate the categories that emerged.

Findings

This section reports on the participants' professional growth as revealed by their interview responses at two stages of the TP experience: at the end of the school attachment phase and at the end of the main teaching practice phase.

Professional growth during the school attachment phase

The participants reported gaining a basic understanding of the teaching approaches and classroom management techniques from observing their mentors' classes. For instance, one participant commented:

> During class observations, I got a grasp of the characteristics of the students, the activities teachers utilize to motivate the students and the techniques teachers adopt to manage the classroom.

The participants also commented on gaining an understanding of the teacher-student relationship in the teaching context, which is critical to effective classroom management. One participant pointed out:

> I observed some classroom management techniques, *eg* how the teacher dealt with overactive students, how the teacher built relationships with the students and the kind of relationship the teacher maintained with the students.

The participants also reported observing a diversity of teaching approaches at the school and developing a more flexible mindset towards the pedagogies to be applied in future teaching practices:

> Each class is different and the teaching approaches the teachers adopted are different too. I got the idea that I could adopt different approaches in my teaching.

> I observed the differences between students of different ages and the differences within each class. Although we discussed class differences at university lectures, only then did I realise what the differences meant and how complex they were. Observing the classes of different language teachers led me to reflect upon the teaching approaches I could adopt when I teach Chinese... I aim to take in the different teaching approaches of these teachers and apply them in my teaching in future.

For most of the student-teachers, the international school context was unfamiliar to them. The unfamiliarity posed a level of uncertainty that could threaten their comfort level of teaching in such contexts. The participants reported that the school attachment phase enhanced their understanding of the context and hence increased their confidence in teaching in this unfamiliar environment:

> During class observation I got to know the school and the students, and also let the students get familiar with me. Without the understanding and familiarity, I would not be very confident.

> School attachment helped me and the students to reach an initial level of mutual understanding. When I finally got to teach them, they would be more receptive to me.

The participants also observed some pedagogical approaches discussed in their university classes being enacted by their school mentors, and such observations strengthened their belief in the value of the approaches and increased their confidence in implementing the pedagogies in their TP contexts:

> During this stage I saw the enactment of 'focus on meaning and then focus on form' in the classroom and started to believe firmly in it, which gave me the confidence to try it out during TP.

> My educational experience was very traditional, very teacher-centred and knowledge-driven. When I was in the international school, I found, although the teacher did do didactic teaching, they set aside most of the time for student discussions and debate. There was a lot of interaction with the students, which made me reflect on whether traditional Chinese teaching could adopt some of these approaches to make traditional Chinese teaching more meaningful and give students more room for self-expression.

Observing the characteristics and attributes of the students also made some participants rethink the nature of the pedagogical and interpersonal relationships with their students:

> I never expected Grade 8 students to be so full of ideas and to be so expressive. When I was their age, it was quite different. This made me feel that I, as a teacher, need to have a lot of fresh ideas and engage in conversations with them. By doing so, I may be able to gain their acceptance.

Furthermore, observing the educational approaches at their TP schools changed some participants' conceptualisation of the aims and foci of teaching:

> The students in the local schools focused a lot on exam results. I was like that when I was at school. But what I observed in the

international schools was that they focused not only on exams but also on personal development. I hope I could help foster the mindset highlighted by the IB among my students.

Thus, at the school attachment phase, the student-teachers gained a general understanding of the appropriate teaching approaches and classroom management techniques in the TP contexts that involve cross-cultural teaching. This general understanding enhanced their confidence in teaching in unfamiliar school contexts and reoriented them towards an internalisation of the educational aims of an IB education.

Professional growth during the main teaching practice phase

In the main teaching practice phase, student-teachers developed a more fine-grained understanding of teaching and focused on its nuances and complexities. One participant commented on how things that seemed very simple during class observations could turn out to be very complex and difficult to handle during TP: 'But when I began to teach, I found things were not that simple, and even the simplest design involved a lot of careful thinking about issues like how to group students and so on.' Another participant was surprised to find that even copying the mentor did not necessarily guarantee success due to the different interpersonal dynamics between her, as a student-teacher, and the student:

> I thought I could teach in the same way that my mentor had taught and things would go very smoothly. It turned out to be much more complex. Unlike me, my mentor had already established authority and could manage the students well.

Thus, participants started to realise that teaching demands a lot of attention to detail:

> When I actually started teaching, I found there were many details I needed to pay attention to. Designing activities is only the first step. I need to plan carefully what to do step by step to get through the activity. Things got tougher when it was my turn to teach.

The student teachers also started to pay greater attention to the coherence of the teaching activities and the connections between teaching sessions:

> I started to understand how to design and, more importantly, how to sequence activities step by step so that they can build on each other in a coherent way.

> It is important to have a clear understanding of the scheme of work for the whole semester. If not, the classes designed will be very incoherent. You will get lost on how the current lesson connects with the previous lessons.

Furthermore, they started to develop a more adaptive approach towards teaching pedagogies and started to find the principle for the selection and utilization of different teaching pedagogies to suit the students. As one participant put it:

> I feel every type of pedagogy could fit a certain context. In practice if I found one type of pedagogy does not work well, I can change to another.

> During the class observations, I observed different teaching pedagogies and how the teachers utilized different teaching pedagogies. At the TP stage, I started to think carefully about what teaching pedagogy would suit me and my students and whether the teaching pedagogy could facilitate the development of the intended skills and qualities among the students.

Thus, they no longer evaluated and selected teaching pedagogy for its own sake, but rather developed a situational view towards the appropriateness of the teaching pedagogies. For example, one participant pointed out that she used to fancy all kinds of creative ideas at the onset of the TP, but after the TP, with the help of the mentor, she got 'more practical and started to consider all the preconditions for the implementation of these ideas (availability of resources, the characteristics of the students, *etc*)'.

In addition to the advancement in their pedagogical understanding, they also felt that the TP boosted their confidence and interest in teaching in international schools, which had a school culture that was different from the one they were used to.

One participant commented that prior to the school experience, she 'was afraid of not being able to interact well with the students and not being able to gain their respect'. But after she started the TP, she realised that the students 'would treat [her] sincerely when [she] treated them with care'. This realisation made her change her perceptions about the school culture of international schools and made her more 'confident in becoming a teacher in international schools'. Another participant found that teaching in international schools gave her a greater sense of accomplishment:

> I feel that their focus on developing students' values and traits and guiding student's personal development was really different from what I experienced in Mainland China. That gave me a sense of accomplishment as a teacher.

They also started to develop a broadened view towards what it means to be a teacher. They came to the realisation that an effective teacher is not just a pedagogical expert but also a well-rounded person who knows how to deal with interpersonal relationships with people around them:

> A teacher is not just a class instructor. He/she needs to know how to handle relationships with parents, with other colleagues and with students.

Furthermore, they realised that an effective teacher is not just a teacher worker who could keep everything well organised and in good order, but rather an educator who aimed at making an impact on students' future lives:

> I used to think that a good teacher is the one who gets students to like him/her and to cooperate in his/her class. Now I feel that a good teacher needs to have a long-term plan and focus on developing among the students the things they can use their whole life.

Based on these responses, a trajectory of student-teacher professional growth can be traced, progressing from an idealised and oversimplified view of teaching to a more nuanced and sophisticated view of teaching for life-long learning, and from an abstract understanding of the pedagogies to a more context-specific and student-centred understanding of them, over the course of the two phases of the TP.

Moreover, closer interactions with the students during the TP had enhanced the student-teachers' enthusiasm for teaching in international school contexts and helped them develop a more sophisticated understanding of what effective teaching meant. To gain a better understanding of the complex interplay of the different factors that lead to professional growth via TP experiences, this study will now examine the views of three student-teachers describing their unique TP experiences.

Case study - Student A: an active participant

During school attachment, Student A went to his mentor's school whenever he could. Keen to familiarise himself with his mentor and students (and *vice versa*), he visited the school for up to five days a week (the minimum requirement is one day per week) in hope of building mutual trust and acquiring more teaching opportunities through active engagement in various school activities.

> I (visited the school) five days a week... I wished to show my mentor the sort of person I was as soon as possible, and then get to know the students, in hopes of gaining more opportunities to teach.

> The school actually welcomed my participation in any of its activities... You just have to hustle, you have to be proactive ... she (the mentor) isn't going to spoon-feed you. You can show up, or not show up. She says it doesn't matter, but if you've shown up you should strive to listen and learn.

Staff and students of the school were very friendly towards Student A, which provided him with a sense of belonging. The democratic school culture allowed Student A to conduct lesson observations in all subjects whenever he wished, and his mentor even offered to share her office space with him. Other teachers were equally friendly and helpful, and the participatory environment motivated him to be more active.

My mentor told me, you're not just here to audit classes – you have to immerse yourself in the school's activities... If I'm busy, if I don't have time to take care of your needs, approach teachers directly in a polite manner – tell them that you find their classes interesting and ask if you could sit in, and they'll let you. You don't have to restrict yourself to Chinese classes – you could audit Theory of Knowledge (TOK) classes, because some of the teachers are incredibly good at what they do ... you could listen to them teach English ... a whole range of different subjects ... so I don't have to hold your hand.

My mentor was very supportive, telling me that I could tell him if I encountered any difficulties, and she would talk it through with me... She also said, you have to take the initiative in doing things. Now that you've come to this school, you have to take the initiative ... because I'm very busy, and I can't cater to every single one of your needs. If you're here you would have to interact with other people on your own.

She also managed to maintain a good relationship with his mentor. Student A said her mentor was like a friend to him, who offered him many tips on being a nice mentee, such as being polite to the teachers, learning from the principal and other teachers, actively reaching out for help.

Student A appreciated her advice and exposure to the real workplace, and soon he was able to integrate into the school environment. He reported gaining many opportunities to learn through both formal and informal communication at his mentor's school. He was invited to sit in on staff meetings, and the conversations taking place during lunchtime were inspiring.

A mentor-mentee relationship is like a friendship ... everything progresses through mutual communication and discussion.

They have a practice of having everyone (teachers) gather around the table at lunch and interacting with one another ... once they start chatting, it could go on for as long as an hour. At first, I only listened because I didn't have a common topic, but as I grew familiar with their conversations, I found myself chatting with them about my situation or learning about wider developments at the school. If you see expatriate teachers gathered together, don't feel self-conscious or shy – start by joining their group and listening in. Eventually, they'll ask for your opinion from time to time, and you'll slowly become part of their group. I also got to hone my English speaking skills.

Many opportunities actually arise during lunch hour. You might be chatting with someone, and he might say that a class is going out for community service in the afternoon, and invite you to join them. I've joined in quite a few times.

While spending a lot of time outside the classroom during his visits, Student A was involved in teaching-related tasks by his mentor as part of his school attachment. His mentor required him to recite the teaching plans and revise them with his own ideas before setting specific teaching objectives for each stage. As a student-teacher or mentee, Student A was also asked to design a unit of teaching on his own:

> She would entrust me with the work for an entire unit of teaching –
> that consisted of the designing and planning for three periods worth
> of lessons. She would say that she was handing over the entire tract of
> time to me, so that was relatively systematic. She wouldn't tell me to
> sandwich a period of teaching between two periods of her teaching –
> perhaps she felt she could trust me!

> It might be because I've observed many lessons in progress, but what
> I now do is look at the teacher's lesson plan after observing each
> lesson, and then duplicate it. My mentor also said I had to create a
> teaching aim, for example, to establish the goals I wished to achieve
> at every stage of teaching – relatively specific, concrete goals.

The knowledge transfer from demonstration of assignment grading and passing on of teaching techniques led Student A to believe that he had been successful in building a trustful relationship with his mentor, alongside the opportunity given to teach complete units in both Language A and Language B at the school:

> She doesn't just encourage you to listen and watch more – she even
> tells you the little techniques and strategies she uses in teaching.
> She coaches the students on the examinable content for their final
> exams, the Individual Oral Presentation and the Individual Oral
> Commentary. The guidebook our university teachers gave us only
> delineated some very general standards for marking, with alphabetical
> classifiers, but how one is to go about assessing the performance of
> outliers – one learns this in the classroom. By listening and observing
> more, one would eventually be able to gauge what it takes for a
> student to achieve full marks.

Formal teaching started with submission of a teaching plan for a complete unit before actual facilitation in class, while the mentor stayed to observe Student A's teaching throughout the process. Post-teaching self-reflections and discussions were also facilitated with coordination from the mentor. The respectful attitude of both the mentor and his students was reassuring, and in a way boosted Student A's confidence and expectations of himself. Toward the end of the school attachment, Student A attained Stage 3 of professional growth (A Shift in Attention), *ie* teacher's attention is shifted from self to the students while concentrating on what the students are learning (see Figure I later in this chapter).

Case study - Student B: a discouraged mentee

Student B also went to her mentor's school whenever she could, but at less frequent intervals. Her visits were meant to familiarise her with her mentor and students (and *vice versa*), to understand the role and duties of a teacher, and to learn more about teaching (*eg* lesson planning, classroom management skills, discussions after lesson observation).

'I guess I wish I could properly immerse myself in their classroom!'

While Student A and Student B both appeared to have had mentors who had busy work days, the students perceived and reacted to this in different ways. Student A seemed to have taken this in stride, demonstrating a mature understanding that the onus of responsibility for her own learning and development fell on herself as the engaged, proactive mentee in the professional mentoring relationship.

Student B, on the other hand, seemed to have put a negative spin on things, claiming that her mentor was 'crazily busy'. She complained that she had been asked to do what she felt were menial tasks for her mentor, such as photocopying, supervising students in completing their assignments, and decorating classrooms. Her dissatisfaction suggests that she approached TP with a sense of entitlement, along with unrealistic preconceived notions of the role of a trainee teacher.

Her attitude towards TP appears to have clouded and limited her outlook, and this is made apparent when her reactions towards her tasks are compared with that of Student C, another student-teacher who took on similar tasks during TP, and whose experiences will be discussed in detail in the next case study. By contrast, Student C displayed an ability to appreciate the place and value of even the most prosaic of tasks in a school, citing her experience of decorating a Chinese subject notice board as having shown her how teachers and schools could create and use different modes and methods to facilitate and foster learning.

Student B was disappointed with the fact that she had few opportunities to observe a complete lesson, as she had been asked from time to time to do clerical work during her observation. She also complained about not having the opportunity to observe her mentor's class preparation for a complete unit.

Moreover, she claimed that she was given no opportunity to discuss anything related to the classes or teaching in general with her mentor. However, Student B did not mention having made any attempt on her part to remedy or improve what she felt so strongly was an unfavourable situation, and in the absence of remedial efforts on her part, had put herself in the position of a passive and unreflective learner who was not quite ready for active inquiry and critical thinking in the process of experiential learning. Student B lamented:

There are many things happening every day; everyone is crazily busy. The mentor just gives me loads of work every day... she'd say, "Quick, help me get this or that printed", "Quick, go and finish up the classroom decorations", or if the students have yet to complete their assignments, she'd say "Help me watch the students complete their assignments while you have lunch" and so on. I feel like I've taken up the work of a Teaching Assistant, a gofer, and a personal counsellor for students... I feel that I had to do a lot of work that required little input of professional skills or know-how.

Even midway through observing a lesson, the teacher would still ask you to help with something else. For example, I was listening intently to a 7th grade class when the teacher told me that preparations for a class in the afternoon had not been completed and that I should help him to type it up. It turned out that there was a lot to type up, so I was away from the classroom for almost half an hour... So I feel that I had to do a lot of work that had nothing to do with observing or auditing lessons... I seldom got a chance to sit through an entire lesson without interruption.

She described that she was like an assistant to her mentor, and suspected that the mentor was taking it for granted.

It's like a master-apprentice relationship, that is, the apprentice has to help the master with whatever he is tasked with, no matter how important or trivial the task!

While spending an enormous amount of time doing hands-on administrative tasks for her mentor, Student B also felt neglected during her school attachment.

I only got to work on the very trivial matters, such as picking out the students' misspelled words when grading their assignments and writing the correct words on the side, *etc.* I did not get to witness the process of his teaching preparations, and did not get to engage in post-lesson evaluations and discussions with her.

Student B felt that her mentor adopted a very traditional and authoritative teaching style that aimed at familiarising the students with IB assessment rubrics.

She is a very traditional teacher – if you don't spot the foreign students amidst the students, or if you don't know that you're in an international school, you would feel as though you were in a local classroom or in a classroom we used to be in back in the Mainland. Many of her lessons have little classroom interaction or activities. For example, if she's teaching Grade 4, she would only tell the students to open their books and read aloud after her.

She is very strict with the students – she doesn't permit noise or disruptions in her classroom, and uses very traditional methods to discipline her students.

Again, Student B found herself in a position similar to a teaching or clerical assistant rather than a mentee or student teacher:

> I felt like her personal assistant. I now know how to fix a printer, print on card paper and everything ... but as for teaching, I have not had the chance to engage in in-depth discussion.

Student B experienced a series of challenges during her formal teaching too. Before teaching, she had difficulty finding a time to discuss her teaching plan with her mentor. She claimed that when she was finally given an opportunity to teach a lesson, her mentor interrupted her during observation and took up the teaching role while managing student discipline. She found it particularly harsh when she was made to follow her mentor's preferred practice of copying words on the blackboard – her mentor did not like her initial teaching design of using word cards.

She found it hard to say 'no' in multiple contexts as she was only a mentee there, and she agonised over not being respected by both her mentor and the students. The knowledge transfer was kept minimal, and she regretted that there was insufficient mentor-mentee communication.

Comparing her feedback with those of Student A and Student C, it can be inferred that it is important for a student-teacher to adjust his/her frame of mind before participating in TP, so as to approach the experience with an open mind, creating space for the exploration and generation of fresh insights when given the opportunity to test the waters of the day-to-day life of a teacher and educator.

This enables one to experience the real-world's resolute defiance of the idealised neatness and reductive apple-pie order that exists only in the textbook classroom. Toward the end of the school attachment, Student B barely reached Stage 1 of professional growth (An Increase of Metacognition), *ie* coming up with idealised views of students and an oversimplified picture of classroom practice, while being obsessed with designing instruction to discourage disruptive behaviour instead of promoting students' learning (see Figure I).

Case study - Student C: a proactive learner

Student C, also an active participant like Student A, took every opportunity to be integrated into her mentor's school. Her approach was taking the initiative to offer her help to others, and this included helping her mentor with daily teaching routines (preparing teaching materials, photocopying, marking students' assignments, decorating the classrooms, and arranging tables and books before lessons) and getting involved in the preparation of the school's events and activities (Chinese speech training, Fashion Week *etc*).

> We helped the teachers with assignment marking, went to meetings with the teachers, and participated in school-wide events. We also helped them decorate the Chinese subject notice board – such activities taught me about the different modes and methods, apart from teaching, in which a school facilitates their students' learning.

> We also attended parent-teacher meetings in order to learn more
> about the interactions among teachers, students and parents – I feel
> that this is very important.

As well as being proactive in offering a helping hand, she also took up an
observer's approach for learning. She firmly believed school is a place that
helped her to integrate theory into practice:

> I think (TP) is a process of integrating theory and practice. What
> we learn in the university is theoretical. We learn pedagogies and
> IB theory and framework there. But in school, you can observe how
> these pedagogies and IB philosophy are put into real practice, and
> you can reflect upon it.

She reported that she would observe how the mentor conducted her
lessons, managed the classes, dealt with students' discipline problems and
enhanced students' motivation. She would also observe the students at the
same time, and see how they responded to her mentor and interacted with
their fellow counterparts.

Notes were taken regarding outstanding teaching techniques and other
interesting things from her observations, before she sought, in a humble
manner, to make an appointment with her mentor for a discussion on
the classes. On top of observing her mentor's classes, she felt that it was
important to observe and learn from teachers of different levels and subjects.

> I observed the lessons of all the teachers in the Chinese department,
> as well as that of every grade from Grade 7 to Grade 11. I also
> observed two periods of Spanish, two periods of French, one period
> of music, one period of physical education, and basically I learnt
> more about the different subjects, the relationships between teachers
> and students, as well as that amongst the students themselves. I only
> visited the school once a week, so it was a long process of gradual
> assimilation – you begin to know what the school is like, and then you
> slowly work yourself into the organisation.

As for the formal teaching sessions, Student C reported that she would
make sure she was fully prepared before entering the classroom. Before
teaching, she memorised students' names and learnt about their abilities
through class observation and assignment marking. She also did her best
to send her lesson plan to her mentor well ahead, which was around two
weeks in advance.

After teaching, she reflected first on her merits and shortcomings, and
then sought to discuss the lesson with her mentor while patiently taking
her advice for improvement of teaching skills. To show one's capabilities to
handle a complete unit on her own, she also claimed that the most important
factors were sufficient communication with the mentor, and preparing the
lesson plan and teaching materials in advance.

Towards the end of the school attachment, Student C attained the highest level of professional growth among the three. She reached Stage 4 (The Development of Standard Procedure), *ie* developing standardised routines that integrate instruction and management (see Figure I).

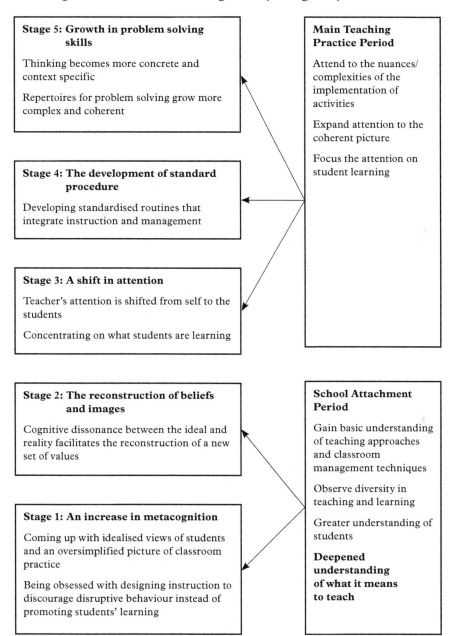

Figure I – Stages of Professional Growth (Kagan, 1992).

Conclusion

In this study, we examined a group of pre-service IB Chinese language teachers' professional development trajectories during their TP at IB schools. We found that this group of teachers demonstrated a progression from a general understanding of their cross-cultural teaching contexts and the diversity of teaching practices at these sites to a more sophisticated, fine-tuned understanding of the complexities of teaching and an increasing tendency towards placing students at the centre of curriculum and pedagogical decision-making. The two phases of the TP afforded different professional development opportunities.

The school attachment phase, with its primary focus on observing current classroom practices and getting familiar with school cultures, served as a bridge that connected these pre-service Chinese teachers to the teaching contexts that were predominated by Anglo-European cultures with ideological and social normative practices that were different from the ones they were used to. It further provides students with opportunities to observe the pedagogical and interpersonal discursive practices in these teaching contexts.

This prolonged period of time observing classes from a third person point of view helped them see the big picture and not become immersed in the details of teaching right from the beginning. This is particularly important in teacher induction in cross-cultural teaching contexts. The observation of different techniques used by their mentors and other teachers to assert professional and social authority also helped to enrich and reshape the repertoire of practices they could utilize to function in the unfamiliar cross-cultural teaching settings. Thus, this class observation phase of the school TP was critical to smoothing the pre-service teachers' transition to the cross-cultural teaching contexts.

The main teaching practice phase, with its primary focus on engaging them in experiential learning and 'reflection in practice', affords these pre-service teachers the opportunities to experiment with the repertoire of diverse practices they picked up from their university courses and from the mentor teachers at the TP sites, and to develop a critical understanding of teaching and learning from such experimentation as a 'reflective practitioner' (Schön 1982, 1987). Hence, the cascading design of TP experience with a prolonged learning by observation phase preceding the learning by doing phase is essential to the development of IB pre-service Chinese language teachers who would be confronted with cross-cultural teaching situations upon entering the profession.

Furthermore, the different functions of the two phases of the TP demand different types of support from the university teachers. In the school attachment phase, the pre-service teachers need to be guided on what to be focused on during the observation, and this guidance needs to reflect the various dimensions of ideological and social normative differences between Chinese cultures and Anglo-European cultures.

Moreover, the pre-service teachers need to be directed to pay attention to the various practices and techniques both Chinese and Western mentor teachers are utilizing to address issues arising from these ideological and normative differences. Some mechanisms are needed to help pool together the pre-service teachers' focused observation during this phase so that they can have a rich repertoire of practices and techniques that they could draw upon to address the various issues in cross-cultural teaching.

In the main teaching practice phase, communication mechanisms need to be provided to enable these pre-service teachers to offer emotional, pedagogical and social support and consultation to each other. Furthermore, they need to be guided to actively reflect on their teaching practices and entertain alternative practices so as to develop a more critical and reflective approach to teaching.

This study also found that these pre-service teachers' professional development varied depending on their TP contexts and their own agency. On the one hand, the mentoring structure at the school and individual mentors' styles directly determined the nature and amount of learning that these pre-service teachers could possibly obtain at the TP sites.

On the other hand, the mentoring quality is not a fixed thing but rather a result of pre-service teachers exercising personal agency in making the most out of each encounter, experience, situation and relationship. Pre-service teachers can only benefit from facilitative and enabling environments if they exercise individual agency in their interactions with their practicum school and mentor, proactively making the best of every situation and environment. How these pre-service teachers position themselves in their interactions with the TP sites and their mentors largely shapes the quality of the mentoring they could receive during a TP.

Thus, to enhance the quality of the TP experience, university teacher training programmes should not only work with TP schools to build mechanisms that support mutual professional growth, in both the pre-service teachers and also the mentoring teachers, but also help their pre-service teachers to exercise a sense of agency in creating a favourable TP environment and supporting them in making the most out of their TP experience.

References

Behets, D. and Vergauwen, L. (2006). Learning to Teacher in the Field. In D. Kirk, D. MacDonald and M. O'Sullivan (eds). *The Handbook of Physical Education*. London: Sage.

Brouwer, N. and Korthagen, F. (2005). Can Teacher Education Make a Difference? *American Educational Research Journal* 42(1): 153-224.

Chambers, F. and Armour, K. (2012). School-university Partnerships and Physical Education Teacher Education Student Learning: A Fruitful Division of Labour? *European Physical Education Review* 18(2): 159-181.

Coolahan, J. (2003). *Attracting, Developing and Retaining Effective Teachers: Country Background For Ireland*. Dublin: Department of Education & Science and the Organisation For Economic Cooperation and Development (OECD).

Cozza, B. (2010). Transforming Teaching Into a Collaborative Culture: An Attempt to Create a Professional Development School-Univeristy Partnership. *The Educational Forum* 74(3): 227-241.

Darling-Hammond, L. (2006). *Powerful Teacher Education: Lessons from Exemplary Programmes*. San Francisco: Jossey-Bass.

Edwards, A. and Mutton, T. (2007). Looking Forward: Rethinking Professional Learning through Partnership arrangements in Initial Teacher Education. *Oxford Review of Education* 33(4): 503-519.

Gram, N. and Karlsen, G. E. (2004). Teacher Education Reform in Europe: The Case of Norway; Trends and Tensions in a Global Perspective. *Teaching and Teacher Education* 20(7): 731-744.

Hodkinson, H. and Hodkinson, P. (1999). Teaching to learn, learning to teach? School-based non teaching activity in an initial teacher education and training partnership scheme. *Teaching and Teacher Education*(15): 273-285.

Kagan, D. M. (1992). Professional Growth among Preservice and Beginning Teachers. *Review of Educational Research Association* 62(2): 129-169.

Kwan, T. and Lopez-Real, F. (2005). Mentors' perceptions of their roles in mentoring student-teachers. *Asia-Pacific Journal of Teacher Education* 33(3): 275-287.

Lewin, K. M. (2004). The Pre-Service Training of teachers: Does it meet it's objectives and how can it be improved? *2005 Education for All Global Monitoring Report: The Quality Imperative*. Paris: UNESCO.

Maynard, T. (1996). The limits of mentoring: The contribution of the higher education tutor to primary student teachers' school-based learning. In J. Furlong & R. Smith (eds.), *The role of higher education in initial teacher training*. London: Kogan Page: 101-118.

McCullick, B. (2001). Practitioners Perspectives on Values, Knowledge and Skills needed by PETE participants. *Journal of Teaching in Physical Education* 21(1): 35-56.

Neville, K. S.,Sherman, R. H., *et al*. (2005). Preparing and Training Professionals: Comparing Education to Six Other Fields. *The Finance Project*. Retrieved on 4th March, 2015, from http://www.financeproject.org/Publications/preparingprofessionals.pdf.

Pollard, A. & Tann, C. (1993). *Reflective teaching in the primary school: A handbook for the classroom*. London: Cassell.

Schön, D. A. (1982). *The reflective practitioner*. New York: Basic Books.

Schön, D. A. (1987). *Educating the reflective practitioner*. San Francisco: Jossey-Bass.

Shum, M. S. K. & Law, D. Y. K. (1998). Reflections of Professional Growth of Chinese Language Student-teachers in a School-University Partnership Scheme in Teacher Education. *Curriculum Forum* (May): 45-59.

Sutherland, L. M., Scanlon, L.A., *et al*. (2005). New Directions in Preparing Professionals: Examining Issues in Engaging Students in Communities of Practice Through a School-university Partnership. *Teaching and Teacher Education* 21: 79-92.

Chapter 4

Experiential Chinese: authentic immersion and interactive language learning

Malcolm Pritchard

Abstract

Language learning forms an essential part of the IB's core educational strategy to promote understanding across cultural groupings and enhance international mindedness. Contemporary language acquisition theories, however, emphasise the educational benefit of authentic input and social interaction, features that are difficult to replicate in the controlled classroom settings found in most IB schools.

Classrooms typically lack the realism, memorability, and linguistic richness of learning settings in the 'real world' beyond schools, which may undermine the effectiveness of school-based language learning as a means of achieving intercultural communication and understanding.

For our first language(s) (L1), the experiential mode of learning through immersion in authentic settings, rich with social interaction, is universal across all cultures. Language acquired experientially is ultimately captured in durable, multi-sensory and context-dependent long-term memory known as episodic memory.

For second language learners (L2), acquisition of language experientially in authentic settings outside of the classroom similarly benefits from strong retention, recall and communicative competency reinforced by rich linguistic contextual cues and cultural 'scaffolding'.

Set in a Vygotskian-Deweyan framework of learning experientially through social interaction in unique and memorable settings, and drawing on Krashen's 'comprehensible input' hypothesis for language acquisition, this chapter explores the theory, design, and practice of experiential language learning, with particular reference to learning Chinese. It proposes that language acquisition activities set in authentic, language-rich settings, where learners engage in direct, personally purposeful interaction with L1 speakers, are more effective in developing culturally and linguistically competent L2 communicators in the target language.

Part 1: Language and learning: an overview

1. Language learning in the IB world

In classrooms across the world, learners studying in International Baccalaureate (IB) programmes experience the challenges and rewards of acquiring multiple languages as an obligatory part of their curriculum. A key section of the IB's Language Policy states:

> The International Baccalaureate (IB) is committed to supporting multilingualism as a fundamental part of increasing intercultural understanding and international-mindedness...
>
> (International Baccalaureate, 2014)

Language learning forms an essential part of the IB's strategy to promote understanding across cultural and linguistic groupings and enhance *international mindedness.*

Overwhelmingly, the setting for courses of study in languages in IB World Schools, whether as first (L1) or second (L2) language learners, is the school classroom. However, the learning environments and pedagogical approaches adopted in schools aimed at the acquisition of a second language typically lack the realism, memorability, and effectiveness of more experiential settings beyond the classroom (Krashen, 2009).

For L2 Chinese language learners, who lack the linguistic and cultural reinforcement of home and community, there are additional, unique challenges. The acquisition of even basic literacy in the unique logographic/ ideographic Chinese script, for example, requires memorising several thousand unique characters, a task that draws heavily on memory function and learner commitment for success.

In classroom settings largely bereft of rich linguistic contextual cues and cultural 'scaffolding' to support and reinforce language acquisition, the task of mastering written Chinese for communicative competency is challenging indeed.

L2 experiential language study undertaken in culturally authentic settings allows learners to use the target language as a communicative tool to solve problems and meet personal needs while interacting with a wide range of native or competent speakers of the target language. Language acquired experientially through social interaction in novel settings is retained and consolidated through rich, multi-sensory and context-dependent memories, captured and recalled through episodic memory – the enduring and autonoetic aspect of long-term memory. Language acquired experientially benefits from a robust, context-reinforced scaffold of memorised perceptual cues derived from the cultural and physical setting in which the language was learned.

Set in a Vygotskian-Deweyan framework of learning experientially through social interaction in unique and highly memorable settings, and drawing on elements of Krashen's 'comprehensible input' hypothesis for language acquisition, this chapter explores the theory, design, and practice of experiential Chinese language learning.

An important distinction is drawn at this point between *knowing about* a language as the focus of study, and *language acquisition,* which refers to the learned capacity to use a language as a medium of communication (Halliday, 2004 [1980]; Romeo, 2000). This chapter focuses primarily on the application of experiential learning approaches to the acquisition of language for communicative purposes by L2 learners of Chinese.

2. Key concepts of learning

Research into the ways in which humans learn language has undergone many paradigm shifts in the past 100 years or so. Indeed, the most complete model of learning increasingly incorporates findings from other disciplines, including genetics, psychology, neuroscience, and cultural psychology. Current evidence still supports the contention that, in contrast to the imitative systems of communication observed in other animal species, only humans seek to *understand* the world as they experience it (Vonk & Povinelli, 2012).

The way in which we construct understanding of our world is shaped by the unique characteristics of the languages we use to describe our experiences (Halliday, 1993). It is through language that the connection is made between human experience and the corresponding knowledge that is constructed:

> Language is the essential condition of knowing, the process by which experience becomes knowledge.
>
> (Halliday, 1993, p.94)

Based on our experience of the world, we utilise the artifact of language in a systematic and sustained way to create knowledge and make meaning about the world (Bruner, 1997, pp.63-71; Cole & Hatano, 2007, pp.113-115; Jonassen, 2009, pp.13-25; Richardson, 2000, pp.1-4, 122-123). Thus, language learning is the critical step in the development of the learner as a social being. In every sense, language shapes the way we think and interact with others (Wells, 1999, p.101).

Learning theory and, by extension, theories of language learning or *language acquisition*, can be divided into two categories: learning from without, otherwise known as the *transmission* model of learning; and learning from within, known as the *constructivist* model of learning (Dewey, 1997 [1938], p.17; R. Mayer, 2005). Historically, transmission of content through teacher-centered instruction has been the principal pedagogy of formal programs of learning. In the latter half of the 20th century, *constructivism* became the dominant paradigm in Western educational philosophy (R. Mayer, 2004, p.14).

Constructivism, described briefly below, forms the theoretical foundation of the approaches to language learning discussed in this chapter. It is also a fundamental plank of the pedagogy adopted in all IB programmes.

In learning theory, constructivism places the learner as an active participant in *constructing* his/her own *viable* version of the external 'real' world experientially, as perceived through successful interaction with the immediate environment, society and knowledge artifacts (Tobin & Tippins, 1993, p.3; von Glasersfeld, 1995, pp.7-8). The learner does not *acquire* knowledge and experiences in the external world; they are perceived and cognitively reconstructed through what Bruner describes as a *logical calculus*

(Bruner, 1997, p.66). Because each person's specific set of experiences and encounters is unique, each person's logical calculus will also be unique.

Learning is initiated when the learner encounters something unexpected or novel that does not accord with previous experience: this is in fact the driving force of all learning – the 'question' or 'problem'. Learners construct knowledge in response to gaps in their understanding, in their experience:

> Before all else, we have to be able to pose problems ... problems do not pose themselves... All knowledge is an answer to a question. If there has been no question, there can be no scientific knowledge. Nothing is self-evident. Nothing is given. Everything is constructed.
>
> (Bachelard, 2002 [1938])

As social beings, human learning requires some form of interaction with others, either directly through social interaction, or indirectly through semiotic mediation (Tharp & Gallimore, 1988, p.19). Vygotsky asserts that learning takes place on two levels or planes: first, on the social plane, and only then, on the individual plane (Amin & Valsiner, 2004, p.87; Vygotsky, 1978, p.57). The social nature of human activity is adopted here as a fundamental point of departure for explaining the process of acquiring knowledge and language. Thus, Vygotsky states, 'Through others, we become ourselves.' (1987, p.105)

Language acquisition, whether first or subsequent, therefore, is an inherently social undertaking, where individual members of a community are part of an on-going network of social interactions, or *conversations* (Ernest, 1995, p.480). The role of language at an intrapersonal level is central to constructivism, as language provides the very building blocks, the means, by which inner speech is structured (Daniels, 1996, p.10). Learning takes place through the medium of language, which results in *deep transformations* as learners are connected to the social and cultural environment into which they were born (Vygotsky & Luria, 1993 [1930], p.171).

2.1. Learning languages in IB Schools

Drawing on the leading educational theorists of our time, such as Vygotsky(1978, 1986 [1934]), Bruner (1997), Cummins (2008), Corson (1999), and Halliday (1993), the IB places language at the centre of all education (International Baccalaureate Organisation, 2008b). Its impact extends well beyond mastery of a particular language:

> (L)anguage is a strong enculturating force... Language shapes our thinking... Language plays a vital role in the construction of meaning and provides an intellectual framework to support conceptual development ... the role of language is valued as central to developing critical thinking, which is essential for the cultivation of intercultural awareness, international-mindedness and global citizenship.
>
> (International Baccalaureate, 2011)

IB language learning, undertaken through interaction with rich and varied linguistic genres, leads to cognitive, affective, academic and social benefits (International Baccalaureate Organisation, 2008b). In practice, language learning ideally is learner-centred and inquiry-based, drawing on prior understanding, it scaffolds knowledge creation and meaning making, and affirms individual identity (Cummins, J. Cited in International Baccalaureate Organisation, 2008b).

In its broadest sense, IB language learning philosophy is informed by Halliday's notion of learning language, learning through language, and learning about language (Halliday, 2004 [1980]; International Baccalaureate, 2011). Two key concepts that further refine the IB's espoused principles and practice of language learning as a learning continuum from basic acquisition to high-level academic competency are Cummins' Basic Interpersonal Communicative Skills (BICS) and Cognitive Academic Language Proficiency (CALP) (2008).

On this foundation rests one of the IB's core programme requirements, *additive bilingualism*, which promotes the parallel and mutually supportive development of proficiency in both mother tongue and an additional language. This ideal of additive bilingualism (or multilingualism) also affirms the IB's fundamental statement of educational values, the Learner Profile, particularly the attributes of balanced, communicators, knowledgeable, and open-minded (International Baccalaureate Organisation, 2008a).

2.2. Acquisition of language: Krashen and comprehensible input

In considering how learners actually go about acquiring a language, theories abound. The discipline has been shaped by many insightful and influential thinkers, such as Chomsky, Pinker, MacWhinney, and Krashen, who have revolutionised the way in which we think about language acquisition (Chomsky, 1965, 1986; Krashen, 1994, 2009; MacWhinney, 2004; Pinker, 1994, 2004).

A detailed overview of the theories of language acquisition, however, lies beyond the scope of this chapter. Krashen's 'comprehensible input' (CI) hypothesis, which describes the nature of the language environment that is most conducive to effective language acquisition, is directly salient to this discussion of the experiential approach to the learning of Chinese language and is described briefly below (Krashen, 2009).

Krashen's CI hypothesis, while not universally accepted, is powerful in its description: '(it) captures features of the second language acquisition process that teachers intuitively recognize as important (Johnson, 1995).' The notion of CI focuses on the nature of the language materials accessed, their content, context, and complexity, as a vital part of language acquisition. The CI hypothesis states:

> ...if input is made comprehensible to the learner, either through the context within which it is used, or as a result of simplified input, acquisition will follow.
>
> (Johnson, 1995)

The CI hypothesis suggests that language learning is achieved by exposure to comprehensible input that is slightly beyond the current level of language competency of the learner, a feature based on Vygotsky's notion of the Zone of Proximal Development (Vygotsky, 1978).

A further hypothesis advanced by Krashen, the Affective Filter (AF) hypothesis suggests that attitudinal variables have a direct impact on the rate and level of language acquisition. Motivation, self-image, social need, and the integration imperative – wanting to be 'like' the speakers of another language – are all seen as strong motivating factors for language learners (Romeo, 2000). The AF hypothesis is particularly germane to language acquisition involving immersion in culturally and linguistically authentic learning contexts.

Krashen confirms that the real advantage of the informal environment is that it supplies authentic comprehensible input in great quantity (2009). The main disadvantage of the outside world as a learning environment, according to Krashen, is its inability to provide controlled comprehensible input for the L2 learner at a lower level of competency. The adult world is complicated and the range of vocabulary and topics is hard to understand for L2 learners (Krashen, 2009, p.59). The classroom, however, is quite limited in what it can provide by way of range and variety of discourse.

2.3. Challenges in school-based language learning

While constructivism is the current dominant theoretical paradigm in educational philosophy, critics suggest that much of what is done in schools does not reflect the demand for knowledge and skills in the world beyond school. Some assert that institutional education largely reflects the oversimplified thinking of behaviorism, which is largely concerned with cause and effect and, particularly, observable results through testing and reproduction of content (von Glasersfeld, 1995, pp.4-5).

The *transmission* mode of education is claimed by some to dominate pedagogical practice (Mok, 2003, p.2; Parkinson, 2003, pp.230, 236; Perkinson, 1984, p.165). Others suggest that much of the current debate on education has not moved much beyond previous attempts at reform, such as Dewey's failed Progressive Education Movement from the early 20th century (Dewey, 1909; Garrison, 2003).

Schools tend to emphasize the more *visible* achievements of individuals, focusing on competencies and functions that are easily measured and often disconnected from the learner's own experience of reality and the processes of personally relevant knowledge construction (Daniels, 2001; Scardamalia & Bereiter, 1994, p.268).

Such metrics allow for a more accessible form of accountability than might be afforded by an approach to learning that stresses implicit 'life-long' outcomes. Others criticise the alleged impracticality of constructivism directly for its failure to impose rigour and pedagogically structured approaches to education needed in institutions (Kirschner, Sweller, & Clark, 2006; Osborne, 1996).

For language learning, this often means that learners are participants in teacher-centered programs of content-driven semantic learning, disconnected from the real world, and producing *inert* knowledge (Wells, 1999). Collins *et al* also express concern over the nature of school-based education:

> Conceptual and problem-solving knowledge acquired in school remains largely unintegrated or inert for many students... Although schools have been relatively successful in organizing and conveying large bodies of conceptual and factual knowledge, standard pedagogical practices render key aspects of expertise invisible to students. Too little attention is paid to ... carrying out complex or realistic tasks.
>
> (1989)

Schools that have not found a way of connecting semantic learning with authentic experience are in danger of become precincts of an 'exotic kind of practice contextually bound to the educational setting' (Lave, 1997, p.33).

Schools are often beholden to societal, and often governmental, constraints that emphasize accountability and certainty of outcomes:

> To fulfill the cultural desire for certainty, the conventional practices of schooling often discourage playful curiosity and experimentation and insist on the existence of the one right answer.
>
> (Chrenka, 2002)

The espoused ideals of learning language in contexts such as IB World Schools are potentially compromised by these institutional phenomena. If 'real world' communicative ability is a key intended outcome in language learning, these criticisms give cause for fundamentally rethinking how language courses are designed and operationalised. The next section discusses experiential learning as an approach that offers a potential solution to this dilemma.

2.4. Experiential learning: Dewey, Hahn and beyond

Often oversimplified as *learning by doing*, experiential learning is the most historically pervasive form of learning in human society (Rogoff, Paradise, Arauz, Correa-Chavez, & Angelillo, 2003). It is also the first and most powerful learning engaged in by all infants.

First, what is meant by the term 'experience'? In this chapter, *experience* is defined as:

> the sum total of impressions and other input from our sensory network that connects the brain, and particularly the memory, to the perceived world beyond the individual.
>
> (Jarvis, Holford, & Griffin, 2003)

From ancient times, experience has been seen as a key part of education in both East and West (Henson, 2003, p.6; F. Mayer, 1960, p.99; Perkinson,

1984). One well-known quotation from 'The Analects' by Confucius invokes an almost Vygotskian view of socially mediated learning by direct experience:

三人行必有我師焉，擇其善者而從之，其不善者而改之
(Confucius, 1983, Book 7:22)
(Where three are gathered together, isn't one my teacher? From their virtues I shall learn, from their vices, I shall correct.

Trans. author

In *The Republic*, Plato's cave invokes an early theory of experience-based education (Barker, 1959; Plato, 1952, Book VII, 540, Trans. B. Jowett). John Locke, in *An Essay on Human Understanding*, asserts:

All reason and knowledge have but one source: *experience*.
(Locke, 1952 [1689], p.122, emphasis in original).

Immanuel Kant, in exploring the boundaries of knowledge and reason, agrees that human cognition, knowledge and experience are inseparably linked (Kant, 1996, pp.44-52, 752-753, Trans. W. Pluhar; Kitcher, 1996, p.xxviii). Jean Jacques Rousseau, in one of his key statements regarding education, suggests:

The gift of education ... comes to us from nature, from men, or from things. The inner growth of our organs and faculties is the education of nature, the use we learn to make of this growth is the education of men, what we gain by our experience of our surroundings is the education of things.
(Rousseau, 1957 [1762], p.6)

Significantly, Rousseau also recognizes the importance of interaction with the learning setting – the *surroundings* – in education (Duffy & Cunningham, 2001; Rousseau, 1957 [1762], p.6).

One of the key educational theorists in the field of experiential learning, John Dewey, asserts that *knowing* experience is the *organising force* of all learning (Garrison, 2003):

Education ... is that reconstruction or reorganization of experience which adds to the meaning of experience, and which increases ability to direct the course of subsequent experience.
(Dewey, 1921)

He adds:

Every experience is a moving force ... all human experience is ultimately social.
(Dewey, 1997 [1938])

While experience and learning have an inseparable connection, it is important to emphasize that they are in fact two discrete entities that must not be conflated. Not all experiences lead to learning, although all human activity yields experience.

(Dewey, 1998 [1897], pp.231-233; A. Kolb & Kolb, 2008, p.2).

Dewey states:

> The belief that all genuine education comes about through experience does not mean that all experiences are genuinely or equally educative. Experience and education cannot be directly equated to each other.
>
> (Dewey, 1997 [1938])

Experience that leads to learning requires more than an instinctive reaction to a set of novel stimuli. According to Dewey, thinking about an experience – reflection – is the essential step in transforming a set of sensory stimuli into learning:

> Thought or reflection … is the discernment of the relation between what we try to do and what happens in consequence. No experience having a meaning is possible without some element of thought.
>
> (Dewey, 1921, p.169)

For Dewey, reflection is:

> (T)he explicit rendering of the intelligent element in our experience. It makes it possible to act with an end in view.
>
> (Dewey, 1921, p.171).

Action is a necessary consequence of experience for Dewey, as it distinguishes between presumptive and habitual acceptance of the routine and a genuine learning experience, the latter of which implies uncertainty (cognitive dissonance) and a responsibility to respond in a rational way:

> Reflection is the acceptance of responsibility for future actions arising out of an experience.
>
> (Dewey, 1921, p.171)

Reflection is therefore the considered, purposeful conjecture that follows the experience of uncertainty, incompletion, and doubt. Dewey's notion of reflection dovetails neatly with the IB's position on reflection:

> Reflection and critical thinking in all learning is necessary for the development of international-mindedness and intercultural awareness. Investigating possible interpretations of any situation and consequent available choices is part of being interculturally aware.
>
> (International Baccalaureate, 2011)

Building on the work of Dewey, the emergence of contemporary theories of experiential learning is often traced to the work of Kurt Hahn (Hahn, 1960; Hattie, Marsh, Neill, & Richards, 1997, p.44), who pioneered an approach to learning that focused on outdoor adventure and survival. Hahn believed that many fatalities in World War Two were the result of a flawed educational system that failed to provide learners with the resources to cope when faced with challenges; Outward Bound is a direct result of Hahn's ideas (Outward Bound International, 2004).

His notion of learning through experience led to the inclusion of community service in the IB diploma (first at Atlantic College, Wales when it opened in 1962) and in other programs such as Round Square and The Duke of Edinburgh's Award (Round Square, 2010; The Duke of Edinburgh's Award, 2011).

Experiential learning allows learners to acquire and apply skills and knowledge through active participation, solve problems, take calculated risks to learn from trial and error, and reflect on their learning (Dewey, 1997 [1938]; D. A. Kolb, 1984; Neill, 2006; Spera, 1996).

Experiential learning also aims to develop self-confidence, analytical skills, risk recognition and management, teamwork and leadership (Neill, 2006). Experiential learning may make intentional use of settings that are distinctive, sometimes unusual, and often challenging, to present problems to learners that support learning outcomes (Neill, 2006).

2.5. Role of episodic and semantic memory in learning and experience

In the fields of education, psychology, and neuroscience, the relationship between learning, knowledge, and memory is complex. Socrates is said to have claimed that 'all learning (knowledge) is recollection' (Plato, 2002, p.111, Trans. G. Grube).

Contemporary criticisms of traditional, didactic education, however, often de-emphasize the role of memory in learning, favoring 'critical thinking'. *Rote learning*, the memorization of content reinforced through repetition, has acquired a pejorative connotation for educational progressives, who see this as a tension between memory and intelligence (Concordia Online Education, 2012), although new research is beginning to question the mind-set against the role of memorising in certain types of learning (Brean, 2014).

In the context of language acquisition, progressive mastery is marked by the emerging automaticity of recall and communicative manipulation of the language. Critical thinking in a target language logically follows acquisition of its vocabulary and grammar, remembered or recalled incidentally or intentionally (Hulstijn, 2003). Reflection on or in a language similarly requires the capacity to recall experiences and the vocabulary to make meaning out of those experiences. Thus, memory is an essential tool in language learning.

In 1972, the Canadian neuroscientist Endel Tulving produced an influential paper, *Episodic and Semantic Memory*, hypothesising the existence of a type of memory that stored information relating to personally-experienced actual past events, which he described as 'episodic memory'

(Tulving, 1972, 2002). Episodic memory is a form of long-term memory with close connections to semantic memory; it is the stronger of the two types and is related to setting and circumstance, with a rich set of sensory cues and stored contextual impressions to aid recall (Sutton, 2004).

There are different memory encoding, storage and retrieval functions applicable to *knowing* as opposed to *remembering*; with the former associated with *semantic* memory and learning and the latter more closely related to *experiential* learning (Tulving, 2004). The creation of knowledge relies entirely on learning and memory: the two are tightly interconnected, mutually reinforcing, but have separate identities (Howard, 1995, p.3).

The role of memory is a significant part of experiential learning because it is only those elements of an experience that are stored in memory that will be available at a later time for retrieval, reflection, and perhaps cognitive construction and personal growth (Howard, 1995; Willingham & Preuss, 1995).

Semantic memory allows the subject to recall factual knowledge about a particular subject, but in a *noetic* sense, that is without self-awareness of the memory as an actual experience, and without any temporal and spatial context (Tulving, 2002). Thus, semantic memory may be useful for the learning of lexical items in a new language, but such learning would be without the experiential scaffold of recalled personal context.

Episodic memory allows learners to re-experience past events through autonoesis – an awareness of self participating in a remembered event – which is strongly associated through recollection with a specific time and place (Tulving, 2002, 2004). Episodic memory has a special relationship to time and place that semantic memory does not: an individual might know of an event that occurred at a particular time and place through semantic memory, but they can only remember it as a part of their own lived experience through episodic memory (Tulving, 2004, p.18). In the context of language learning, episodic memory allows the learner to recall a word or phrase in a language reinforced by the setting and circumstances in which it was experienced.

Due to the particular encoding, storage and recall functions associated with episodic memory, autonoetic experience tends to activate a distinct process of capturing and storing memories in the form of a complete *episode*, containing an interconnected set of sensory data, which are more likely to leave a deep residual impact on the learner (Herbert, 1999). An experiential framework or scaffolding of a learning activity therefore assists learners to organize and categorize retained knowledge (Herbert & Burt, 2004).

2.6. The 'where' of experiential learning: setting

A key distinction between classroom-based 'semantic' learning and 'experiential' learning is setting (Pritchard, 2010). The *setting* is the immediate physical location in which learning takes place, including the tools, artifacts and objects present; each setting has an embedded emotional, social and cultural dimension (Marsh, 2004, p.125).

The evidence of experiential learning is found in the meaning constructed and behavioral changes arising from the learner's exposure to a range of novel sensory input captured through the interaction between the learner, the problem (learner's cognitive gap), and the setting in which the problem is encountered (Pritchard, 2010).

While setting is seen by some as theoretically unproblematic (Van Note Chism & Bickford, 2002), acting as a *container* of human behaviour (Engeström, 1993, p.66), others, such as Vygotsky, see it as *changeable* and *dynamic* – and not a *static entity* to be taken for granted (Marsh, 2004, p.125; Vygotsky, 1994 [1934], p.346). The setting in which learning takes place holds historical, cultural, institutional, or psychological significance for learning (Engeström, 1993, pp.66-67; Engeström & Miettinen, 1999, pp.1-13; Wertsch, 1991). Authenticity is an essential attribute of the ideal learning environment from a constructivist perspective: in authentic settings, learning problems can be *complex and challenging* (Loyens & Gijbels, 2008).

There are, however, practical difficulties in creating theoretically ideal environments that offer a degree of authenticity and present learners with realistic, complex problems. Conventional classrooms are settings constructed within an institutional context and as such are not necessarily aligned with the theory-driven demands of student-centered learning (Land & Hannafin, 2000, pp.2-16). The inertia of existing setting design and institutional practice results in compromise, as new approaches are heavily modified to fit into existing infrastructure (Land & Hannafin, 2000, p.16).

Ideally, the setting for learning should be memorable, offering sharp discontinuity with the previous life experiences of the learner; such settings generate discontinuous experiences (Williams, 2005). This discontinuity may not necessarily involve personal risk or particularly confronting problems, but it should offer stark contrast (Theobald & Tolbert, 2006, pp.271-274). Such settings exert affective influence on the learner's experience, generating feelings of unfamiliarity, isolation, dissonance, and mild anxiety (McKenzie, 2000, pp.20-21; 2003, p.14). Natural or realistic settings introduce a greater degree of reality and uncertainty to the learning activities (Hoberman & Mailick, 1994).

A further important aspect of the setting of learning is the extent to which the context and artifacts associated with learning are designed or selected to *afford* certain possibilities of opportunities for learning. The setting should not just be memorable and offer a contrast to the learner's routine environment: it should also create possibilities for certain kinds of intended learning outcomes.

In setting, an *affordance* is an invariant property of an object or artifact, not of the learner or subject, although the affordance is perceived visually by the learner (Gibson, 1986, p.139). Setting affords the learner the potential to undertake certain actions or engage in certain experiences. The learner must have the requisite skills or knowledge, or be guided, to exploit what is afforded by the setting (Zhang & Patel, 2006, p.335). The property of a setting or object, itself, may therefore play a role in the deployment of human intelligence, drawing out latent capabilities and making possible certain types of developmental activity that might remain dormant in a different setting with a different set of affordances (Pea, 1993, pp.51-53).

In language learning, learning about food culture, for example, would be facilitated by an experience in a restaurant that afforded the opportunity to see, hear, taste, and feel an important venue in which food culture is expressed. Chinese cultural artifacts, such as chopsticks and writing brushes, afford certain opportunities to have language learning reinforced.

Language learning in realistic settings offers promise, but it is recognized that one of the major practical difficulties in creating authentic language learning opportunities in the real world is the difficulty in controlling the level of language to which the learner is exposed (Krashen, 1994). This question is examined more closely in the following discussion on program design and setting selection.

3. Summary of experiential learning

Based on the foregoing discussion of learning theories and experience, in summary, experiential learning requires three elements: learner, problem (cognitive gap or dissonance) and setting (Pritchard, 2010). Furthermore, experiential learning:

a) Places the learner at the centre of scaffolded, realistic problem-solving activities (Bruner, 1996, p.65; Gordin, Hoadley, Means, Pea, & Roschelle, 2000).

b) Comprises socially and culturally mediated interaction with others (Henson, 2003; Piaget, 1952; Vygotsky, 1978, trans.).

c) Creates strongly autonoetic memories that are encoded and stored in episodic memory (Tulving, 2002).

d) Relies on intentional interaction with a learning environment or activity setting (Miller & Boud, 1996), including its
   1 physical environment;
   2 socio-political milieu;
   3 economic context;
   4 chronological frame (Cole & Wertsch, 1996); and
   5 cultural setting (Lutterman-Aguilar & Gingerich, 2002).

e) Requires risk-taking as an integral part of learning process, with learners expected to make and learn from mistakes to develop self-reliance (Bruner, 1966; Dewey, 1997 [1938]).

f) Concludes with reflection on experience which is an integral element of learning (Dewey, 1921, 1997 [1938]; Fenwick, 2000).

g) Transforms learners and generates personal growth (Dewey, 1997 [1938]; Miller & Boud, 1996); and

h) Leads to the acquisition of new skills and the construction of new knowledge (Wells, 1999).

Part 2: Experiential learning programs (ELP) design: the essential elements

1. Overview

This section summarises the essential elements of ELPs and discusses the design and implementation of L2 learning programs based on the principles of experiential learning. The design parameters and practices featured here are derived from a study of ELP, including Chinese language-based programs, undertaken in Australian secondary schools (Pritchard, 2010).

Building on the summary of experiential learning theory, experiential learning programs (ELPs) are ideally founded on the following essential elements:

    a) Challenging settings;
    b) constructed (facilitated) social interaction;
    c) taking risks; and
    d) enduring learning and reflection.

ELPs should engage or accommodate each of these essential elements as an intentional element of program design and implementation. This ELP model is highly compatible with the demands of experiential learning with a language focus. Each of the essential elements is briefly discussed from a program design perspective below.

2. Challenging settings

The most important design choice in experiential programs is the setting, which affords the Rousseau-type education of the 'surroundings' or acts as the 'third teacher' in Reggio Emilia philosophy (Gandini, 1998). As discussed above, it is an active part of the learning process. The setting is the total physical, cultural, geographical, political, social, economic and chronological context in which a program is situated.

Program settings should offer some form of separation or isolation from home or community – physically, socially, culturally, and linguistically. Experiential settings may heighten emotional responses as they interrupt the learner's sense of security and certainty. Learners may initially feel uncertainty, vulnerability, exposure, and alienation in a novel setting. The emotional energy generated by challenging experiential settings creates an adventure described as intensified and accelerated. This adds to the memorability of the learning in context.

As noted, realistic settings in experiential programs for L2 learners are linguistically rich and authentic. Managed appropriately, they may be superior to the contrived, artificial environment of the classroom, which often strives to recreate what is readily available beyond school boundaries. Authentic settings are often challenging because they are essentially *uncontrolled*, and as such may pose genuine risks to learners; these risks require careful management through program design (Fenwick, 2000).

For L2 learners of Chinese, settings must offer experientially rich immersion in Chinese language and culture. This not only provides exposure to the target language, but also provides the multisensory cognitive scaffolding to reinforce any language acquired in context. Settings selected for specific purposes, such as a market, train station, restaurant, or shopping precinct, afford the possibility of targeted exposure to, and acquisition of, Chinese lexical items and grammatical structures, strengthened by the autonoetic 'first-person' memory of actually being there.

Ultimately, authentic settings offer an experience that cannot be replicated in the classroom (Krashen, 2009).

3. Constructing social interaction

In language learning terms, native or L1 speakers of the target language provide a rich cultural and linguistic resource for L2 learners in authentic settings. It is the possibility of extensive and intensive interaction with L1 speakers of Chinese within a culturally authentic setting that sets the ELP apart from other modes of learning. Social interaction without preparation, purpose, or control, however, is educationally undesirable and most likely ineffective.

One way of shaping social interaction is through the judicious selection of settings in which targeted, focused interaction takes place. Limiting L2 learner exposure to social interaction by controlling the number of L1 speakers encountered or the context in which interaction takes place assists with focusing preparation and the execution of the activity itself.

Providing L1 speakers encountered during an activity with some information about the learning context of the interaction is also an important aspect of constructing meaningful and effective interaction. Allowing the L1 interlocutor to understand the purpose of the interaction can reap enormous benefits for the learner.

The role of the teacher in constructing social interaction is crucial. Schön's notion of the mentor as a facilitator of the learning practicum offers a useful model (1987). When seen as a practicum the ELP approximates the real world in its presentation of actual problems in all their complexity, with the teacher/mentor acting to mediate, reduce, or remove some of the risks, pressures and consequences that attach to real world tasks. Experiential educators take on the role of practicum mentors, assessing and managing the learning setting and the risks in real time (Schön, 1987).

4. Taking risks: the Learner Profile in action

Taking risks is the third essential element of all ELPs and is a particular feature of experiential language acquisition for L2 learners. Risk is a necessary part of moving a learner from their zone of competence into a zone of uncertainty, possibility, and risk. When working in the Zone of Proximal Development (ZPD), previously learned coping strategies may not be reliable; experimentation and risk taking must be embraced, mistakes similarly tolerated, if not celebrated.

Risk tolerance is a contentious and problematic area for schools and educators. Schools in many countries have reported an increasing growth in risk aversion at both a parental and regulatory level due to changes in community values. Parents are accustomed to rescuing their children and schools have become much more sensitive to the risk of litigation.

When risk results in adverse outcomes, communities look for accountability. Ironically, accountability, along with resilience to endure adverse outcomes, is one of the key attributes developed by this type of learning. The culture of the school is particularly important in measuring the risk appetite of parents, teachers, and school boards.

Institutional risk *aversion* minimizes or eliminates risk of error as a matter of policy. If translated into classroom practice, the learner may find that achieving the correct solution to any problem is the goal. Thus, learners may be encouraged to avoid mistakes by not taking risks.

Experiential learning, on the other hand, relies fundamentally on novel experiences and this logically entails risk taking and exposure to the possibility of errors. The corollary of this is the need for learners to develop problem-solving skills to recover from their mistakes.

School settings typically do not develop real world problem-solving skills in learners because teachers and other adults tend to solve learner problems for them. The reasons for this are many, but include time constraints, resourcing and supervision constraints, duty of care issues, timetables and scheduling, among other institutional factors. It is simply more *efficient* for adults to intervene.

In order to overcome this potential institutional predisposition towards risk aversion, teachers in experiential programs must adopt an approach of self-control that allows learners some leeway to wrestle with problems and potentially make mistakes. Intervention should only be sufficient to move the learner forward, not to solve the problem. It is a fine balance.

Risk tolerance juxtaposes the experiential dichotomy of *suffering* and *safety*: these are the two extremes of the experiential risk spectrum. Risk arises from tough challenges and confronting experiences leading to potential *suffering*, with varying degrees of *safety* or protection afforded through a supportive scaffold of teacher intervention. The measurement of risk and its associated risk appetite varies greatly across ELP, with each seeking a balance between *risk* and *safety*.

5. Reflection and memorable learning

The aim to ensure that experiential learning has an enduring and memorable impact on learners is the fourth essential element. For the impact of any single experience on the student to be enduring educationally, it needs to create vivid and durable autonoetic memories, that is ones in which there is a strong self-awareness of personal participation in the experience.

Setting, interaction and risk-taking, through a combination of isolation, novelty, challenge, and conflict, create intense reactions in students, which in turn assist in creating lasting autobiographical memories. Learning arising from these experiences lies in the construction of knowledge, or the making of meaning. Learning is thus manifested in the transformation of memories of an experience into understanding, attitudinal transformation, and skill acquisition.

In these programs, the essential process employed to shape and reinforce the encoding of student memories is the use of formal and informal reflection. Reflection may be facilitated by teachers, who provide students with scaffolding through guided questioning, or direct tasking, during dedicated reflection sessions.

Time is also allocated to students for written self-reflection in programs. Reflection is practiced in both written and verbal modes, utilizing a variety of different genres. Written reflective practices are intended to capture the individual insights of students while the experiences are fresh in their minds. Some written reflections are unguided *self-reflections*, which serve as a self-guided assessment of learning outcomes.

The form of reflection is significant in structuring memories of an experience: a common phenomenon is that students turn their experience into a form of personal narrative, story or tale. For L2 learners, the extent to which such a reflection might be constructed in the target language will depend largely on the language level of the learner. The ability to place language learning in a reflected context in the learner's mother tongue, however, is just as powerful in consolidating the making of meaning in the L2.

The way in which an experience is recorded and encoded in memory is influenced by the way in which the experience itself affects the student at the time. The absence or presence of reflection as a form of scaffolding influences the memories retained about a particular experience. The way in which the experience is encoded in memory relies on the presence or absence of teacher direction in the forming of a personal narrative.

Reflection is commonly practiced in ELPs as a means of allowing students to construct durable memories from their experiences, both individual and collective. These enduring memories are a significant part of the process to construct new knowledge, develop new attitudes, or effect behavioral change, all of which are evidence of learning.

These programs are each designed around an expectation that student experiences are memorable because they are confronting, challenging, unexpected, or demanding. The learning arising from these enduring memories is linked inseparably to the memories of the experience and is thus expected to extend for years beyond the formal program conclusion.

6. Parameters of program design
This final section on ELP design discusses the application of the four essential elements in the design of Chinese language focused ELPs.

Choice of setting
The choice of setting for L2 Chinese ELPs is somewhat constrained geographically, but should also consider aspects such as:

a) Overall language objectives of ELP (literacy, oracy, cultural): spoken competency as an intended outcome lends itself to more informal, public settings; exposure to more literary Chinese language implies access to a more formal or institutional setting.

b) Choices within 'Greater China' (People's Republic of China, Taiwan, Singapore, other South East Asian Chinese communities).

c) Potential influence of local dialects or accents on verbal communication: many interesting settings in Chinese speaking communities pose difficulties for less competent L2 learners because of regional or dialect influenced pronunciation.

d) Public and personal safety for participants.

e) Ease of transportation access.

f) Quality and cost of accommodation.

g) Freedom of movement and access to L1 speakers.

h) Cultural significance of setting; and

i) Intrinsic interest of the specific settings for activities (*eg*, Great Wall of China, Silk Road, *etc*).

Authentic learning problems

Designing authentic learning problems allows learners to encounter something novel or unexpected that creates the potential for learning. Embedded in the setting, the learning problem, activity, or challenge, forms the core of the experiential adventure. Educationally effective ELP learning problems tend to have the following characteristics:

a) Problems are authentic: classrooms are seen as 'fake' or contrived learning environments by many learners; ELP problems must be connected to the actual needs of learners, such as arranging transport, navigating to an activity site, ordering a meal, arranging services.

b) Problems are recognised, and to an extent defined, by learners within the constraints of the target learning activity: beyond setting the broad parameters for an exercise, it is not the role of the teacher to point out what is required.

c) Authentic problems require learner intervention: they require action, not passive observation; learners must not be left with the option not to participate.

d) Learners must be required to plan, coordinate, organise and allocate resources to achieve the set objectives: for example, learners exercise leadership in assigning specific roles to members of a group to manage an aspect of the activity, such as budgeting, transport, site/activity background research and information, group leadership, and group welfare – headcounts.

e) They require negotiation and social interaction: problems always have a social context.

f) They involve real consequences: from the learner perspective, if the problem is not solved, or if mistakes are made in solving the problem, there must be some form of managed, yet real consequence that impacts on learners personally.

The sequencing of learning problems, moving from rudimentary to complex, should also act as a coherent whole across an ELP, creating the sense of a learning 'journey'. Coherency of structure in an ELP can be generated through the following:

a) Rite of passage at the commencement to mark the transition from the learner's 'normal' context to the ELP setting.

b) Repetition of activities to promote a perception of growth: activities conducted at an early stage, repeated when learners are more confident and competent, offer a contrastive perception of development.

c) Cascading: allowing skills developed and knowledge acquired in one activity to flow into the next; for language learning this allows the learner to acquire and consolidate language sequentially.

d) Bookending: placing key experiences at the beginning and end of an ELP to mark the transitions from and back to the routine world of the learner.

Teachers as mentors in ELPs

Experiential learning is often not step-by-step, where the outcome is already known. ELP activity teachers work with ambiguity and uncertainty, because novel situations (for learners) must logically give rise to the potential for novel reactions (from learners).

One of the philosophical values embedded in ELPs is that learners take responsibility for their own learning, seeking answers to their own questions. This requires the locus of control to move to the learner in a controlled, managed way. ELP teachers should never undertake a task on behalf of the learner that the learner, working in his/her ZPD, could manage with support.

For L2 learners, teacher intervention or scaffolding typically consists of the following:

a) Development of L2 communication strategies to resolve a miscommunication: working with L2 learners to practice specific strategies such as reiteration, repetition, simplification, non-linguistic communication.

b) Resource support: teachers identify potential resources to solve language problems, *eg* dictionaries, bilingual local citizens, internet resources, *etc.*

c) Lexical support: teachers monitor progress and offer 'just in time' limited linguistic support through the provision of lexical items to allow L2 learners to move past a communication block.

d) Support in context: teachers offer scaffolding by informing local interlocutors of the educational purpose of the learning activity.

Residential experiential programs in particular provide an intensively social immersive learning setting, which can produce memorable and unique challenges for learners. Learners are able to participate cooperatively in the management of learner living arrangements and environments. Learners are able to manage:

a) Accommodation: bookings, room allocation, management of group members where commercial accommodation is used, coordination of accommodation logistics – check-in and check-out, management of personal documentation, management and security of valuables.

b) Finances: budget allocations, cash management, expenditure control, accounting, receipt handling, production of accounting reports.

   c) Transportation: planning transport routes, identifying modes of transport, accessing public transport, management of groups of learners when in transit, navigation to specific sites, negotiation and payment for transport.

   d) Catering: planning for meals, venue selection, purchasing supplies, managing catering budgets, monitoring group welfare in food and water consumption, preparation of self-catered meals, food hygiene.

   e) Group wellbeing: headcounts, group scheduling and movement, meetings, study and journal times, free-time.

   f) Education: researching background information on sites and activities, preparation of vocabulary and grammar needed for planned activities, consolidation of language learning from previous activities, presentation to other learners on aspects of L2 culture, site activities and site histories.

Activity design

Activities to be undertaken in a challenging setting must connect philosophically with the program objectives, but must also connect in a meaningful way with the specific learning objectives attaching to the activity.

In language acquisition, local residents are a precious language learning resource. Given Krashen's concerns about lack of control over comprehensible input in such settings, one mechanism to shape and filter the language likely to be generated for learners is for the activities to be designed to elicit certain responses from respondents.

For example, a visit to a produce market might offer learning objectives on many different levels, from bargaining practices (social interaction, retail culture, economics, and mathematics) through to selection of produce (food culture, unique foodstuffs, and management of quantities). Some simple examples of programmed constructed social interaction with L1 speakers of the target language in limited settings are:

   a. Personal survey in a public place: name, place of residence, occupation, date of birth.

   b. Employment survey in a public place: type of employment, starting and finishing times, attitudes to work, qualifications, salary (cultural caution is necessary as this is a taboo topic in some cultures).

   c. Produce market survey: produce types, prices, competition.

   d. Transport survey (at a transport hub, bus station, railway station): types or modes of transport use, commuting times (if relevant), costs, convenience, safety issues.

   e. Commodity surveys: checking on the price of common items or commodities in settings without pricing controls; this activity may include a focused comparison with the prices of similar commodities in the learner's home country.

As a follow-up activity, many of the suggested surveys also yield statistical data that can be aggregated and used to discern trends or make comparisons with other settings where comparable data may be available (working hours, salaries, commodity prices, for example).

Interaction with Chinese language artifacts is also an important dimension of experiential learning. Learners will be immersed in a rich textual environment and may encounter many unfamiliar characters during the ELP. Capturing this phenomenon through the regular, intentional, scheduled collection of unfamiliar characters which are then shared in plenary forums with other learners offers L2 learners with a structured way of noticing things that are unfamiliar, researching these characters, and sharing their learning with other learners.

Part 3: Summary: ELP learning outcomes

All genuine learning has the power to shape behaviour, change attitudes and generate new knowledge. Experiential learning, by virtue of its enduring and highly personal nature, extends its influence over many years in the lives of learners. Because experiential learning is autonoetic, it cannot be made obsolete by new experiences; each learning experience adds to existing cognitive structures or generates new ones, but all remain an integral element of the learners constructed reality.

For L2 learners, ELPs offer an opportunity to acquire authentic language and develop cultural understanding in a highly memorable way. Language acquired in a real world setting remains intimately connected to the memories of the context in which the language was experienced. Recall of experientially acquired language is enhanced by the 'first-person' nature of the memories accessed. Learners can picture themselves listening, speaking, reading, and writing in the host country, interacting with L1 speakers.

By tapping into the enduring power of experience as a mode of learning, there are many benefits and skills that may potentially accrue to the learner:

a. Memorable and enduring learning.
b. School retention through personal relevance of experience.
c. Engaged learners post-program.
d. Accommodation and development of a wider range of individual learning styles and standards.
e. Real world applications of experiential learning.
f. Greater connectivity between the classroom and the real world.
g. Relevance of experience to personal needs and interests.
h. Closer connection between school experiences of education and community standards.
i. Direct cross-generational exchange of knowledge.
j. Direct transfer of sub-cultural knowledge – *eg* workplace culture
k. Competence in facing real problems to develop real solutions.
l. Leadership skills.
m. Personal development: resilience, courage, commitment, patience, open-mindedness, international mindedness, self-determination.

n. Greater flexibility developed in learners.
o. Development of specialised skills and knowledge in context.
p. More focused targeting of some educational resources.
q. Enhanced learning from errors and mistakes.
r. Life-long or independent learning skills developed.
s. More reflective and objective in self-appraisal.
t. Potential savings in resource expenditure on learners with specific learning difficulties.

This list provides something of a sketch and no more, and one of the reasons for this is the highly individualised nature of experiential learning outcomes that reflect a unique interaction between the learner and the experience itself.

All learning is ultimately experiential and all learning arises from the question in the mind of the learner. The intelligent design and implementation of experiential learning, which pose authentic and meaningful questions for learners, when effectively integrated into a wider program of learning, has power disproportionate to the time and resource allocation to shape learning. ELPs are thus educational amplifiers.

In the context of language learning, the vivid and enduring memories of interaction with L1 speakers in authentic settings potentially produces positive outcomes in both the affective and cognitive domains that extend well beyond the conclusion of the program itself.

References

Amin, T. G., & Valsiner, J. (2004). Coordinating Operative and Figurative Knowledge: Piaget, Vygotsky, and Beyond. In I. M. Carpendale & U. Miller (Eds.), *Social Interaction and the Development of Knowledge*. Mahwah, NJ: Lawrence Erlbaum Associates, (pp.87-109).

Bachelard, G. (2002 [1938]). *The Formation of the Scientific Mind: A Contribution to a Psychoanalysis of Objective Knowledge* (M. McAllester Jones, Trans.). Manchester: Clinamen Press Ltd.

Barker, E. (1959). *The Political Thought of Plato and Aristotle*. New York: Dover.

Brean, J. (2014, 21 August 2014). Math Wars: Rote Memorization plays a crucial role in teaching students how to solve complex calculations, study says. *National Post*. Retrieved from http://news.nationalpost.com/2014/08/21/math-wars-rote-memorization-plays-crucial-role-in-teaching-students-how-to-solve-complex-calculations-study-says/-__federated=1

Bruner, J. S. (1966). *Toward a Theory of Instruction*. Cambridge, MA: Belknap Press.

Bruner, J. S. (1996). *The Culture of Education*. Cambridge, Massachusetts: Harvard University Press.

Bruner, J. S. (1997). Celebrating Divergence: Piaget and Vygotsky. *Human Development*, 40(2), 63-73.

Chomsky, N. (1965). *Aspects of the Theory of Syntax*. Cambridge, MA: MIT Press.

Chomsky, N. (1986). *Knowledge of Language: Its Nature, Origin, and Use*. Westport, CT: Praeger.

Chrenka, L. (2002). Constructivism and the Role of the Teacher: Misconstructing Constructivism. *Phi Delta Kappan*, 82(1), 694-695.

Cole, M., & Hatano, G. (2007). Cultural-Historical Activity Theory. In S. Kitayama & D. Cohen (Eds.), *Handbook of Cultural Psychology* (pp.109-135). New York: Guildford Press.

Cole, M., & Wertsch, J. V. (1996). Beyond the Individual-Social Antimony in Discussions of Piaget and Vygotsky. *Human Development, 39*(5), 250-256.

Collins, A., Brown, J., & Newman, S. (1989). Cognitive Apprenticeship: Teaching the Crafts of Reading, Writing, and Mathematics. In B. Resnick (Ed.), *Knowing, learning, and instruction: Essays in honor of Robert Glaser.* New Jersey: Lawrence Erlbaum Associates, (pp.453-494).

Concordia Online Education. (2012). What is Rote Learning? A Battle Between Memory and Intelligence. Retrieved 26 February, 2015, from http://education.cu-portland.edu/blog/curriculum-instruction/what-is-rote-learning/

Confucius. (1983). The Analects (論語). Retrieved 23 February, 2015, from http://www.cnculture.net/ebook/jing/sishu/lunyu_en/07.html

Corson, D. (1999). *Language Policy in Schools: A Resource for Teachers and Administrators.* Mahwah, NJ: Lawrence Erlbaum Associates.

Cummins, J. (2008). BICS and CALP: Empirical and Theoretical Status of the Distinction. In B. Street & N. H. Hornberger (Eds.), Encyclopedia of Language and Education (2nd ed., Vol. 2, pp.pp.71-83). New York, NY: Springer Science + Business Media. Retrieved 24 February 2015 from http://www.researchgate.net/profile/Jim_Cummins5/publication/226699482_BICS_and_CALP_Empirical_and_Theoretical_Status_of_the_Distinction/links/0deec534e935d7a289000000.pdf.

Daniels, H. (1996). *An introduction to Vygotsky.* London ; New York: Routledge.

Daniels, H. (2001). *Vygotsky and Pedagogy.* London: RoutledgeFalmer.

Dewey, J. (1909). *Moral Principles in Education.* New York: Houghton Miffin.

Dewey, J. (1921). *Democracy and Education: An Introduction to the Philosophy of Education.* New York: MacMillan.

Dewey, J. (1997 [1938]). *Experience and Education.* New York: Touchstone.

Dewey, J. (1998 [1897]). My Pedagogic Creed. In L. Hickman & T. Alexander (Eds.), *The Essential John Dewey: Pragmatism, Education, Democracy,* Bloomington: Indiana University Press, (Vol. 1, pp.229-235).

Duffy, T. M. & Cunningham, D. J. (2001). Constructivism: Implications for the Design and Delivery of Instruction. In D. H. Jonassen (ed.), *Handbook of Research for Educational Communications and Technology.* Retrieved 25 February, 2015 from the Association for Educational Communications and Technology website: http://www.aect.org/edtech/ed1/07/index.html

Engeström, Y. (1993). Developmental studies of work as a testbench of activity theory: The case of primary care medical practice. In S. Chaiklin & J. Lave (Eds.), *Understanding Practice: Perspectives on Activity and Context,* Cambridge: Cambridge University Press, (pp.64-103)

Engeström, Y., & Miettinen, R. (1999). Introduction. In Y. Engeström, R. Miettinen, & R. Punamaki (Eds.), *Perspectives on Activity Theory,* Cambridge: Cambridge University Press, (pp.1-18).

Ernest, P. (1995). The One and the Many. In J. Gale & L. Steffe (Eds.), *Constructivism in Education.* Hillsdale, NJ: Lawrence Erlbaum Associates, (pp.459-488)

Fenwick, T. (2000). Experiential Learning in Adult Education: A Comparative Framework. Retrieved 14 May, 2005, from http://www.ualberta.ca/%7Etfenwick/ext/pubs/aeq.htm

Gandini, L. (1998). Educational and Caring Spaces. In C. Edwards, L. Gandini, & G. Forman (Eds.), *The Hundred Languages of Children: The Reggio Emilia Approach - Advanced Reflections*. Greenwich: Ablex, (pp.161-178).

Garrison, W. (2003). Democracy, Experience, and Education: Promoting a Continued Capacity for Growth. *Phi Delta Kappan*, 84(7), 525. http://www.questia.com/PM.qst?a=o&d=5001512002

Gibson, J. J. (1986). *The Ecological Approach to Visual Perception*. Hillsdale, NJ: Lawrence Erlbaum Associates.

Gordin, D., Hoadley, C., Means, B., Pea, R. D., & Roschelle, J. (2000). Changing How and What Children Learn in School with Computer-Based Technologies *The Future of Children*, 10(2), 76-101.

Hahn, K. (1960). Outward Bound: Address by Dr. Kurt Hahn at the Annual Meeting of Outward Bound Trust on 20th July, 1960. Retrieved 20 July, 2010, from http://www.kurthahn.org/writings/obt1960.pdf

Halliday, M. A. K. (1993). Towards a language-based theory of learning. *Linguistics and Education*, 5, 93-116.

Halliday, M. A. K. (2004 [1980]). Three Aspects of Children's Language Development: Learning Language, Learning through Language, Learning about Language. In J. Webster (Ed.), *Language of Early Childhood*. London, UK: Continuum, (Vol. 4, pp.308-326).

Hattie, J., Marsh, H. W., Neill, J., & Richards, G. (1997). Adventure Education and Outward Bound: Out-of-Class Experiences That Make a Lasting Difference. *Review of Educational Research*, 67(1), 43-87.

Henson, K. (2003). Foundations for Learner-Centered Education: A Knowledge Base *Education*, 124(1), 5-16.

Herbert, D. (1999). *What do students remember from lectures? The role of episodic memory on early learning*. Paper presented at the Australian Association for Research in Education - New Zealand Association for Research in Education Conference.

Herbert, D., & Burt, J. (2004). What do Students Remember? Episodic Memory and the Development of Schematization. *Applied Cognitive Psychology*, 18, 77-88.

Hoberman, S., & Mailick, S. (1994). *Professional Education in the United States: Experiential Learning, Issues, and Prospects*. Wesport, CT: Praeger Publishers.

Howard, R. (1995). *Learning and Memory: Major Ideas, Principles, Issues and Applications*. Westport, CT.: Praeger.

Hulstijn, J. (2003). Incidental and Intentional Learning. In C. J. Doughty & M. H. Long (Eds.), *The Handbook of Second Language Acquisition*, Malden, MA: Blackwell Publishing Ltd, (pp.349-381).

International Baccalaureate Organisation. (2008b). *Learning in a language other than mother tongue in IB programmes*. Cardiff, Wales: International Baccalaureate Organization.

International Baccalaureate Organization. (2011). *Language and learning in IB programmes*. Cardiff, Wales: International Baccalaureate Organization.

International Baccalaureate Organization. (2014). Language Policy: Information on the International Baccalaureate's support for languages, language courses and languages of instruction. Retrieved 23 February, 2015, from http://www.ibo.org/globalassets/ib-language-policy-en.pdf

Jarvis, P., Holford, J., & Griffin, C. (2003). *The Theory & Practice of Learning*. London: Kogan Page.

Johnson, K. E. (1995). *Understanding Communication in Second Language Classrooms* Cambridge: Cambridge University Press.

Jonassen, D. (2009). Reconciling a Human Cognitive Architecture. In S. Tobias & T. Duffy (Eds.), *Constructivist Instruction: Success or Failure?*. New York: Routledge, (pp.13-33).

Kant, I. (1996). *Critique of Pure Reason* (W. Pluhar, Trans.). Indianapolis: Hackett.

Kirschner, P. A., Sweller, J., & Clark, R. E. (2006). Why minimal guidance during instruction does not work: An analysis of the failure of constructivist, discovery, problem-based, experiential, and inquiry based teaching. *Educational Psychologist*, 41(2), 75-86.

Kitcher, P. (1996). Prefaces and Introduction: Kant's Central Problem *Critique of Pure Reason*. Indianapolis: Hackett, (pp.xxv-lx).

Kolb, A., & Kolb, D. (2008). Experiential Learning Theory: A Dynamic, Holistic Approach to Management Learning, Education and Development. Retrieved 5 September 2010 from Learning From Experience website: http://learningfromexperience.com/media/2010/08/ELT-Hbk-MLED-LFE-website-2-10-08.pdf

Kolb, D. A. (1984). The Process of Experiential Learning. Retrieved 9 December, 2005, from http://www.learningfromexperience.com/images/uploads/process-of-experiential-learning.pdf

Krashen, S. (1994). *The Comprehension Hypothesis and its Rivals*. Paper presented at the Eleventh International Symposium on English Teaching, Taipei.

Krashen, S. (2009). *Principles and Practice in Second Language Acquisition* Retrieved from http://www.sdkrashen.com/content/books/principles_and_practice.pdf

Land, S., & Hannafin, M. (2000). Student-Centred Learning Environments. In D. Jonassen & S. Land (Eds.), *Theoretical Foundations of Learning Environments*. Hillsdale, NJ: Lawrence Erlbaum Associates, (pp.1-23).

Lave, J. (1997). The Culture of Acquisition and the Practice of Understanding. In D. Kirshner & J. Whitson (Eds.), *Situated Cognition: Social, Semiotic, and Psychological Perspectives*. New Jersey: Lawrence Erlbaum Associates, (pp.17-36).

Locke, J. (1952 [1689]). An Essay Concerning Human Understanding. In R. M. Hutchins (Ed.), *Locke Berkley Hume*. Chicago: Encyclopedia Britannica Inc., (Vol. 35, pp.318).

Loyens, S., & Gijbels, D. (2007). Understanding the effects of constructivist learning environments: introducing a multi-directional approach. *Instructional Science*, 36, 351-357. Retrieved 25 February, 2015 from http://publishing.eur.nl/ir/repub/asset/14906/2008120300307.pdf from http://www.dofe.org

Lutterman-Aguilar, A., & Gingerich, O. (2002). Experiential Pedagogy for Study Abroad: Educating for Global Citizenship. Winter. Retrieved 11 June, 2005, from http://www.frontiersjournal.com/issues/vol8/vol8-07_luttermanaguilargingerich.htm

MacWhinney, B. (2004). A unified Model of Language Acquisition. In J. Kroll & A. De Groot (Eds.), *Handbook of Bilingualism: Psycholinguistic Approaches*. Oxford, UK: Oxford University Press, (pp.49-67).

Marsh, C. (2004). *Key Concepts for Understanding Curriculum*. London: RoutledgeFalmer.

Mayer, F. (1960). *A History of Educational Thought*. Columbus, OH: Charles E. Merrill Books.

Mayer, R. (2004). Should There Be a Three-Strikes Rule Against Pure Discovery Learning? The Case for Guided Methods of Instruction. *American Psychologist*, 59(1), 14-19.

Mayer, R. (2005). Introduction to Multimedia Learning. In R. Mayer (Ed.), *The Cambridge Handbook of Multimedia Learning*. New York: Cambridge University Press, (pp.1-16).

McKenzie, M. (2000). How are Adventure Education Program Outcomes Achieved?: A review of the literature. *Australian Journal of Outdoor Education*, 5(1), 19-28.

McKenzie, M. (2003). Beyond "The Outward Bound Process:" Rethinking Student Learning. *The Journal of Experiential Education*, 26(1), 8-23.

Miller, N., & Boud, D. (1996). Animating learning from experience. In D. Boud & N. Miller (Eds.), *Working with Experience: Animating Learning*. New York: Routledge, (pp.3-13).

Mok, I. (2003). *A "Teacher-Dominating" Lesson in Shanghai: The teacher's and the learner's perspectives*. Paper presented at the Learner's Perspective Study, University of Melbourne. Retrieved 25 May 2005 from The University of Melbourne Faculty of Education website: http://extranet.edfac.unimelb.edu.au/DSME/lps/assets/lpswebupdates/Teacherdominating.pdf

Neill, J. (2006, 10 May 2006). Experiential Learning & Experiential Education. Retrieved 7 July, 2010, from http://wilderdom.com/experiential/

Osborne, J. (1996). Beyond Constructivism. *Science Education, 80*(1), 53-82.

Outward Bound International. (2004). Kurt Hahn - The Founder's Story. Retrieved 24 February 2015 from http://www.outwardbound.net/about/history/kurt-hahn.html

Parkinson, J. (2003). *Improving Secondary Science Teaching*. New York: RoutledgeFalmer.

Pea, R. (1993). Practices of distributed intelligence and designs for education. In G. Salomon (Ed.), *Distributed Cognitions*. New York: Cambridge University Press, (pp.47-87).

Perkinson, H. (1984). *Learning from Our Mistakes: A Reinterpretation of Twentieth-Century Educational Theory*. Westport, CT: Greenwood Press.

`Piaget, J. (1952). *The Origins of Intelligence in Children* (M. Cook, Trans.). New York: International Universities Press.

Pinker, S. J. (1994). *The Language Instinct*: How the Mind Creates Language. New York, NY: Harper Collins.

Pinker, S. J. (2004). Clarifying the logical problem of language acquisition. *Journal of Child Language*, 31(2004), 949-953.

Plato. (1952). *The Republic* (B. Jowett, Trans. Vol. 7). Chicago: Encyclopedia Britannica.

Plato. (2002). *Phaedo* (G. Grube, Trans.). Indianapolis: Hackett.

Pritchard, M. (2010). *Experiential Learning Programs in Australian Secondary Schools*. (PhD Thesis), University of Melbourne, Melbourne, Australia. Retrieved 23 February, 2015 from http://hdl.handle.net/11343/35988

Richardson, K. (2000). *The Making of Intelligence*. New York: Columbia University Press.

Rogoff, B., Paradise, R., Arauz, M., Correa-Chavez, M., & Angelillo, C. (2003). Firsthand Learning through Intent Participation. *Annual Review of Psychology*, 54, 175-203.

Romeo, K. (2000). Krashen and Terrell's "Natural Approach". Retrieved 26 December, 2014, from http://web.stanford.edu/~hakuta/www/LAU/ICLangLit/NaturalApproach.htm

Round Square. (2010). Round Square. Retrieved 6 March, 2011, from http://www.roundsquare.org/index.php?id=11

Rousseau, J. J. (1957 [1762]). *Emile* (B. Foxley, Trans.). New York: Dutton.

Scardamalia, M., & Bereiter, C. (1994). Computer support for knowledge-building communities. *The Journal of the Learning Sciences*, 3(3), 265-283.

Schön, D. (1987). *Educating the Reflective Practitioner: Toward a New Design for Teaching Learning in the Professions*. San Francisco: Jossey-Bass.

Spera, V. (1996). Experiential Education: Just What Do We Mean? Retrieved 7 July, 2010, from http://www.aypf.org/forumbriefs/1996/fb092796.htm

Sutton, J. (2004, 10 May 2004). Memory. *The Stanford Encyclopedia of Philosophy (Summer 2004 Edition)*. Summer 2004. Retrieved 9 April, 2005, from http://plato.stanford.edu/archives/sum2004/entries/memory

Tharp, R., & Gallimore, R. (1988). *Rousing Minds to Life: Teaching, learning, and schooling in social context*. Cambridge: Cambridge University Press.

The Duke of Edinburgh's Award. (2011). The Duke of Edinburgh's Award. Retrieved 6 March, 2011 from http://www.dofe.org.

Theobald, P., & Tolbert, L. (2006). Finding Their Place in the Community: Urban Education outside the Classroom. *Childhood Education, 82*(5), 271-274.

Tobin, K., & Tippins, D. (1993). Constructivism as a Referent for Teaching and Learning. In K. Tobin (Ed.), *The Practice of Constructivism in Science Education*. Hillsdale, NJ: Lawrence Erlbaum Associates, (pp.3-21).

Tulving, E. (1972). Episodic and Semantic Memory. In E. Tulving & W. Donaldson (Eds.), Organization of Memory. New York: Academic Press, (pp.381-403).

Tulving, E. (2002). Episodic Memory: from mind to brain. *Annual Review of Psychology*, xvi.

Tulving, E. (2004). Episodic Memory and Autonoesis: Uniquely Human? In H. S. Terrace & J. Metcalfe (Eds.), *The Missing Link in Cognition: Origins of Self-Reflective Consciousness* New York: Oxford University Press, (pp.1-56).

Van Note Chism, N., & Bickford, J. (2002). *The Importance of Physical Space in Creating Supportive Learning Environments* (Vol. 92). San Francisco: Jossey-Bass.

von Glasersfeld, E. (1995). A Constructivist Approach to Teaching. In J. Gale & L. Steffe (Eds.), *Constructivism in Education*. Hillsdale, NJ: Lawrence Erlbaum Associates, (pp.3-16).

Vonk, J., & Povinelli, D. (2012). Similarity and Difference in the Conceptual Systems of Primates: The Unobservability Hypothesis. In T. R. Zentall & E. A. Wasserman (Eds.), *The Oxford Handbook of Comparative Cognition*. New York, NY: Oxford University Press, (pp.552-578).

Vygotsky, L. S. (1978). Mind in Society : *The Development of Higher Psychological Processes* (M. Cole, Trans.). Cambridge, MA: Harvard University Press.

Vygotsky, L. S. (1986 [1934]). *Thought and Language* (A. Kozulin, Trans.). Cambridge, MA: MIT Press.

Vygotsky, L. S. (1987). The Genesis of Higher Mental Functions. In R. Reiber (Ed.), *The History of the Development of Higher Mental Functions*. New York: Plenum, (Vol. 4, pp.97-120).

Vygotsky, L. S. (1994 [1934]). The Problem of the Environment. In R. van de Veer & J. Valsiner (Eds.), *The Vygotsky Reader*. Leiden: Blackwell, (pp.338-354).

Vygotsky, L. S., & Luria, A. R. (1993 [1930]). *Studies on the History of Behavior: Ape, Primitive, and Child* (J. E. Knox & V. I. Golod, Trans.). Hillsdale, NJ: Lawrence Erlbaum Associates.

Wells, G. (1999). *Dialogic Inquiry: Towards a Sociocultural Practice and Theory of Education.* Cambridge: Cambridge University Press.

Wertsch, J. (1991). *Voices of the Mind: A Sociocultural Approach to Mediated Action.* Cambridge, MA: Harvard University Press.

Williams, I. (2005). Creating a Capacity for Relatedness Through Discontinuous Experiences. *Journal of Cognitive Affective Learning*, 1(2), 13-19.

Willingham, D. B., & Preuss, L. (1995). The Death of Implicit Memory. 2(15). Retrieved 9 April, 2005, from http://psyche.cs.monash.edu.au/v2/psyche-2-15-willingham.html

Zhang, J. J., & Patel, V. (2006). Distributed Cognition, Representation, and Affordance. *Cognition & Pragmatics*, 14(2), 333-341.

Part two:

Implementating IB philosophy in classroom practice and teaching materials development

Chapter 5

Implementing international mindedness in the International Baccalaureate Diploma Programme: a qualitative case study in a Hong Kong second language Chinese classroom

Kwok-ling Lau

Abstract

The aim of this chapter is to examine the enabling factors for the successful implementation of international mindedness (IM) in the International Baccalaureate Diploma Programme (IBDP) in a Chinese as a second language classroom in an international school.

The research questions are: (1) How successfully do the teachers of IBDP Chinese B teach the concept of IM in Chinese lessons? (2) How successfully do the students of Chinese B perform in class work in the teaching and learning cycle? Hayden, Rancic and Thompson (2010:107), UNESCO (2002), Oxfam (2006), and Hill (2007:33-34; 2012:258-259) have contributed new insights on IM which form part of my theoretical framework.

This IB school is a typical example of the implementation of the IB Chinese B Diploma Programme by an expert teacher. The research methodology includes classroom observation and classroom discourse analysis (Christie, 2005). The enabling factors that promote IM in teaching and learning include scaffolding, inquiry-based learning, research skills, critical thinking, collaborative learning, student-centered teaching, discussion of global citizenship and intercultural understanding. Students demonstrated IM by making moral judgments and applying interdisciplinary knowledge relating to social issues.

I hope that this study will contribute a framework to promote IM and that such insights can inform and drive change and improvement in IB curriculum development and teacher training.

Keywords: International mindedness, inquiry-based learning, international education, International Baccalaureate Diploma Programme, Chinese as a second language

Introduction

Human core values and human civilisation are learnt through world languages. UNESCO (1974:4) emphasises the importance of teaching foreign languages, civilizations and cultural heritage 'as a means of promoting international and inter-cultural understanding'. Hill (2001:50-53) indicates that intercultural understanding is greatly assisted by language learning which, in turn, helps students to respect different values and attitudes through the discussion of global issues.

Duff & Lester (2008:5) emphasise that people need to use different languages in communication because of globalisation and human migration. As a growing number of people are using Chinese around the world, Chinese (Mandarin) has become one of the world's most important languages. Hong Kong is an international city with a large number of international companies that have set up or expanded their operations within its territory. The population is multicultural and the official languages are Chinese and English.

I believe a good teacher not only teaches a syllabus (subject matter and skills) but also inspires students to develop moral values which are part of an IB education. Thus, this study attempts to demonstrate how IM is implemented in the teaching of IBDP Chinese as a second language in Hong Kong.

Although IB advocates IM as a key concept in IB philosophy, it seems that stakeholders do not give sufficient attention to the treasure of IM. As a result, the promotion of IM and the IB mission statement may not be fully carried out.

There are very few in-depth studies examining the presence of IM in a Chinese B classroom. This study seeks to reduce that gap as it attempts to answer the following research questions:

1. How do the teachers of IBDP Chinese B teach the concept of IM in their lessons?
2. How do the IBDP students of Chinese B demonstrate concepts related to IM in their class work in the teaching and learning cycle?

Table 1 below indicates the research methodology applied to these two questions.

Research Questions	Research methodology	Theoretical underpinning
How do the teachers of IBDP Chinese B teach the concept of IM in their lessons?	Classroom observation, in-depth interview with students, using semi-structured questions.	Classroom discourse analysis (Christie, 2005). Systemic functional linguistics (SFL) (Halliday, 2000) are used.
How do the IBDP students of Chinese B demonstrate concepts related to IM in their class work in the teaching and learning cycle?	Classroom observation, in-depth interview with students, using semi-structured questions.	Classroom observation, In-depth interview of students, using semi-structured questions. Classroom discourse analysis (Christie, 2005), systemic functional linguistics (SFL) (Halliday, 2000) are used.

Table 1: research methodology for the two research questions.

The next section seeks to define the nature of IM so we can identify it in the classroom.

International mindedness (IM)

Hayden (2006:7) points out that there is no simple definition of IM. In summary she states that international education is defined as being entirely related to IM and to a formal curriculum. With the aim of analysing and comparing students and teachers regarding their perceptions of international education, Hayden, Rancic and Thompson (2010:107) grouped 32 items into nine catagories: international experience and international-mindedness; parental factors; type of institution attended; second language competence; neutrality; open-minded flexibility of thinking and action; attitude towards own value system and culture; respect for others; tolerance of the behaviour and views of others.

Cambridge and Thompson (2004:167-168) find that international education is presently in a dilemma between ideological and pragmatic interests. The ideological 'internationalist' identifies international education with the moral development of individuals, which has positive effects towards peace, international understanding and responsible world citizenship.

However, the pragmatic 'globalist' connects international education with the process of economic and cultural globalisation, educational qualifications and global quality assurance, such as accreditation in the global educational market. Oxfam (2006:4) and UNICEF (2013:3) state that the goal of Education for Global Citizenship (which has many similarities with IM) is not only to encourage young people to explore, develop, and express their own values and opinions, but also to respect other people's points of view.

The key elements of IM comprise a collection of concepts and ideas which can then be expressed in terms of knowledge, skills and values – these are the fundamental parts of an IB curriculum, in fact of any school curriculum.

IM concepts and ideas

Students need to know about learning other languages, global citizenship, intercultural understanding, civic education (community service, the consequences of intolerance, cooperation), and global issues such as human rights, social justice and equity, diversity, peace, conflict resolution (UNESCO, 2004:95) ecologically sustainable development, critical thinking, debate over issues, co-operation, sense of identity, self-esteem, and empathy. Notions of life-long learning and learning to live together [Delors (1996:37)] are also fundamental to IM. UNESCO (2004) classified the objectives of international education into three groups:

> the development of the human personality;
> human rights and fundamental liberties; and
> international understanding, and the promotion of peace.

> (p.87)

Harrison (2013:95-96) indicates that intercultural understanding is an important component of IM. Students develop intercultural understanding by learning through experience and languages. Harrison also emphasises that it is important to develop internationally-minded curricula in order to understand other cultures and respect for cultural diversity under the impact of globalisation. Cambridge (2000:26) indicates that it is very important to have sustainable development and intercultural dialogue in a global village.

UNESCO (2013:10) identifies intercultural competences and concepts that include cultural diversity, peace, relationships, self, other, globalization, adaptation, and empathy. Numerous possible interpretations arise, connected with the diversity of our worldviews, opinions, languages, cultures, disciplines, beliefs, *etc.*

These components of IM can be grouped according to whether they relate to acquiring knowledge, developing skills or forming attitudes – this is the way we think of curriculum in education. Some of the components will belong to more than one of those three groups

Knowledge

Students need knowledge about many of the IM components. The most important revolve around the notion of global citizenship, which means knowing vocabulary and grammar to learn additional languages, and also learning about other cultures and the way people think and act differently in those cultures. This is the intercultural understanding that has been described above. Being a global citizen means being aware of global issues, knowing the points for and against, knowing where opposing views are coming from – what are the cultural, historical, economic, scientific, sociological, religious, *etc* reasons for different views.

We require knowledge about the interdependence of nations in relation to so many aspects of life on our planet such as living in peace, human rights, the flow of wealth and poverty, telecommunications, climate, pollution, sustainable development, territoriality, international crime, international travel, and the distribution of electricity, fresh water and oil supplies.

Skills

Once knowledge is acquired, students then need to develop skills which enable them to use that knowledge. Vocabulary and grammar need to be learned, but then students need to practice the skills of listening, speaking, reading and writing in order to make use of the new language. Relating effectively to people in other cultures should be a natural consequence of knowing about their ways of living; being able to analyse why they act and think differently in some ways is a skill to develop.

Critical thinking is one of the most important skills in IM: not to accept all that you hear, see and read but to reflect wisely and deeply before arriving at conclusions and acceptance or rejection of ideas, proposals and explanations. Research skills are an essential component in inquiry-based learning programmes like the IB.

The ability to work cooperatively with others of different or the same cultural origins, to have well-articulated debating skills, to be able to comprehend multiple perspectives about the same event, and to be sufficiently articulate to defend causes such as social justice and equity (once knowledge of them has been acquired) are indicators of IM.

Values (or attitudes)

The International Bureau of Education (1999: 4) stresses the importance of teaching core values and attitudes: human rights and democracy, cooperation and solidarity, preservation of cultures, the self and others' internationalism, protection of the environment, and spirituality.

These are important in the curriculum framework for peace education. Oxfam (2006: 2) states that the goal of Education for Global Citizenship is not only to encourage young people to explore, develop, and express their own values and opinions, but also to respect diversity and other people's points of view. We are now in the realm of values education to guide our utilisation of knowledge and skills.

UNESCO (2002:24) Asia-Pacific Network for International Education and Values Education (APNIEVE) believes that there are eight core values in human and social development: health and harmony with nature, truth and wisdom, love and compassion, creativity and appreciation of beauty, peace and justice, sustainable human development, national unity and global solidarity; and global spirituality. All these values converge around the central value of respect for human dignity.

It seeks an integration of the learner's knowledge, values and attitudes, abilities and skills to bring about his/her full development. This is very much in line with the value dimension of IM in an IB education.

Values education is flagged when we see such words as respect, commitment, concern, empathy, compassion, appreciation. A person can have vast knowledge, excellent skills to exploit that knowledge (language and critical thinking skills about sustainable development, for example), but an attitude which is not conducive to sharing solutions that would benefit the future of the planet. Such a person might act in a way which benefits the individual or a particular company wishing to sell more natural fuel.

The same could be said of someone who decides to use their knowledge and skills to act in ways that promote intolerance and racially prejudiced ideas rather than intercultural appreciation and respect for other human beings. A student could learn conflict resolution skills but decide to apply them badly or not at all if he/she wanted to perpetuate a conflict for economic gain (sale of arms and post-conflict reconstruction, for example). So the attitudinal, or values, dimension of the IBDP Chinese B curriculum is essential if students are to fulfill the criteria for being fully internationally minded.

Cambridge & Thompson (2004: 162) indicate that intercultural understanding, appreciation of other cultures and languages, and different perspectives are important components in an IBDP Curriculum.

Theoretical framework of IM

Based on the literature review and the preceding discussion, Figure 1 shows that the key components of IM can be described in terms of knowledge, skills and values.

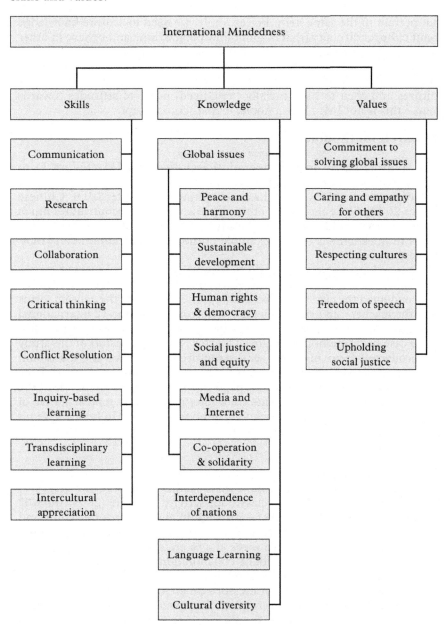

Figure 1: Theoretical framework of international mindedness.

This conceptual framework, drawn from the preceding discussion and literature review, allows us to identify the components of IM that appear in the case study documentation later in this chapter.

It is important to recognise that a number of items above should appear in two or more columns because you can have knowledge and skills and values that pertain to the same item. For example, we need to acquire knowledge about cultural diversity (that is about how people think and behave in other cultures); then we need skills to communicate with other cultures; but we also need an attitude of empathy towards other cultures in order for IM to operate effectively. It is possible to have knowledge and skills about other cultures and then to have racially prejudiced, negative attitudes towards them – this is not IM. IM is a noble, empathetic concept.

Research methodology
Choice of case study
This study is based on the theoretical framework of IM (Figure 1) to analyse School C which was opened in 1983. It is one of the English School Foundation institutions and it has been authorised to offer IBDP Chinese B since 2000. Since the choice of the representative case contributes much to the external validity of a case study, it is important to show that the school in question is a typical example of the implementation of an IBDP Chinese B course.

I focus on Christie's classroom discourse analysis – curriculum macrogenre (see below) – in the Year 12 Chinese classroom. The average age of students is 17. I conducted the classroom observations after obtaining the consent forms from the teacher and principal with assent from their Year 12 international school students. The classroom observation was conducted over four lessons.

The case study method is employed for this paper. The results of this study were collected from in-depth semi-structured interviews and classroom observations carried out in March 2011. A teacher and two to four students were interviewed in school C. This paper focuses on the result of one of the schools only, where four students were interviewed. It is representative of responses from the other two schools, although we need to be wary about generalising from such a small sample. The interviews were tape-recorded and transcribed.

Curriculum macrogenre
I applied the model of curriculum macrogenre to explore the stages of the teaching cycle in school C classroom activity. Christie (2005:100-101) examines a prototypical model of a curriculum macrogenre of teaching and learning activities in terms of curriculum initiation, curriculum negotiation, and curriculum closure. These three stages are shown in Figure 2 which also indicates that teacher-student collaboration and interaction among students constitute the major parts of teaching for IM.

The school C teacher spent four lessons (of 60 minutes each) teaching for IM at the curriculum macrogenre level. The teacher set the tasks and gave instructions about the aims in the curriculum initiation phase. Students presented their findings by collaborative groups during curriculum negotiation in lesson 3 and the teacher and students gave comments on the presentation during curriculum closure in lesson 4. They had revision for examination at the end of the teaching cycle as shown in Figure 2.

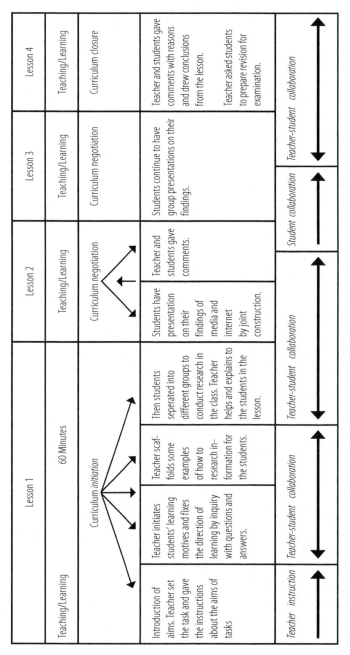

Figure 2: *Curriculum macrogenre in School C (Christie: 2005:131, Shum, 2010: 140); each lesson is 60 minutes.*

In Figure 2, the teacher set the tasks and gave instructions and expectations about the aims; students were expected to understand the focus of the task and write down key points in their notebooks. The teacher initiated students' motivation through inquiry-based learning. Students were separated into groups and were asked to collect data about current global issues from the internet and public media. The teacher had given examples of varied interpretations of some events by the media on the internet. The teacher then gave scaffolding support so students could research the information in lesson one. Students presented their findings about the media and internet in group presentations. The teacher and students gave comments from lessons two to four. At the end of lesson four the teacher drew conclusions and asked students to prepare revision for the examination.

Selected IM components
The following IM components were selected to inform the analysis of the classroom interactions.

Inquiry skills by scaffolding
In the teaching cycle, the teacher implemented an inquiry-based approach. Spronken-Smith *et al* (2011: 15-16) identified inquiry skills having three scaffolding levels:

> *Structured inquiry* where the teacher probed the open-ended questions relating to media reporting on the internet of certain events in different nations and encouraged students to engage in classroom interaction in order to arouse their curiosity and encourage their participation.
>
> *Guided inquiry* where the teacher provided questions to stimulate inquiry but students are self-directed in terms of exploring these questions. The class discussed the internet issues with the teacher, posing questions in order to enhance students' understanding of multiple perspectives.
>
> *Open inquiry* where students formulated the questions as well as going through the full inquiry cycle themselves (after Staver and Bay 1987).

Teacher:
OK. Actually, we are exploring the global influence of the internet. For example, the relationship between the internet and the economy, its influence and the benefits it brings, or the influence of the internet on the cultural exchanges and its contribution in promoting information regarding culture. Let us think about the characteristics of internet for two minutes. Discuss this with your classmates. If you know now, you can also speak out.

In the discussion, the teacher guided students to think about the influence of internet on global and social development by group discussion and she encouraged students to express their opinions.

One student indicated that the internet represents internationalism.

学生：很快，很有效率，没有地域的限制。
Student:
    Very fast, very effective, it is not restricted by geography.

The teacher further elaborated that internet is global even though some countries controlled internet access. She also indicated that the internet functions as media.

师：还有呢？好，我分析一下，请你们做笔记。做笔记的话，第一点，互联网是全球性的，它不是某个地区才有的网站。如果某个国家不拦截，你可以浏览任何国家的网站。互联网是全球性的东西，不属于某一个国家。第二点，互联网就是传媒。

Teacher:
    Is there anymore? Good, let me analyse. Please take down the points... Now the first point. The internet is global. The internet is not only available as websites in the country where you are. If there is no restriction by any country, you can surf to the websites of any country. The internet is global and does not belong to any country. Now the second point. Internet is the media.

In order to develop communication skills, the teacher analysed internet interpretation of events and she asked students to make notes and expand their vocabulary for further discussion.

Collaboration and research skills

The Teacher set the research tasks on the impact of the Internet on culture and gave guiding questions The students then undertook collaborative analysis of the points in order to reach conclusions

老师：现在我要你们收集资料，两三个星期之后做口头报告，主要关于文化方面，即互联网对文化交流带来什么影响。

Teacher:
    Now, I want all of you to search for information in both Chinese and English and after two to three weeks present an oral report. Its main theme is related to culture, that is, the influence of the internet on cultural exchanges.

老师：我把这个问题留给你，你回家思考。下个星期我会留部分时间给你们讨论互联网与文化的关系。关于互联网给经济带来的好处与冲击，是不是都是好处？不是，那不是的是什么，要有例子，我要你们找这方面的资料。

Teacher:
> I will leave these questions to you. Please think at home. Next week, I will give you some time to discuss the relationship between internet and culture. There is also an impact of the internet on the economy. Is the internet beneficial all the time? If it is not, then what exactly is it? There must be examples. You are required to research the related information.

The teacher expects students to develop research skills through collaborative and critical reflection which are the key components of ways of knowing. They are applying new knowledge in real-life situations. This research-based practice and critical reflection can help students develop IM in terms of problem-solving skills and research skills through collaborative learning.

The teacher divided the students into three groups after the discussion. Students were expected to prepare for lessons and were required to have enough ideas to start the discussion by working in teams. This can cultivate students' confidence, inquiry skills and critical thinking skills. Students have to analyse the link between internet and culture, and the knowledge is interdisciplinary and inter-related in the group discussion and group presentations. They have to research the relevant facts about the internet, and then prepare the discussion, setting out arguments for and against, and ending with oral presentations of their own views.

Intercultural and international understanding

Harrison (2013:95-96) has highlighted the importance of intercultural understanding for IM. Hill stresses that intercultural understanding is an essential component of IM:

> I think the most important element is intercultural understanding/ awareness and what we sometimes call intercultural literacy. It is absolutely fundamental; without that you can't have IM.
>
> (Interview, Hill 2012)

UNESCO (2004) states:

> The acquisition of knowledge is based on the principle of mutual understanding between nations, of peaceful coexistence, of international understanding and by understanding the growing world interdependence of States with different social political systems.'
>
> (p.95)

So UNESCO advocates the main goal of international education in terms of knowledge about the interdependence of nations, skills of mutual understanding between countries, and values which are committed to world peace. These are all aspects of international understanding (that is, understanding between nations).

In the following group presentation, students discussed the impact of the Internet on intercultural understanding around the world. They also learn about multiple cultural perspectives on the same issue.

Chris:
We will talk about the good and bad influences of the internet.

Chris:
还可以看其他国家，如美国的新闻，因为不同国家对同样事情的观点会不同。我们看到别国对一些事情的看法，譬如美国对埃及的看法，可能跟香港的看法不同，从别国的看事情的角度可以看到它们的文化。

Chris:
We can also watch the news from other countries like American news because different countries have different opinions regarding the same issue ... for example, the American view of Egypt is likely to be different from the Hong Kong one. From the way other countries look at certain issues, we can also see their culture.

In the group discussion, students analysed that there were multiple perspectives from different countries on the same issue because of different cultures and values. Students indicated that they can understand different cultures by travelling and using the internet:

Student H:
The point is that the internet makes touring even more convenient. Right now, we only need to surf the internet, we are able to perform many such tasks. Furthermore, touring a country is the best way to understand the cultures of other countries. If touring is made even more convenient, we will gain greater understanding of the cultures in other countries.
Moreover, internet promotes learning cultural heritages such as Cantonese Opera and Chinese Opera around the world. It can also promote and preserve cultural heritages.

Student C:
The fourth point is that we can use internet to admire the essence of the cultures of all other countries. For example, people from other countries can also watch the Cantonese or Beijing opera.

Students learn intercultural understanding by appreciation of cultural heritage (in this case Cantonese and Chinese Opera). This leads to understanding the importance of preserving cultural heritage.

In the following discussion, the teacher asked students to think about cultural invasion and endangered cultures.

老師：同学们都讲过，大国文化侵略小国文化，对不对，其实他们是从哪些国家移民到哪些国家？肯定是，怎么样？多元文化。

Teacher:
> Students have also mentioned that the cultures of some larger countries invade the cultures of smaller countries. Right? Actually, from which countries are those cultures migrating and to which country? This is multiculturalism.

某男学生：国际地位

A male student:
> Countries whose international standing is important.

老师：对，国际地位高的国家，政治和经济能力高的国家，对不对？然后他们，引用美国的例子，很好，因为美国的文化遍布全世界，所以，肯定是政治和经济的关系的影响有关，同学都没有讲到，大国文化我们可以讲到美国，可是小国文化呢，就是小文化吧，有同学大文化小文化这样分，这样分也可以，所以小文化慢慢被侵略了。

Teacher:
> Yes, the countries with high international standing, strong economic and political influence. Right? After that, we can use the United States as an example. This is very good because the culture of the USA is prevalent throughout the world. So, it must be related to the influence of economics on politics. So, the regional cultures and other endangered cultures may disappear because of cultural invasion.

In the group presentation, students have to identify facts, opinions, values or ethics in controversial issues. They observed that the internet is dominated by Western countries and English language. Students develop mutual respect, ethics, rights and responsibilities through the presentation. The teacher indicated the danger to minor cultures because of the pervasiveness of Western cultures and the English language on the internet.

The teacher stated that people will be influenced by languages and ideology. It is very important to preserve endangered cultures and languages.

Critical thinking

The teacher guided the students towards critical thinking on global issues. She indicated that the present internet is multi-directional and communication can be interpreted in many ways. Students can understand the global issues from different points of view and they can participate, interacting and sharing their views. They can make their own judgements and seek the 'truth of history' from different cultural interpretations against the backdrop of human rights, using human values as a framework.

某女学生A：互联网也可以给人们有自由言论的好处，它可以让我们可以自由发表对不同国家对政治方面，或者是社会方面的意见和经济方面的问题。

A female student A:
> The internet is also beneficial in giving others the freedom of speech. It enables us to express freely opinions regarding political aspects of other countries and their societal aspects and economic problems.

某女学生B:还有我们过度依赖网页的资料,都是不好的,因为有些网路的资料,因为是不准确的,还有会有些误导。

A female student B:
> It is not good that we are overly dependent on the internet for information. Some of the information on the internet is not accurate and can be misleading.

Chris:
> 因为网上大量的信息,所以会导致人们很难分辨信息的真伪,所以会引起误会和错误地接受信息,这就会使网民对其他国家的文化可能有不正确的印象,引起对事物看法的偏差,严重的情况下会引起种族歧视。

Chris:
> The large volume of information on the internet makes it difficult to differentiate between genuine and false information, causing misunderstanding and errors when the information is received. This will lead internet citizens to have incorrect impressions of the cultures of other countries. This will give rise to deviated views. Under more severe conditions, it will lead to racial discrimination.

虽然网上有言论自由,但是我们也要切记网上的并非全部是真实的。另外,互联网会让网民接触到很多新鲜有趣的文化与其他国家的事物,有可能让一些网民忘记自己的文化传统。

Although there is freedom of speech on the internet, we have to always remember that not everything on the internet is authentic. Apart from that, internet allows internet citizens to come into contact with many new and interesting cultures and other things from other countries. It is possible that some internet citizens forget their own cultures and traditions.

老师:好处方面大家讲得都很直接,你们都很了解。关于这两点坏处方面,比如说忘记自己的文化,这是对的,但能不能深入发展一下这一点。如果从全球文化方面说,一些人和民族有追求大文化、比较先进国家的文化趋向,觉得自己的文化没不值得保留,这样会出现什么问题?

Teacher:
> Everybody has talked directly regarding the advantages. All of you understand this well. Regarding the disadvantages, for example forgetting one's culture, this is correct. But, can

we elaborate this point further? From the viewpoint of global culture, these peoples and races adopt more influential cultures, which are the trendy cultures of more developed countries. They feel that their cultures do not deserve to be preserved. What problems will this bring about?

The teacher plays an important role guiding the students to correlate the varying interpretations of world events. Students discuss the impact of the internet on the world in terms of internationalisation and globalisation.

In the group presentation, students critically analysed misleading information on the internet which could lead to misunderstanding and even racial discrimination. Students have to apply reasoning, justification, induction and deduction in order to get rid of biases.

Global citizenship

Harrison (2013:97) indicates that global issues are related to the notion of interdependence in relation to many areas: human rights, economics, politics, the environment, culture, technology, climate change, finite resources, poverty, peace and conflict.

Students develop IM through learning deeper transdisciplinary knowledge of global issues to which they apply skills such as critical thinking and values such as intercultural understanding and respect. The teacher used transdisciplinary approaches to ask students to think about the connections between different types of knowledge in the media and the impact of the Internet on globalisation.

学生：互联网让个人与不同的团体表达他们的意见或信念的系统。因为互联网它不属于个人的控制，这个性能让教育更加包容，更便利彼此的学习，因此互联网能通过教育大大减少不同种族之间的冲突，在社会方面，互联网也可能让不同的人更加融洽。

Student:
>The internet is a system that lets individuals and different organisations express their opinions and beliefs. Because the internet is not controlled by any one person, this characteristic enables education to be even more comprehensive and even more beneficial to studies. Because of this, through the internet, racial conflicts are being cut down drastically. As regards societal aspects, the internet also enables different people to become more integrated.

Students realised that every right has a corresponding responsibility for all individuals, such as human rights and social justice. The teacher commented that students should not only think about the advantages and disadvantages of internet but also consider the preservation of cultural identities and the promotion of cultural diversity under the impact of globalization.

老师：在群体方面，外来文化侵略本地文化，其实外来文化进入本土，也可以带来一个好处，我们有了多元化，所以两面都可以说。

Teacher:
> In the group aspect, external culture invades the local culture. Actually an external culture also brings a benefit. We can speak about the two aspects.

The teacher helped students to develop IM by thinking about the impact of the internet locally, nationally, and globally. During their internet investigations students would see how an event was reported by the media in different countries and thus become aware of multiple perspectives. UNESCO (2014:4) indicates that the acquisition of basic knowledge and cognitive skills (the content of learning) must promote problem-solving and creative thinking, understanding and respect for human rights, inclusion and equity, and a positive attitude towards cultural diversity. It must also foster a desire and capacity for lifelong learning and learning to live together, all of which are essential for the betterment of the world and the realization of peace, responsible citizenship and sustainable development.

Interview with student:

Student C:
> I think we have to do research about global issues but Chinese B is more about finding the words in Chinese and learning more simple ideas. The IB programme aims to teach you how to think. So maybe by teaching individuals how to approach significant global issues you empower the people, empower the students to analyse different problems in our world.

(Student, interview, 2012)

In the interview, students reflected that they were developing IM by group discussion and collaborative learning about global issues. The teacher was a role model to promote IM. She encouraged students to learn and respect different points of view on social issues. Because the teacher is open-minded she helped students to develop IM and critical thinking by inquiry-based learning.

Interview with teacher:

Teacher:
> I think the meaning of the IB mission statement is too general. I hope children are open-minded and have the courage to express their own views in the classroom discussion.

(Teacher, interview, 2012)

Students and the teacher made judgments about the ethics of the internet based on human core values.

The practice of pedagogic discourse between the teacher and the students was focused on promoting IM and self-reflection in the teaching/learning cycle.

Conclusion

The teacher made good use of scaffolding in her teaching. Christie (2006:125) indicates that the concept of 'guidance through interaction' in the context of shared experience can help students solve problems under teacher guidance or in collaboration with more capable peers in group discussion.

Christie (2006:166-167) also indicates that teachers and students should share judgments on the significance of events in the teaching and learning cycle. This study provided evidence that students were not only learning language but also developing IM, and the skills of problem solving and critical thinking through researching media websites in different countries. Students reacted negatively to (perceived) unethical social sanctions and made positive recommendations about the need for caring and understanding.

Halliday (2007a:350-351) recommends 'language learning, learning through language and learning about language'. He indicates that learning is 'learning how to mean'. Halliday (2007b:187) also stresses that second language learning, like first language learning, is a problem-solving activity which involves information processing.

The teacher divided the students into groups after the discussion. The teacher indicated that students had enough ideas to start the collaborative learning discussion in order to cultivate students' confidence and abilities in developing inquiry and critical thinking skills.

International education is facing a dilemma between ideological and pragmatic interests. I urge that education should not just emphasise pragmatic interest and examination results. Teachers are not just transmitting simple knowledge and basic ideas.

In contrast, the teacher should be a role model of the IB learner profile and encourage students to learn from their peers through discussion and open minded critical thinking. Teachers should use probing questions to engage students in self-reflection on personal beliefs and values based on the human core values. The teacher and students were willing to share their points of view based on mutual trust and mutual respect 'to create a better and more peaceful world through education' (IB mission statement).

Teachers are expected to facilitate students' developing global views, critical thinking and independent learning. However, teachers' professional change is a long process. In fact, teachers need a lot of support in using different strategies in different classroom contexts. Thus the IB should not only continue to provide regular professional development, but should also give concrete support to enhance teachers' IM in pedagogic design so as to implement the curriculum objectives successfully via a whole school approach.

This study has attempted to explore the relationships among international education, the International Baccalaureate and Chinese as a second language. It can also help second language teachers and students in the effective teaching and learning of Chinese. Moreover, it is hoped that the relationships between IBDP Chinese B, the goals of international education, and the mission of the International Baccalaureate have been somewhat clarified by this study.

A variety of IBDP professional development opportunities should include inculcating an inquiry-based interdisciplinary approach and development of IM – an attitude of caring and commitment to lifelong learning, intercultural understanding, global citizenship and cultural thinking – in Chinese B teaching as outlined in this case study.

I suggest that curriculum and student evaluation include opportunities to develop and assess creativity, values and commitment. This paper has raised some issues that IB curriculum coordinators and examiners should consider for the betterment of IB Chinese B curriculum planning. Teacher and students need the ability to think globally, work co-operatively and become responsible citizens.

They also need the pedagogical tools to cultivate intercultural understanding, to think in a critical and systemic way, and to resolve conflict in a non-violent manner. The traditional teaching and learning style has been shifted to conceptualise global citizenship as knowledge, skills and values acquisition via a pedagogy that favours autonomous collaborative learning, critical and interdisciplinary thinking, and a constructivist inquiry-based approach on the path to IM.

Confucius and Mencius advocated a perfect world of brotherhood of mankind: equality, union, harmony, welfare, justice and universal peace in an ideal world, or the idea of Utopia 'Da-Tong'. Kahteran (2015:215-216) indicates that neo–Confucian scholars Tu Weiming & Daisaku Ikeda promote the concept of great harmony (Datong) or the harmony of differences in a harmonious society of peaceful coexistence. They advocate the promotion of intercultural dialogue, intercultural understanding and creation of a worldview of harmony and coexistence.

Teachers may not always succeed in developing IM in their students. Teachers can download information and lesson plans for the classroom from the IB Community Theme web pages and they can also discuss global issues among themselves from the IB Global Engage web pages. These will provide opportunities to put into practice the spirit of the IB mission statement.

Finally, I hope this study will contribute to promote effective implementation of IM in teaching and learning Chinese and other languages in IB programmes.

References

Cambridge J. and Thompson J. (2004). Internationalism and globalization as contexts for international education. *Compare* 34 (2). 161-175.

Christie, F. (2005). *Classroom Discourse Analysis: A Functional Perspectives*. London: Continuum: Paperback Edition.

Christie, F. (2006).*Pedagogy and the Shaping of Consciousness: A Functional Perspective*. London: Continuum. Paperback edition.

Delors Jacques. (1996). *Learning: The Treasure Within*. Paris, UNESCO. unesdoc.unesco. org/images/0010/001095/109590eo.pdf   Viewed on 27 February 2015.

Duff, P. & Lester, P. (Eds.) (2008). *Issues in Chinese Language Teaching and Teacher Development*. Centre for Research in Chinese Language and Literacy Education. Canada: University of British Columbia, November, 2008. http://crclle.lled.educ.ubc.ca/documents/ SHProceedings.pdf   Viewed on 27 February 2015.

Halliday, M.A.K. (2000). *An introduction to functional grammar*. Beijing: Foreign Language Teaching and Research Press.

Halliday, M.A.K. (2007a). *The Language of Early Childhood*. Volume 4. Beijing: Peking University Press.

Halliday, M.A.K. (2007b). *Language and Education*. Volume 9. Beijing: Peking University Press.

Harrison, D. (2013). Intercultural understanding: continuity in the international secondary school. In M. Hayden & J. Thompson, (eds) *Exploring Issues of Continuity: The International Baccalaureate in a Wider Context*. London: John Catt, pp.91-106.

Hayden, M. (2006). *Introduction to International Education*. London: Kogan, pp.7.

Hayden , M., Rancic, B. & Thompson, J. (2010) Being International: Student and teacher perceptions from international schools. *Oxford Review of Education*, 26:1, 107-123.

Hill, I. (2001). Curriculum development and ethics in international education. *Education for Disarmament Forum*. Three. 2001 p.49-58. UNIDR (United Nations Institute for Disarmament Research), Geneva. Available in English on the following website http://mercury.ethz.ch/serviceengine/Files/ISN/109160/ichaptersection_ singledocument/79b97c04-1743-463a-ba91-15e885b5077b/en/08_Curriculum+Developme nt+and+Ethics+in+International+Education.pdf   Viewed on 25 February 2015.

Hill, I. (2007). International education as developed by the International Baccalaureate Organization. In M. Hayden, J. Thompson, J. Levy (eds) *Sage Handbook of research in international education* Sage: London, 2007. pp.25-37.

Hill, I. (2012). Evolution of education for IM. *Journal of Research in International Education*. 11 (3) 245-261.

International Bureau of Education. (1999). A Culture of Peace. *Education Innovation and Information*, Number 100, September 1999. http://www.ibe.unesco.org/publications/ Innovation/inno100e.pdf   Viewed on 25 February 2015

Kahteran, N., (2015). Tu WeiMing & Daisaku Ikeda New Horizons in Eastern Humanism: Buddhism, Confucianism and the Quest for Global Peace. *DISPUTATIO PHILOSOPHICA*, pp.213-218 http://www.google.com.hk/url?sa=t&rct=j&q=&esrc=s &source=web&cd=3&ved=0CDAQFjAC&url=http%3A%2F%2Fhrcak.srce.hr%2Ffil e%2F198446&ei=xEcYVfGRL8OumAXAmoH4BQ&usg=AFQjCNHAkWpnJ14p_- qAi4WugGY_4jL-Vw   Viewed on 29 March 2015.

Oxfam (2006). *Education for Global Citizenship: A Guide for Schools*, pp.1-12. http://www. oxfam.org.uk/coolplanet/teachers/globciti/downloads/gcguide06.pdf   Viewed on 27 December 2014.

Shum, M.S.K. (2010). *The functions of language and the teaching of Chinese: Application of Systemic Functional Linguistics to Chinese language teaching*. Hong Kong: Hong Kong University Press.

Spronken-Smith, R.A., Walker, R., Batchelor, J., O'Steen, B., Angelo, T.. (2011). Enablers and constraints to the use of inquiry-based learning in undergraduate education. *Teaching in Higher Education*. Vol. 16, No. 1, February 2011,15-28.

Staver, J.R., and M. Bay. (1987). Analysis of the project synthesis goal cluster orientation and inquiry emphasis of elementary science textbooks. *Journal of Research in Science Teaching* Vol. 24: pp.629-643.

UNESCO (1974). Recommendation concerning education for international understanding. Cooperation and peace and education relating to human rights and fundamental freedoms. Paris: UNESCO General Conference. http://www.unesco.org/education/nfsunesco/pdf/Peace_e.pdf   Viewed on 25 February 2015.

UNESCO (2002). Asia-Pacific Network for International Education and Values Education (APNIEVE), Bangkok: UNESCO Asia and Pacific Regional Bureau for Education.24.

UNESCO (2004). What is International Education? UNESCO Answers, San Sebastian UNESCO Centre, pp.94-95 http://unesdoc.unesco.org/images/0013/001385/138578e.pdf Viewed on 28 December 2015.

UNESCO (2013). Intercultural Competences: Conceptual and Operational Framework. Paris: UNESCO, pp.10

UNESCO (2014). *Position Paper on Education-2015*. UNESCO, pp.4 http://unesdoc.unesco.org/images/0022/002273/227336E.pdf   Viewed on 15 February 2015.

UNICEF (2013). Global Citizenship- A High School Educator's Guide (Grades 9–12), pp.1-54. teachunicef.org/sites/default/.../global_citizenship_hs_final_3-13.pdf   http://teachunicef.org/explore/topic/global-citizenship   Viewed on 10 January 2015.

Chapter 6

Integrating Theory of Knowledge (TOK) thinking skills into the IB Chinese classroom

Cho-yam Lam

Abstract

IB learners are encouraged to apply their TOK thinking skills to their overall IB learning and subject teachers to integrate TOK into their subject. This is expected to be common practice in all IB World Schools. This pilot case study took place in an IBDP Language B Chinese classroom of an international school in Hong Kong.

The aim is to explore how TOK links are made by both the teacher and students and what factors contribute to the facilitation or impediment of the application of critical thinking in their classroom. The analysis is based on the data collected from IB official documents, literature, interviews with an international educator, the IB coordinator, the Chinese teacher, and the students.

The data reveal discernible efforts made by the teacher to integrate not only TOK critical thinking processes but also IB philosophy and pedagogy into her language class. Some of the key factors for her success include an understanding of what TOK is about, careful selection of teaching materials, scaffolding, believing in her students and challenging them with support and guidance.

However, support from school level seems to be absent in this IB endeavour. Though it only provides a glimpse of the picture and further study is needed for a fuller picture, the findings in this study can still shed some light on the matter and inform discussions regarding how TOK critical thinking can be an integral part of Chinese Language B classroom practice and across different subjects.

The chapter concludes with suggestions to include critical reading in the IBDP curriculum and urge schools to provide teachers with extra time for reflection and preparation and ongoing professional training.

Introduction

Since the establishment of the International Baccalaureate (IB) in 1968, Theory of Knowledge (TOK) has always served as an interdisciplinary course. It has stood the test of time and remains an essential feature of the IB Diploma Programme (IBDP). The curriculum structure of six subjects plus three core elements has remained the same with TOK as one of these core requirements (Walker, 2011:5). It shows the original model is a visionary one and its framework is still a preferable model in which the skills and attitudes that it seeks to develop in students are more or less aligned with the general demands of 21st century education (Beard & Hill, 2008).

These include research skills (extended essay), critical thinking skills (TOK) and communication skills (languages, presentation). Reflection on the cultural shifts of the information society brought about by the massive expansion of knowledge made available through information technology is one of the main elements of TOK (IB, 2013b:3). The inclusion of Approaches to Learning and Approaches to Teaching, together with international mindedness, in the new curriculum model across the continuum demonstrates the IB philosophy and educational goals.

TOK at the core underpins all subjects with the central aim of instilling critical thinking in students and ultimately the skills of learning how to learn. Furthermore, it also aims to try to help students to comprehend and make connections with what they come across in their daily lives and in their learning of different subjects. Teachers are expected to relate their teaching to the learning experiences of their students in TOK.

Placed at the centre of the Diploma Programme, TOK aims to foster a spirit of inquiry and develop critical thinking by encouraging students to take a metacognitive stance reflecting on the knowledge that they've constructed based on their own experiences. Alec Peterson, the first Director General of the IB, expressed the aim clearly:

> the purpose of Theory of Knowledge is to make explicit in the minds
> of pupils the differing methodologies of the carefully planned range
> of subjects which they study. It will succeed in its purpose if no holder
> of the International Baccalaureate enters the university unaware
> of the difference between moral and aesthetic and the problems of
> their inter-relation and without having thought about the differences
> between the 'proof' in mathematics, in physics and in sociology.
>
> (Peterson 1972: 41 as cited in Doll, 2001:3)

In the history of the IB, TOK has always been an important component and plays a strategic role. It functions as a vehicle to connect all disciplines in the IBDP and to promote the thinking skills that enable students to understand and act upon the values summarised in the IB mission statement and learner profile throughout their IB journey. Despite its importance, many in the IB community are unclear of what TOK is about (Dombrowski, Mackenzie & Clarke, 2010:5).

To help clarify TOK, the IB commissioned a research paper on it which was completed in late 2010. All new IB subject guides published since then have a section to demonstrate the link between the subject and TOK with a list of suggested questions. The IB has also introduced new workshops such as 'TOK for subject teachers', 'TOK integration around the hexagon', 'TOK integration across the subject' as well as 'A theoretical and practical approach to developing links between TOK and CAS.'

Each workshop for subject teachers aims to provide non-TOK teachers with a basic understanding of TOK, whereas the workshop for TOK integration is for TOK teachers and subject teachers to share their understanding and to discuss ways to integrate TOK across the curriculum. While these workshops are useful for disseminating the idea of TOK within the IB community, they are only useful for those who have the opportunities to attend the workshops.

Unless their schools have an established culture of sharing experience amongst teachers, especially after someone has attended a workshop or seminar, those who do not know much about TOK may still remain confused. In addition, using the words of Judith Fabian when she talked about the practice of Dewey's democratic classroom in reality, she said 'to what extent it is practised is questionable' (2011:24). The same statement can be used to reflect on the extent to which IB philosophy is practised in the IB classroom and in the IB school.

The nature of TOK
Interdisciplinary
On the IB official site, TOK is referred to as 'the interdisciplinary TOK course' which aims to help students to 'develop a coherent approach to learning that transcends and unifies the academic areas and encourages appreciation of other cultural perspectives.' In recent years, efforts made to strengthen this special function of TOK have been evidenced. The latest IBDP evaluation guide and self-study questionnaire requires schools to evaluate their 'collaborative planning and reflection includes the integration of theory of knowledge in each subject' (IB, 2010:25). This was not a requirement in their 2005 publication.

The term 'interdisciplinary' is defined as the integration of knowledge from multiple disciplines (Hammond and McCallum, 2009), or plainly as a 'study of relationship among disciplines' (Doebler, 1980:11). Nissani (1995) and Wood (1997) refer to 'interdisciplinary' as the combinations of two or more disciplines. This integration is open to interpretation which may range from simple communication of ideas to the mutual integration of organising concepts, methodology, procedures, epistemology, terminology, data, and organization of research and education in a fairly large field (Franks *et al*, 2007:170).

Wood further suggests that a thematic approach is a common characteristic of interdisciplinary curricula whereby students have the benefit of studying multiple sources and gaining multiple perspectives. Wraga (2009) categorises TOK as an example of fused curriculum, which is the study of the interrelationships of two or more subjects. However, most definitions focus on what 'interdisciplinary' is and offers no information on the nature of the process. For IB, the definition for interdisciplinary in terms of TOK can be summed up as a 'coherent approach to learning' and 'transcends and unifies the academic areas' through the application of critical thinking skills.

Critical thinking
Critical thinking, as concluded by Huitt (1998), is one of the most essential attributes for success in the 21st century. Although critical thinking has a strong association with TOK owing to the question-based nature of the

course, IB offers no specific definition for either critical thinking skills or the critical thinking process; rather the IB leaves it open to the teachers to decide what they should be. However, the TOK course with its wide range of areas of knowing (AOKs) and ways of knowing (WOKs) concurs with the 'broad-based, cross-disciplinary' requirement of Halpern (1993:246) for an effective critical thinking course.

There is no consensus on its definition amongst experts in this area, albeit the concept has been around for a long time and there is a vast arsenal of research studies on critical thinking. For example, Ennis (2011) defines critical thinking as 'reasonable and reflective thinking focused on deciding what to believe or do', while Astleitner (2002) views critical thinking as a higher order thinking skill. In comparison to lower-order thinking skills, it constitutes interpretation, analysis, evaluation and inference, rather than mere comprehension and knowledge application.

Paul and Elder (2006) define critical thinking as 'the art of analysing and evaluating thinking with a view to improving it'. The essential elements include the ability to ask appropriate questions, select pertinent information, reach well-supported conclusion, examine different perspectives and communicate effectively. Hughes (2014:35) criticises the lack of emphasis on analytical thinking in the TOK assessment criteria and hence deflates the overall aim of TOK as a critical thinking course.

It is apparent that critical thinking in the TOK context is unlikely to match perfectly an array of existing definitions. Thus no dispositions or taxonomy of critical thinking will be used to analyse the data for research question 2 (#RQ2). Instead, the focus will be on whether or not the teacher noted her students applying critical thinking in her lessons and whether or not the students themselves were aware of applying critical thinking when learning Chinese.

Importance of language in the IB

Besides TOK, language development is also valued highly not only in the IB Diploma Programme, but also across the IB continuum. It is the aim of the IB to create globally-engaged students who can communicate in more than one language and have a good understanding of other cultures in the wider world (IB, 2013a:6). The IB recognises the contributions of language in developing students into holistic learners, ones that embrace a good understanding of intercultural differences, show empathy and share humanity, respect others' values, and see the world as whole. It requires all students to take a first language and a second language in all programmes, so that they can also learn to recognise their own cultural identity, value and prejudices. Hill (2010:17) sees language as a link to humanity.

When a linguist employs a language with attitude, namely 'differentiated, dynamic and realistic attitudes', he believes it will maximise intercultural understanding and actualise international mindedness. I prefer the terms used by Deardroff (2006) to identify intercultural competence: respect, openness, curiosity and discovery – they are more straightforward and can be instantly linked to the attributes of the IB learner profile.

Besides serving its purpose as an instrument for communication and as an important means of intercultural understanding, language is also a way of knowing in TOK (IB, 2009:3). Since languages impact on culture, identity and international mindedness, the requirement of the studying of a first and a second language in the IB programmes serves the purpose of preserving the mother tongue, native culture and heritage of the students (Bridgestock, 2009) as well as being a channel to enhance understanding and awareness of differences.

In some IB schools, many of them in Hong Kong, students often take English as their first language, and their mother tongue, Chinese, as their option in Group 2. There are also cases where students take English in Group 1 and an additional language in Group 2, for example, an Indian student who takes English and Mandarin or a Chinese student who take English and Spanish.

However, for the majority, being asked to study two languages allows them to keep close to their mother tongue and heritage culture. Thus, TOK helps students to develop critical thinking skills and learn how to learn; languages enable students to develop an understanding of another culture and to learn to live together. They are both key elements in developing critical thinking and intercultural understanding and an integral part of the IB curriculum. They therefore contribute to the IB aspirational education vision of cultivating internationally minded, globally sensible and responsible citizens.

Language B and TOK

With the essential role of language in mind the new Language B guide, which came into effect as of 2011, provides specific thematic areas for language focus which teachers can use freely in their delivery of the curriculum. The new features in the latest Language B course require students to study three core topics and two optional topics from a choice of five. The core consists of communication and media, global issues, and social relationships.

Two of these topics are concerned with how people interact and behave in the modern world especially under the influence of technology. Global issues, in particular, allow students to gain awareness of dilemmas that transcend geographical borders. The study of global issues offers students the opportunity to utilise their critical thinking skills and examine them from a global perspective.

Hanvey's (1982:162) classification of global perspective includes five dimensions, of which 'perspective consciousness' is the most important for fulfilling the aim of cultural awareness in both IB language teaching and TOK:

> The recognition or awareness on the part of the individual that he
> or she has a view of the world that is not universally shared, that this
> view of the world has been and continues to be shaped by influences
> that often escape conscious detection, and that others have views of
> the world that are profoundly different from one's own.

The five general topic areas are cultural diversity, customs and traditions, health, leisure and science and technology. These topics are closely related to students' real-life experience and offer opportunity to students to draw on their prior knowledge gained from other subject areas as well as their background knowledge and experience.

These thematic areas are not too dissimilar to the areas of knowledge (AOKs) identified by TOK. They are 'mathematics, natural sciences, human sciences, history, the arts, ethics, religious knowledge systems and indigenous knowledge systems'. The last two have been added in the new 2013 guide after the TOK curriculum review, though the guide also suggests that exploring any six of them would be adequate. The new thematically structured Language B course lends itself well to TOK, as it offers limitless opportunities for discussions and debates over different topics under the prescribed theme.

> I think language teaching is wonderful for critically discussing global issues from a TOK perspective because you can use virtually any content. The door is wide open. You can bring in all sorts of issues to do with intercultural understanding, for example. There is a plethora of things that you can do. Almost all literature is about the human condition and can lead to discussions, plays or scenes which can be acted out in class dealing with social issues and with global issues – language teaching offers more opportunity than any other subject to explore dimensions of international mindedness.
>
> (Hill 2014 taped interview)

In addition, the selection of topics can be flexible to match the interest of the students and their real-life experiences, a good starting point for an inquiry (Kahn & O'Rourke, 2004).

To strengthen links between TOK and subject disciplines, a list of suggested TOK and subject-related questions is included in all latest subject guides. However the list in the Language B guide is problematic. The fact that it recommends teachers make links between their language and the four ways of knowing (reason, emotion, perception and language) relies on two assumptions:

> All Group 2 teachers are familiar with TOK and its terminology, which we know is not the case.

> That teachers will go beyond discussing TOK questions that are associated with the subject area itself, and move on to questions such as: 'Do we know and learn our first language(s) in the same way as we learn additional languages?' (IB, 2013:8). This could be construed as precluding meaningful discussion on a range of topics pertaining to the content of the Language B course and be seen as irrelevant and time-consuming by the language teacher.

Finally, the exclusion of the four newly-introduced ways of knowing (intuition, memory, faith and imagination) can cause confusion to non-TOK teachers. Although this is likely to be an oversight, at the time the

Language B guide was updated, the new TOK guide had been in circulation for months. Most importantly, this does not help teachers understand how to integrate TOK into their subject; rather it appears like asking teachers and students to spend their valuable lesson time for extra TOK lessons. Though these questions are second language related, none of them are related to the topics of the core or options. This is inclined to confuse non-TOK language specialists and discourage them from incorporating TOK in their teaching.

Mandarin and the curriculum

In order to set the context of this study, we need to understand the importance of Mandarin and its special status in the school curriculum in Hong Kong. Other than enabling cultural understanding, language is a useful tool for interaction and communication. Especially in the 21st century, being competent in a foreign language is regarded as beneficial for providing an economic edge and ensuring national security in addition to improving brain development and enhancing intercultural understanding.

Since China opened up its market to the world in 1978, the growing demand for learning Mandarin is apparent and persistent. After more than 20 years of economic reform, China's presence in the world's economy nowadays is prevailing. Mandarin is ranked as a desirable language in relation to employability, trade and even national security by many expert groups such as the Expert Group on Future Skills Need (EGFSN) (2012:12) in Ireland and the National Security Language Initiative in the United States.

Furthermore, mastering Mandarin is the key to understanding Chinese people and the Chinese culture. After the handover in 1997, the Hong Kong government has introduced the 'biliterate and trilingual' language policy and promoted the use of Mandarin in the business sectors. As Hong Kong and China's economic ties get closer and contact between the people of Hong Kong and mainland China grows more frequent, Mandarin has become an important second or foreign language to the locals and the expatriate community in Hong Kong.

This is one of the reasons why Mandarin is added to the curriculum in nearly all international schools in Hong Kong, including IB World Schools. Most of them make it a compulsory subject for all year groups, while some offer it as an option, but the number of students taking Mandarin is proportionally much higher than other foreign languages in almost all schools.

TOK, language, IB learner profile and IB philosophy

Hill (2001:50) indicates that intercultural understanding helps people to respect different values and global issues; he also stresses that languages can help students to respect different values and attitudes. Policy and practices in all IB schools are expected to reflect and support the IB educational philosophy that is spelled out in the IB's mission statement and learner profile (IBLP). In the latest TOK guide, it has provided a table to show the link between TOK and the IBLP.

Such are the qualities of TOK that they can be identified in all of the learner profile characteristics. 'Thinker, reflective, inquirer and knowledgeable' are obvious in their connection to knowing. 'Open minded, balanced and risk-taker' link with the consideration of all perspectives and rational considerations related to an issue. 'Principled and caring' rely very much upon emotion and ethics as a base for positional thinking. 'Communicator' demands an understanding of value-laden and cultural specific vocabulary and how this is used to convey knowledge.

However some literature indicates that the teaching and implementation of the attributes of the IB learner profile and mission statement are flawed (Starr 2009:122), and that the reality in schools does not match the stated aims of the IB mission statement (Nette, 2006:8). Moreover George Walker (2010) in his paper entitled *East is East and West is West* adds further discussion to the importance of Chinese expansion in the IB programme and questions the underpinning approach to the educational philosophy of the earlier IB. He suggests that it might be beneficial to consider Asian philosophical principles alongside the Western principles as what may be good for a Western based curriculum may not be ideal in the Asian context.

In a study that took place in an IB primary school in Hong Kong, Mcleod Mok (2009) commented that specialist teachers, especially Chinese language teachers, are less approving of the inquiry approach and reluctant to collaborate in the planning of the IB curriculum. In the absence of another case study in a Western country for comparison, it is hard to pinpoint whether it is due to a mismatch of Chinese upbringing to the Western teaching approach of IB or to other factors. However, the study does show a glimpse of IB Chinese language teachers in Hong Kong.

In recent years, there has been a growing interest in investigating the impact of the IBDP. The research findings of Coates, Rosicka and MacMahon-Ball showed that most university representatives recognised the value of DP in fostering critical thinking and academic skills for tertiary education readiness (2007:20). Cole, Gannon, Ullman and Rooney (2014:41) further investigated the topic of TOK and critical thinking and found that second year IB students displayed stronger critical thinking skills than those in their first year.

Nevertheless, the student participants were uncertain whether it can be attributed to their learning of TOK. Furthermore, they also pointed out that lack of time and apprehensiveness towards TOK were two common concerns of non-TOK teaching staff. This is possibly the reason for their reluctance to integrate TOK into their teaching. The following quote from Hill (2014 taped interview) rightly highlights the urgency of demystifying and making TOK accessible to all IBDP teachers:

> Teachers don't have the time to actually get together and find out what TOK is about, unless it's really structured and organised. So they really do need to understand the fundamental concepts of TOK. It's not philosophy, it's epistemology, to a certain extent.

Indeed, TOK is often perceived as a philosophy course and the 'mystery' view of TOK has been in existence for quite a while, especially in the eyes of non-TOK teachers. A very important IB research paper was published in 2010 by TOK experts about what TOK is (and is not). However, IB teachers who do not frequent the IB's Online Curriculum Centre might not have heard of the document.

As Dombrowski *et al* (2010:5) announced in their introduction to this research paper, in order to achieve the aims of TOK and further those of the IB, the teachers and students must have a clear understanding of what TOK can achieve and how. For an important paper as such, the most straightforward way to reach the teachers is to dispatch it through the IB coordinator in all schools and to seek that person's assistance in bringing it to the attention of all IBDP subject teachers.

Although the amount of research related to the IB and its three programmes is increasing, there has been little discussion about TOK. Moreover, at the time this study took place, no research studies had been found that survey the integration of TOK in any specific subject area; thus looking at the integration of TOK in the language classroom is worth doing.

Research questions and methodology

This pilot study focuses on the integration of IB Theory of Knowledge (TOK) thinking skills into the teaching and learning of Language B Chinese in international schools in Hong Kong. The study set out to answer the following research questions:

1. To what extent do Chinese language teachers of the IBDP integrate TOK into their teaching?

2. What are some of the factors that facilitate or impede the application of critical thinking by second language Chinese students?

A case study approach was employed in this study to address the research questions. The school participating in this case study is one of the oldest co-educational international secondary schools in Hong Kong. It offers an international education through the medium of English. Students follow the UK GCSE and IGCSE curriculum, and then progress to study the IBDP or the BTEC Vocational course in Years 12 and 13. The school was authorised to offer the Diploma Programme in December 2006.

The teacher research participant has been teaching the Chinese Language B course since it was launched at the school and it was her second year as a TOK teacher. The target class was a Year 12 Chinese Language B Standard Level class comprising 14 students of mixed gender and from different nationalities.

By the time the observation took place, the students had already been taking both TOK and Chinese Language B courses for almost half a year. Chinese Language B is chosen as the target rather than Language A here because there are a greater number of Language B learners, compared to a handful of Language A, which will ensure higher reliability. Data collected from a standard level class will help to determine if language proficiency is a factor that hinders students in applying critical thinking skills.

A total of seven lessons of a full teaching cycle based on a sub-topic was observed. The topic 'Poverty' was introduced as a sub-topic of the core 'Global Issues'. The observation from the introduction of the new topic until the last lesson lasted about three weeks. Towards the end of the teaching-learning cycle, the students were asked to write an essay about poverty problems in China. A focus group that consisted of students representing high, medium and low Chinese ability and a student with special education needs was invited to participate in a 20-minute interview to talk about their IB learning experience with the focus on TOK and Chinese.

In-depth semi-structured interviews with the Chinese teacher who was observed, and the IB coordinator of the school, were carried out. A personal interview with Dr Ian Hill, former Deputy Director General of the IB who worked with the organisation for nearly two decades, were also conducted. This would allow a better understanding of different perspectives on the research focus and provide for data triangulation. The interview of the teacher and the IB coordinator complemented each other and formed a fuller picture of the operational side of the Chinese classroom together with an overall picture of the school with regard to the integration of TOK across the curriculum. It also helped to form a more comprehensive view of educational practice in the school.

The first research question was answered by the data collected from the interview with Dr Hill, the IB coordinator and the Chinese teacher of the school. Data for the second research question came from the interviews with the Chinese teacher and the student representatives. Owing to the limited word allowance here, the analysis of the observation and essay is not included in the chapter.

Results and discussion
Discussion of case study findings for RQ#1
To what extent do Chinese language teachers of the IBDP integrate TOK into their teaching?

The new TOK knowledge framework provides step-by-step guidance for both the TOK teachers and students as they examine knowledge questions through the use of different ways of knowing (WOKs) that associate with each of the areas of knowledge (AOKs). This guidance has been criticised by some as being too prescriptive. IB has identified eight WOKs, namely language, sense perception, emotion, reason, imagination, faith, intuition, and memory but it is sufficient to just learn any four of them in detail.

This interdisciplinary approach as defined by Newell and Green (1982:24) enables learners to make 'inquiries which critically draw upon two or more disciplines and which led to an integration of disciplinary insights'. The TOK knowledge framework provides a structured overview for TOK teachers, especially those new to TOK, to unpack the knowledge questions and make links to WOKs and other disciplines across the curriculum.

Although the new guide looks more prescriptive than before, it is explicitly announced at the beginning of the guide that there is no obligation to follow the guide to the letter, and it is not a limitation for teachers as they have the autonomy to deliver the course providing that it fits the TOK aims and objectives. However the likelihood of a successful delivery of TOK largely depends on knowledge of the TOK curriculum by its TOK teachers. If some TOK teachers themselves have difficulty in grasping the essence of TOK and limited support has been provided in school, it is unlikely that the course would be delivered effectively.

> We don't use the framework, it is too complicated. I don't have time. The other problem of course is the TOK teacher; even though I was in the TOK team. Except for the first year, I was supported. It really takes a lot of time to teach TOK... The problems is, even teachers who have taught TOK, I don't know whether they have complete understanding.
>
> (Chinese teacher)

There is obviously a gap between what IB expected and what is happening in schools. However, why were measures only taken in the past few years to improve classroom practice?

> Because the IB has realised that in schools people are not integrating TOK as we thought they would and as we would like them to. TOK is so central to the whole essence of IB so the IB wanted to provide more support for teachers, but the consultation process takes time. I also see critical thinking skills as an important component of international mindedness, a concept which has been with the IB since its inception but which practitioners and scholars have been struggling to define.
>
> It's only in the last eight or nine years that IB curriculum documents have really focused on this and bring it out in the subject guides. For example, the columns to be found in the recent maths and sciences DP subject guides indicating where TOK ideas, relationships with other subjects (interdisciplinarity), and intercultural awareness information occur for particular syllabus topics.
>
> (Hill 2014 taped interview)

Cole *et al* (2014:32) reported that schools differed in their approaches to fulfil the TOK requirement. Schools that made the development of thinking skills a whole-school initiative enjoyed greater success in the integration, while those which offered training to subject specialists only, received both positive and negative responses. According to the study, a whole school approach seems a vital element in the success of integrating TOK thinking skills across a school curriculum.

In addition, Long, Moran & Harris (2010:29) argue that promoting an interdisciplinary approach is essential for nurturing successful learners as it helps students develop the ability to integrate knowledge gained from other subject disciplines. Jones (2009:76) states that the interdisciplinary approach can strengthen the understanding of the students and raise their attainment in all disciplines but it requires time and effort from the teachers in collaboration and preparation.

In other words, in order to reap the benefits of applying an interdisciplinary approach and achieving the intended aims and purposes of TOK, it needs collaborative effort from all teachers and support by the school to make room for this to happen. However, the Chinese teacher was somewhat frustrated:

> Collaborative learning, frankly speaking, in this school, even though they are talking about it, up till this moment, we don't have any...

Nonetheless, all interviewees were optimistic about the likelihood of a successful integration of TOK into the wider curriculum. Hill stressed that understanding TOK is a prerequisite for its success and all three interviewees mentioned that the lack of time was another hindrance in actualising the integration:

> I think that it can be done ... it has to be done first of all by teachers knowing what TOK is about. And this is the first problem in most schools. In most schools the pace is frenetic.
>
> (Hill 2014 taped interview)

> We have at least one teacher from each subject involved in the teaching of TOK. That's the best we can do... Unfortunately, you know it is impossible as staff and teachers have no time.
>
> (IB coordinator)

> Actually, if you are really dedicated to do your lesson plan, it takes a lot of time. How do you interpret IB and TOK philosophy? I will say, No 1, time is very limited.
>
> (Chinese teacher)

When the teacher was asked about her opinion regarding the usefulness of the 'Group 2 and TOK' section in the subject guide, it elicited the following response:

> They never talk about TOK, how to integrate it. Even the Chinese workshop tells us nothing about how to integrate TOK into the Chinese language classroom.

So, what has the Chinese teacher done to incorporate TOK in her lessons?

> I think actually providing them with scaffolding, then skills to expand not only the vocabulary, grammar, and also actually including that they read some UNESCO, United Nations' literature. Then they cultivate critical thinking through global issues. Collaborative skills are very important too.

From the interview with the Chinese teacher, it is apparent that she is enthused by IB philosophy and dedicates her teaching to achieving the IB mission statement and helping students to become real IB learners. She chooses her teaching materials deliberately to stretch the ability of her students, even though her students are Language B standard level learners. In her lessons, she used a lot of open-ended questions to steer students to think in the direction she intended to explore whether it was a topic specific terminology or an idea. She often encouraged elaboration by asking follow-up questions which required students to think critically.

> Teacher: Let me ask you, why is education so important? To a poor family, is education important?
>
> Students: Important.
>
> Teacher: Why?
>
> Student A: Because ... um ...they have to...
>
> Teacher: Alleviate poverty. Say it again "tuo pin" (alleviate poverty).
>
> Teacher: OK, let's have a look at the global issue. With so many poor, for example in Hong Kong, China, India, so many poor, listen, what is the importance of education to an individual, why is education so important? To them, to an individual, why is education so important?

She asked questions to elicit ideas from students until they were able to come up with the idea that education can help them to expand their knowledge. She then pointed to the common belief that education can change lives and the world. In addition, she also intentionally pointed out the difference between Western and Chinese values, and built in group presentations and essay writing in each teaching cycle.

> We talked about democracy, because it is holistic education, we talk about the differences between Western and Chinese values... There are students who can do the presentation and show that they can explore the issue critically.
>
> (Chinese teacher)

The other strategies she used to help foster the critical thinking skills of her student were through scaffolding and providing them with a list of carefully-selected websites, guiding them to gather relevant information, to explore different perspectives and reminding them frequently and explicitly to explain their point of view with reasons and supporting evidence just like they are required to in TOK. Here are some extracts from her lessons which showed her constant and unequivocal way of linking TOK to her teaching:

> In TOK, you first look at a claim, then find evidence.
>
> There should be supporting evidence, where is the evidence?

In TOK, you make a claim with proof to support it. In Chinese, you also have to think of the logic... TOK is not just for an exam, it's for everyone, it is for you to apply in your research, and to show proof.

She believed that the students:

need to do the research and explain why. They are not only reading, they need to understand what it is. They may need to think, of course, they think about the issue. So I asked them to read different perspectives because they need to think about, for example, the United Nations and human rights, shared human values, such as the shared values of different religions. I think they can evaluate what is right, what is wrong.

Nonetheless, she also commented on the belief of a colleague who saw deeper and broader understanding of topics as unnecessary for Language B since it is a language acquisition course:

One teacher asked me if we have to teach our students to write about global citizenship, because they are foreign language students.

The study of Lai, Shum & Zhang (2014) reveals a similar picture as displayed in the above interview. They conclude that concern with examination outcomes means that pedagogical beliefs and interpretations of the concept of international mindedness are hindrances to the integration of international mindedness in teachers' classroom practices. By the same token, based on the interview, they are also likely to be obstacles to the integration of TOK in subject disciplines. However, further study will have to be done to confirm this assumption.

Discussion of case study findings for RQ#2

What are some of the factors that facilitate or impede the application of critical thinking by 2nd language Chinese learners?

All three students agreed that TOK is helpful in the development of critical thinking skills. In general, it helps them to think more logically, see other points of view rather than their 'own egotistic point of view'.

The Chinese teacher believed that her students exercise critical thinking skills and their comparatively limited Mandarin competency is not a barrier for her to ask higher order thinking questions:

I think they have the, I would say, prior knowledge. I know that they have Model United Nations; this way, they have prior knowledge and common sense.

She encourages them to think critically, even if they have to think in English, or their own mother tongue, but 'they should have their own point of view, this is what I emphasise'. However, she also suggested that assessments should include explicit criteria that require students to think critically:

I think they need to, in their assessment, frankly speaking... The most important thing is (that) students have the ability to explain logically, reasonably with evidence.

When the students were asked about what strategies they use to integrate TOK in the learning of Chinese Language B, the responses mostly revolve around multiple perspectives:

Exploring arguments from different sources and different points of view.

I don't think of TOK when I am making my comparison and looking at different points of view, but I think, in a way, I am integrating TOK because I try to ask questions, and think in different ways before I come to conclusions.

Being able to explore arguments from multiple angles is something everyone can do; the benefit of TOK is that it provides more starting points to base an argument on.

However, the constant reminders from the Chinese teacher and the guidance provided to the students are also mentioned:

My Chinese teacher always reminds us to think like in TOK, provides us links to do research on the topics we discuss. It is a lot of work, and sometimes I do not understand, but it is helpful in developing my knowledge of the topic.

TOK itself is a method of improving the overall thinking process... I am now more aware of thinking an issue through different perspectives, especially when I am reminded. I have never done it before I took TOK.

My Chinese teacher always reminds us to think of TOK, to research and give evidence.

It seems the constant reminders given by the teacher is a crucial factor that supports and enhances the integration of TOK into teaching and learning in her Chinese classroom.

However, besides their Chinese teacher and TOK teacher, 'most of the teachers never mentioned TOK in class' or 'TOK is not strongly suggested in class but it is occasionally referenced where applicable'. It is worth noting that one of the students made a very acute observation which provided a snapshot of the reality in their classroom:

To say most would be very generous, unless teachers are subconsciously incorporating TOK within our learning. However, unlike our Chinese teacher, it is rarely ever discussed explicitly 'if you think about it from a TOK perspective' but never in any detail as teachers mainly work through the syllabus and don't tend to go out of their own way if the information is unnecessary.

These responses yet again confirm that the teacher's beliefs and the teaching pedagogy employed are key factors that impede the integration of TOK across the curriculum. In the interviews, the students all agreed that the Chinese teacher has positively integrated TOK into her teaching. Moreover, their responses also mirrored the comments made by the Chinese teacher earlier, that is, little evidence is available in school regarding the promotion of TOK thinking in other subject disciplines, a key factor for the success of TOK integration.

Conclusion

In this chapter we examined integration of TOK in the context of an IBDP Language B classroom in a long-established international school in Hong Kong. Based on the data collected from IB official documents, interviews with Dr Hill, a very experienced international educator, the IB coordinator, the Chinese teacher and the students, it shows that it is possible to transfer IB TOK critical thinking skills to the learning of other subjects and continue to develop these skills outside of the TOK classroom.

In the current era of knowledge explosion, the agglomeration of information flooding the internet today, helping students develop critical thinking skills for discerning biased or untrue information that is widely available on the internet is as important as learning content knowledge. However, as suggested by Hughes (2014:42), with the aim of developing students' critical thinking, the assessment of TOK should require a display of analytical skill. I would like to add that developing students' critical reading skills explicitly in the curriculum is as vital as critical thinking.

While TOK lessons encourage open verbal discussions on knowledge issues and knowledge claims, little or no attention has been paid to critical reading, an ability that is valued as much as critical thinking in tertiary education. The ability to read critically any texts, not limited to printed texts, but in a broader sense such as source-websites, video clips, paintings, data charts and so on, allows students to distinguish facts from opinions, analyse assertions, and justify their understandings with evidence.

Subject specialists need to be prudent therefore in selecting teaching materials or texts that are relevant to the course content and adequate to the ability of their students. At the same time, the teaching materials should also provide opportunity for students to reflect, think and make links to their prior knowledge and understanding. In a Language B classroom, more demanding texts can also be used with the support of technology, such as learning online platforms where students can read and understand an unseen text with the help of an inbuilt dictionary and audio function, or approach the task in collaboration with other students through Google doc and so on.

Discussions after reading should provide an excellent venue for integrating TOK critical thinking explicitly in the classroom. Especially in a Language B classroom, without a basic understanding and knowledge of a topic and the topic-specific vocabulary, it can be difficult to have a meaningful discussion in the target language. Teachers may want to reflect upon this aspect when considering their selection of differentiated texts. These should range from easy to complex to create a classroom environment where students will be encouraged to apply strategies to decode and reconstruct intended textual meaning.

In conclusion, meaningful learning largely depends on the belief of the teachers, their pedagogy and strategies employed in their classroom. Whether it is the integration of TOK, the use of inquiry learning, concept-based learning or technology, teachers must primarily not only have an understanding of what they are doing but have school support in terms of time to be able to plan its integration into lessons, and ongoing professional training to develop this further.

References

Astleitner, H. (2002). Teaching critical thinking online. *Journal of Instructional Psychology*, 29(2), 53-76.

Beard, J. & Hill, I. (2008). How IB prepares students. In *Educational Leadership,65*(8). Retrieved April 8, 2015 from http://www.ascd.org/publications/educational-leadership/may08/vol65/num08/How-IB-Prepares-Students.aspx

Bridgestock, L. (2009). Every teacher is a language teacher. *IB world*. Retrieved March 1, 2015 from http://www.ibo.org/ibworld/jan09/everyteacher.cfm

Coates, H, Rosicka, C, & MacMahon-Ball, M. (2007). *Perceptions of the International Baccalaureate Diploma Programme among Australian and New Zealand Universities*. Canberra, Australia. Australian Council for Educational Research.

Cole, DR, Gannon S, Ullman J, &Rooney P. (2014). *Theory of knowledge (TOK):Exploring learning outcomes, benefits and perceptions*. Bethesda, MD, USA. International Baccalaureate.

Doebler, B.A. (1980). Skinning cats and interdisciplinary studies: A caveat. *Change,12*(8):10-12.

Deardorff, D.K. (2006). Identification and assessment of intercultural competence as a student outcome of internationalization. *Journal of Studies in International Education*, 10 (3), 241-266.

Doll, G.J. (2001). *The IB Theory of Knowledge course: A study of its character, development, perceptions of it, and its potential for students and teachers in United States overseas schools* (Doctoral Thesis). Retrieved from Proquest Dissertations and Theses database. (UMI No. 3004691)

Dombrowski, E., Mackenzie, J., & Clarke, M. (2010). *Perspectives on a curious subject: What is IB theory of knowledge all about?* IB research paper. Cardiff, UK.

Ennis, R. H. (2011). *The Nature of Critical Thinking: An Outline of Critical Thinking Dispositions and Abilities*. Retrieved March 15, 2015 from http://faculty.education.illinois.edu/rhennis/

Expert Group on Future Skills Needs. (2012). *Key Skills for Enterprise to Trade Internationally*. Forfás: Ireland.

Fabian, J. (2011). Principled teaching and learning. In G. Walker (Ed.), *The changing face of international education-Challenges for the IB* (pp.21-37). Cardiff, UK: IB.

Franks, D., Dale, P., Hindmarsh, R., Fellows, C., Buckridge, M., & Cybinski, P. (2007).

Interdisciplinary foundations: Reflecting on interdisciplinarity and three decades of teaching and research at Griffith University, Australia. *Studies in Higher Education 32* (2), 167-185.

Halpern, D. F. (1993) Assessing the effectiveness of critical thinking instruction. *The Journal of General Education*, Vol. 42 (4), 238-254.

Hammond, C., & McCallum, F. (2009). Interdisciplinarity: bridging the University and field of practice divide. *Australian Journal of Teacher Education*, 34(2). 50-63.

Hanvey, R. (1982). An Attainable Global Perspective. *Theory into Practice*, Vol. 21 (3), 162-167.

Hill, I. (2001). Curriculum development and ethics in international education.Education *Disarmament Forum n3. 2001 49-58.* UNIDR (United Nations Institute for Disarmament Research), Geneva.

Hill, I. (2010). Promoting international-mindedness through language acquisition. *International School* magazine (ECIS), Vol.13(1), 16-18.

Hill, I. (2014) Taped interview with the author at the University of Hong Kong.

Huitt, W. (1998). Critical thinking: An overview. *Educational Psychology Interactive.* Valdosta, GA: Valdosta State University. Retrieved March 8, 2015 from http://chiron. valdosta.edu/whuitt/col/cogsys/critthnk.html.

Hughes, C. (2014). Theory of Knowledge aims, objectives and assessment criteria: An analysis of critical thinking descriptors. *Journal of Research in International Education*, 13(1), 30-45.

IB (2009). *Language and learning in IB programmes.*Cardiff, UK: IB.

IB (2010). *Programme evaluation guide and self-study questionnaire: Diploma Programme.* Cardiff, UK:IB.

IB (2013). *Language B guide.* Cardiff, UK: IB.

IB (2013a). *What is an IB education?* Cardiff, UK: IB.

IB (2013b). *Theory of knowledge guide.* Cardiff, UK: IB.

Jones, C. (2009). Interdisciplinary approach-advantages, disadvantages, and the future benefits of interdisciplinary studies. *ESSAI (7)*, Article 26. Retrieve December 14, 2014 from: http://dc.cod.edu/essai/vol7/iss1/

Kahn, P., & O'Rourke, K. (2004). Guide to curriculum design: Enquiry-based learning. *Higher Education Academy*, 30-3.

Lai, C., Shum, M.S.K., & Zhang, B. (2014). International mindedness in an Asian context: the case of the International Baccalaureate in Hong Kong, *Educational Research*, 56:1, 77-96, DOI: 10.1080/00131881.2013.874159

Long, J., Moran, W., & Harris, J. (2010). Following the yellow brick road: Interdisciplinary Practices in the land of Oz. *Issues in integrative studies (28)*,28-68.

Mcleod Mok, W.H.W. (2009). *Teacher learning in a context of comprehensive school change: A case study of an international school in Hong Kong during implementation of the International Baccalaureate Primary Years Programme* (Doctoral Thesis). Retrieved from HKU Theses Online.

Nette, J. (2006, October). *Internationalism - A virtual reality.* Paper presented at the 21st IB Asia-Pacific Annual Regional Conference, Hanoi.

Newell, W.H. & Green,W. (1982). Defining and teaching interdisciplinary studies. *Improving College and University Teaching 30*(1), 23-30.

Nissani, M. (1995). Fruits, salads, and smoothies: a working definition of interdisciplinarity. *The Journal of Educational Thought, 29*(2), 121-128.

Paul, R. & Elder, L (2006). *The Miniature Guide to Critical Thinking Concepts and Tools.* Dillion Beach CA: The Foundation for Critical Thinking.

Peterson, A (1972) *The International Baccalaureate: an experiment in international education.* London: Harrap.

Starr, L. J. (2009, Fall/Winter). A critique of the International Baccalaureate learner profile as a curricular document: context, hegemony, hermeneutics and the four Rs. *PEAR Papers, Essays and Review, 1* (2), 115-124.

Walker, G. (2010). *East is East and West is West.* IB position paper. Cardiff, UK.

Walker, G. (2011). Introduction: Past, present and future. In Walker, G. (Ed.), *The changing face of international education* (pp.1-17). Cardiff, UK:IB.

Wood, K. E. (1997). Interdisciplinary instruction: *A practical guide for elementary and middle school teachers.* Upper Saddle River, NJ: Merrill.

Wraga, W.G. (2009). Toward a connected core curriculum. *Educational Horizons, 87*(2), 88-96).

Chapter 7

International mindedness and teaching materials development in Chinese Language B

Tung-fei Lam

Abstract

This study aims to understand how Mandarin teachers position Mandarin B in relation to IB philosophy, particularly to the notion of international mindedness (IM), and how they make sense of IM through teaching material adaptation. In-depth semi-structured interviews were used to collect data from Mandarin teachers who had taught the Diploma Programme (DP) in Hong Kong. Sixteen teachers from ten International Baccalaureate (IB) schools were interviewed.

The research findings show that two different orientations of understanding IM in relation to the goals of Mandarin B were identified, namely basic understanding and deep understanding. Those who tended to have basic understanding significantly relied on the textbook and adopted a textbook-based approach to adapt materials, whereas those who tended to have deep understanding adopted a textbook-free approach. In the textbook-free approach, strategies teachers used to adapt materials to enact IM evolved around the empowerment of learners and the interplay between text(s) and/or student-centered pedagogy. The result of this study conceptualises Mandarin teachers' understandings of Language B in the IBDP and their practices of material adaptation for developing IM in line with the framework of teacher change proposed by Fullan.

Introduction

The concept of international mindedness becomes increasingly important in the field of international education. Some researchers focused on historical and/or theoretical aspects of the concept, particularly in the evolution and construction of the International Baccalaureate (IB) programmes (Hill 2000; Haywood 2007; Hill 2007; Sylvester 2007; Cause 2011; Hill 2012).

Others were concerned with people's perceptions of the concept in the context of IB schools (Hayden & Thompson 1998; Hayden, Rancic *et al* 2000; Fryer 2008; Gigliotti-Labay 2010; Wilkinson & Hayden 2010; Hersey 2012). This study follows the latter track in this field and aims to understand how Mandarin teachers position Mandarin B in relation to IB philosophy, particularly to the notion of international mindedness (IM), and how they make sense of IM through curriculum planning and materials development.

A recent empirical study about IB Mandarin teachers in the context of Hong Kong showed that the interpretation of the concept of IM in teaching was one of internal challenges to the teachers, but the teachers found various strategies to integrate the concept into practice (Lai, Shum *et al* 2014). Another study also suggested that some teachers took an idealistic approach to adapt teaching materials in the enactment of Language B curriculum in order to promote the notion of IM (Lam 2013).

Both studies tended to agree that different teachers' interpretations of IB philosophy led to different strategies in the enactment of curriculum. Regarding different interpretations of the concept of IM, Lai's study (Lai, Shum *et al* 2014) suggested that:

> Some teachers perceived that international mindedness would develop naturally as a result of studying the subject area. Some teachers focused on promoting international pedagogical arrangements such as engaging students in critical inquiries around the texts and reflections of different cultural settings. Others interpreted international mindedness as achievable through being immersed in a transnational student community and the related international experience.
>
> (p.81)

Based on previous results, the researcher of this study seeks to further develop this observation into the field of materials adaptation in the Mandarin B subject of the IB Diploma Programme (DP).

In the field of materials adaptation, many studies were related to mathematics (Remillard & Bryans 2004; Brown 2009; Mesa & Griffiths 2012) whereas most studies of curriculum material in the subject of Chinese as a Foreign Language were discussed from the point of view of linguistics and aspects of course-books (赵贤洲 1988;李泉 2006;韩萱 2009).

As suggested by Lam (2013), most Chinese teachers did not just choose a textbook but they also adopted some strategies to adapt materials in order to enact the IB curriculum. Such teacher-tool interaction was understood as a significant part of the intended curriculum developed by the teacher to which the following factors contributed: knowledge, beliefs, practices, access to resources and support, knowledge of students and local contexts (CSMC 2012).

Therefore, it is an academic and practical need for researchers to investigate how Chinese teachers interpret the notion of IM and how they may interact with teaching materials accordingly. Precisely speaking, there are two main research questions here:

1. How do IBDP Mandarin B teachers in Hong Kong interpret IB philosophy and the notion of IM in relation to the subject?

2. How do they make sense of IM through adapting teaching materials in the subject?

IB Perspective: international mindedness and Mandarin B

As stated in all IB curriculum documents, IB programmes aim to eventually develop learner's IM. The concept of IM is articulated in different attributes of the learner profile (IB 2006) and highlighted in the *Learner Profile Booklet* (IB 2008) as principal guidance for teaching and learning in IB schools.

As a key cross-programme component, the learner profile will become the central tenet of the IB programmes and central to the definition of what it means to be internationally minded. (p.2)

Singh and Qi (2013:15) further argued that three attributes – communicators, open-minded and knowledgeable – listed in the learner profile were respectively associated with three core elements of IM – multilingualism, intercultural understanding and global engagement – despite the fact that other researchers had a different view (Castro, Lundgren *et al* 2013).

In order to enhance IB learner's IM and related constructs, all students are required to learn more than one language throughout the programmes. The importance of learning language has been stated in *Language and Learning in IB programmes* (IB 2011a) as follows:

In the case of IB programmes, the role of language is valued as central to developing critical thinking, which is essential for the cultivation of intercultural awareness, IM and global citizenship.

(p.3)

Language B plays a key role for the purpose of promoting intercultural understanding as manifestly contributing to IM, so it is one of the core ingredients in the Middle Years Programme (MYP) and the Diploma Programme (DP). In the DP, Language B emphasises 'the importance of understanding language acquisition as a process that also involves the recognition and understanding of another culture'(IB 2011b:19). In the *Language B Subject Guide*, the notion of intercultural understanding has been mentioned in relation to objectives or aims, learner profile and other forms of constructs in the subject.

In relation to the objectives or aims of the subject, the notion of intercultural understanding is identified and stressed in eight different places such as the mission statement, assessment objectives, and course design. In regards to the learner profile, the concept is identified as a means to be a successful communicator in the section of the Language B guide called 'Nature of the subject' where the subject is designed to 'provide students with the necessary skills and intercultural understanding to enable them to communicate successfully in an environment where the language studied is spoken' (IB 2011a:4).

In relation to other forms of constructs, the notion of intercultural understanding is written as 'intercultural engagement' with the target language and culture, rather than intercultural understanding used to describe the interactive skills in *ab initio* (IB 2011b). It is also written as 'intercultural skills and competencies' in conjunction with the notion of linguistic and metalinguistic, sociolinguistic, pragmatic competencies when Language B is linked with Theory of Knowledge (TOK) (IB 2011a). Finally, it becomes 'intercultural awareness' when Language B is linked with the international dimension itself (IB 2011a).

The terms, 'intercultural awareness' and 'international mindedness' are sometimes difficult for individual IB teachers to put into operation in their classes; the terms may appear abstract and arbitrary although the IB did not intend for them to appear so. Such challenges for IB teachers in different regions (for example, the United States, Australia and Hong Kong) have been discussed in many recent studies (Gigliotti-Labay 2010; Doherty and Mu 2011; Lai, Shum *et al* 2014).

In addition, it has been argued that being multilingual did not necessarily enhance intercultural awareness or international mindedness (Allen 2003; Hall 2005). Poor experience of learning other languages may result in the opposite feeling and resistance to the targeted language and culture. So a question for both teachers and researchers will be how Language B teachers can cultivate intercultural awareness and international mindedness as ultimate goals through language learning (IB 2011b).

IB suggested several strategies for IB teachers to achieve the goals, including activating prior understanding and building background knowledge, scaffolding learning, extending language and affirming identity (IB 2011b). In learning by scaffolding, IB identified a number of strategies such as the use of a mother tongue as a temporary aid, more concrete and less abstract contexts for understanding, *etc* (IB 2011b). How Mandarin teachers employ these strategies to adapt materials to develop IM is one of the key questions in this study.

Research method

In-depth, semi-structured interviews were used as the research method to collect data from the teachers. Sixteen teachers from 10 IBDP schools were interviewed. (See Appendix 1 for details about the roles and experience of the teachers.) Only Teacher A, who was responsible for the curriculum development, had not taught Language B in the past. The coverage of IB schools and interviewed participants is wide and sufficient to address the research questions in this study.

Recruiting interview participants was done in two stages, *ie* first stage and second stage shown in Appendix 1. In the first stage, the researcher emailed invitations to the heads of Chinese in all 17 IBDP schools offering Mandarin B at the time of the research. Seven schools accepted the email invitation and nine teachers participated in the interviews at this stage.

In the second stage, the researcher continued to email the invitation to those who were recommended by interviewed teachers in the previous stage. As a result, even more teachers from six schools were interviewed. All recruited participants had to fulfill the following criteria:

had been trained by the IB through official workshops;

were involved with the subject DP Mandarin B in an IB school either as a leader or as a teacher or both;

were willing to share thoughts and experiences with regard to the research questions.

Each interview took 30 to 60 minutes. Except teachers from Schools 6 and 7 who undertook the interview in pairs, all other interviews were conducted individually. Interview questions addressed four aspects:

their teaching background and school context;

their interpretation of IB philosophy and international mindedness;

their attitude towards textbook use in Mandarin B;

their strategies of material adaptation in the subject.

Interview questions for each teacher were raised not in exact order or wording. The order and wording of interview questions were adapted according to the interviewees' responses in order to minimize the effect of leading and to allow teacher participants to talk as freely as possible.

All interviews were audio-recorded except the interview data from Schools 6 and 7 which was only recorded in note form. The interview transcripts and notes were sent to teacher participants for audit checking. The transcripts were coded in the same fashion. The coding system for transcripts worked as follows:

Transcript is numbered line by line.

Teacher's response(s) is grouped or divided into units in relation to the research questions.

Each meaningful response is perceived as one coding unit.

Each coding unit is presented as six digits (the first three digits show the starting line of a unit and the last three digits show the final line); for example, if a response starts at Line 15 and ends at Line 20, it will be presented as 015020.

Each unit is summarised into short phrases with the six-digit code at the end.

Each transcription was read reiteratively. Relevant data from the transcriptions were summarised and coded. Different codes were aggregated into different categories reiteratively with the researcher's reflection as an insider's perspective. This is a process of deduction and induction to gradually generate important meaning from interview data.

The generated meaning was then cross-checked within the text of each transcription and re-visited through empirical evidence or examples. Such a repeated process of coding and analysing allows the researcher to investigate how IBDP Mandarin B teachers interpreted and adapted materials accordingly. The clarity of the coding system here aims to attain a high level of trustworthiness as well as a high level of responsiveness and sensitivity, which are significant in qualitative research.

Mandarin B teacher's perspective: findings and discussion

The interview data illustrated an interesting phenomenon in which the notion of IM was examined in a subject, specifically in terms of material adaptation in DP Mandarin B. The study explored how respondents interpreted Language B in relation to IM, through adapting curriculum materials. The respective findings and discussions will be presented in accordance with our two key research questions.

1. International Mindedness and Mandarin B

Regarding the first research question, the interview data shows that the respondents tended to have two different understandings of the notion of IM in relation to the goals of Mandarin B. Some respondents perceived Language B as a structural component of being internationally minded whereas others perceived Language B as a pedagogical means to be internationally minded.

The former perception tended to focus on mastery of language skills and understanding the culture of the target language only, rather than the concept of intercultural understanding across several cultures. The latter perception tended to focus on different dimensions of IM such as knowledge, skills, attitudes and/or action as suggested in the analytical framework of IM (Castro, Lundgren *et al.* 2013). In this article, we call the former basic understanding of IM whereas the latter is called deep understanding of IM.

1.1. Findings

With regard to the orientation of basic understanding, Teachers H and I asserted that the ultimate aims of the IB curriculum were too demanding and sometimes even unachievable. For the Language B learners, they did not need to learn complicated concepts as long as all linguistic elements of Chinese language could be covered. With regard to the concepts such as international mindedness, it could simply mean that the content of a selected text had to touch on different countries or regions (12T15/T16 Points 6 & 8).

Teacher P, in a similar vein, stressed that Language B learners should be able to have basic understanding of Chinese culture and history as well as verbal and written productive skills at the end of the course. Since learning Chinese is not easy, choosing to learn Chinese was perceived as the embodiment of being a risk-taker, which is one of the IB learner's attributes (06T6022026, 06T6034044).

Teachers who shared a similar thought tended to interpret the relationship between Language B and IB philosophy in a simplified way in which the concept of IM in IB philosophy could be achieved through adding related content into the selected course-book or even taking Chinese as a second language itself.

Teacher E, who was an experienced IB teacher and Chinese curriculum leader, concluded that Group 2 (known as Language B in the Diploma Programme), which aimed to enhance student's communicative competence in a variety of situations and genres, ought to have embodied the concept of international mindedness in the IB curriculum (10E2058070, 10E2070082). This is because the respondent said, 'the establishment of Group 2 Language B curriculum itself manifests the IB programme's philosophy of internationalization' (10E2070082).

In short, this type of response suggests that learning Chinese as a second language was regarded as a structural component of being internationally-minded. In line with such orientation, the respondents did not make authentic changes in regards to the curriculum goals of Mandarin B. They simply perceived the goals of Mandarin B as a subject to understand more Chinese culture, master Chinese language skills and gain confidence in using target language to communicate. These goals are basic and shared by Mandarin teachers in other curriculum contexts.

With regard to the orientation of deep understanding, Teacher K not only emphasised communicative competence but also perceived Language B as a means to nurture a global citizen who will be able to express ideas about personal, regional and global issues (01T8022024). Teacher O took an alternative approach in which the attributes of the IB Learner Profile can be understood through reading Chinese literature and cultural texts. It perhaps was too simple for her students if the terms or concepts were only mentioned superficially in class (03T11060076). Teacher M perceived communicative competence as a bridge between different cultures and as an attribute of being a global citizen who would be able to understand the world and extend their caring from oneself to the world (10T9078091, 10T9065075). She stressed that:

> [Language B allowed learners] to see the world, to understand
> self and other people. [The learners] will start from taking care of
> self [and extend] to his/her local community, [and learn] how to
> communicate, how to exchange ideas, and how to take care of the
> world (10T9201020).

However, both Teacher M and Teacher C shared a view that it had been too difficult to achieve the goal or fulfill all attributes of the IB Learner Profile in teaching due to the pressure of final examinations (10T9065075, 08T10161170). In spite of the difficulty, the interview data shows that the respondents shifted their foci from a mastery of language skills and cultural understanding of the target language to the concept of understanding a variety of cultures as a key component of IM and/or its related knowledge, skills, attitudes and actions.

1.1.1 Knowledge dimension

Some respondents perceived that Mandarin B, as a subject, should include facts about cultural differences and global issues. Teacher B stated that Mandarin B SL focused on daily life culture whereas Mandarin B HL covered the spirituality of a culture, but they all allowed students to understand and accept different cultures (07T120530580). In addition, Teacher N also highlighted that the new component of literature in Mandarin B HL embodied the increasing importance of intercultural awareness promoted by IB (02E3119132).

Teacher L and Teacher M echoed this view but the former respondent highlighted generic higher-order thinking skills of the IB curriculum such as the skill of appreciating literature (06T6034044) whereas the latter respondent focused more on perceiving the literature component as a resource to facilitate communicative competence of the target language as well as the understanding of other cultures in the world (10T9078091).

1.1.2 Skill dimension

In addition to communicative competence, some respondents perceived language as a learning and thinking tool where generic skills such as critical thinking, reflection and literary appreciation were always identified. Teacher L emphasised the importance of critical thinking through reading texts (09T4213216) whereas Teacher O emphasized the importance of literary appreciation through understanding characters inside stories (03T11278281).

In terms of reflection, different respondents reacted in different ways. Teacher P referred to self-reflection about daily practices (06T6146150) whereas Teacher C referred to reflection on his/her role as an IB learner (08T10291292). Teacher N even highlighted the importance of Language B as a context for cultural reflection whereby Language B learners can compare and contrast the culture of the target language with their own cultures (02E3505510). As Teacher O said:

> In the IB Learner Profile, ...one of the attributes is to be reflective. Being reflective people, IB learners should reflect on their strengths and weaknesses in addition to the surrounding environment (03T11270273).

1.1.3 Attitude and action dimension:

Some respondents stressed the affective aspect of learning outcomes such as being open-minded, respectful, inclusive and caring when they were asked to interpret the goal of Language B in relation to IM. Teacher L claimed that:

> I think to be internationally minded means you ought to understand ... such a huge world where every place is different. Difference exists, so you need to respect ... and to be open-minded to accept it (09T4232234).

Apart from differences, Teacher M took another view of intercultural understanding: that cultures do share some common elements such as a sense of caring, developed from self to others as well as to the world (10T9068071). Teacher N, a very experienced Mandarin B teacher, put forward the idea of caring about the target language culture. She concluded that Language B emphasised the use of a language in a cross-cultural context where students were aware of people and issues in other cultures, and eventually accepted such awareness to be part of their responsibilities and actions (02E3099109, 02E3109118). She reiterated that:

> Being internationalised means that [his/her thinking and acting] has been beyond his/her country and nation. Therefore, I think, to nurture such mindedness for L2 learners ... you [L2 learners] should pay attention to the environment outside your mother tongue ... even join the process of transforming it and making it better ... as a return, it would benefit your country, and your personal development. Being such a person is what we call being an internationally minded citizen (02E3111119).

In short, those respondents who tended to focus on knowledge, skills, attitudes and actions in relation to intercultural understanding demonstrated a different orientation, namely the orientation of deep understanding. Along with such orientation, they suggested that learning a second language was regarded *as a pedagogical tool to develop internationally minded learners*.

In other words, their views showed that Language B should not simply be a course of learning a second language in IBDP but rather a course of *learning through language* where the notion of international mindedness and the related construct (such as the attributes of the IB Learner Profile) are consciously conjured up, understood and/or facilitated as a result of language learning.

1.2. Discussion

In this study, two ways of making sense of IM in relation to Language B were found: basic understanding and deep understanding. The findings suggested that these two types of understanding had different foci in terms of the place of Mandarin B in the IB diploma programme profile of subjects, the teaching approach, and the nature of the curriculum objectives.

For the respondents who focused on Mandarin B as contributing to the overall design of the IB diploma programme, this study revealed two types of orientations. Some respondents explicitly or implicitly regarded learning Mandarin B as a *structural component* (part of the IB diploma programme configuration) of being internationally minded whereas the others regarded learning Mandarin B as a *pedagogical tool* for developing international mindedness.

However, the findings should not be simply interpreted as a dichotomy of curriculum perception but rather as a continuum of teacher change. As Fullan (1991) suggested, change in teachers can be observed in three different dimensions:

the possible use of new or revised materials;

the possible use of new teaching approaches; and

the possible alteration of beliefs.

Yin and Li (2008:64) proposed a new framework, based on Fullan's description, to understand how teachers might change in relation to curriculum reform. In this framework, teacher change could vary between 'surface' to 'authentic'. They argued that a teacher's belief was the most difficult element to be changed and an authentic change would only occur if there were changes in all dimensions.

Lam (2013) also suggested a continuum to describe teachers who took different approaches in relation to material adaptation for IB curriculum, *ie* a pragmatic approach versus an idealistic approach. He argued that the former perceived applied language skills as the major goal of the subject whereas the latter perceived the constructs of IM as the goal of Mandarin B teaching, despite the fact that both stressed the attitude of being open-minded to different ideas and respecting different cultures as an IB learner.

With regard to respondents' approaches to teaching Mandarin B, this study found that some respondents focused more on the concept of learning language whereas the others focused more on the concept of learning *through* language. The concepts are not mutually exclusive but rather describe different approaches to language learning at different stages. According to the language-based theory of learning (Halliday 2004; Halliday 1993), there are three strands of language acquisition: learning language, learning through language and learning about language (the last is not pertinent to this study).

The strand of *learning language* refers to 'a child [who] starts learning language from the moment he is born, ...[and is] actively involved in communication, exchanging signals with the other human beings around him' (Halliday 2004:308). The strand of *learning through language* refers to 'language in the construction of reality: how we use language to build up a picture of the world in which we live, ...the part played by language in shaping and transmitting the world view of each and every human culture' (Halliday 2004:317).

The concepts were borrowed to explain the continuum of language learning in IB programmes where the domains such as discrete skills and basic interpersonal communicative skills (BICS) are the foci of learning language whereas the domain of cognitive academic language proficiency (CALP) is the focus of learning through language (Inugai-Dixon 2009; Inugai-Dixon 2013). In the curriculum document, *Language and Learning in IB programmes* (IB 2011b:24), it was clearly stated that CALP can be very onerous for second-language learners due to the fact that teaching often assumes a cultural and academic linguistic background common to all students rather than a diversity of complex multilingual profiles.

In regard to the objectives of teaching Mandarin B, the *DP Language B Subject Guide* states that 'the main focus of the course is on language acquisition and the development of language skills' and 'the material should be chosen to enable students to develop mastery of language skills and intercultural understanding' (IB 2011a:5).

However, it should be noted that a mastery of language skill itself does not necessarily lead to intercultural understanding. Previous researchers indicated that poor experience in language learning could result in an opposite or negative effect on the development of intercultural awareness, in Hall's words: 'new ethnocentrism' and 'new exercise of power' (Allen 2003; Hall 2005).

There were also plentiful academic discussions in regard to the development and/or assessment of intercultural sensitivity, global competence, and other aspects of IM (Bennett 1986; Hammer, Bennett *et al* 2003; Morais and Ogden 2011; Harwood and Bailey 2012). As suggested in the IB research paper by Castro, Lundgren *et al* (2013), the analytical framework of IM comprises five dimensions: assessment, knowledge, skills, attitudes and action.

The findings of this study suggested that the orientation of basic understanding is particularly related to cultural knowledge and linguistic skills of the target language reflected in the objectives of Mandarin B as perceived by respondents. On the other hand, interviewees who were inclined to have deep understanding focused more on IM-related attitudes such as mutual respect, global-mindedness and cultural appreciation as well as the knowledge and skills that could facilitate intercultural understanding and generic higher-order thinking across varied cultures.

It is also worth noting that the assessment and action of IM were rather uncultivated in the respondent's community. For some respondents such as Teacher C and Teacher M, they even perceived the assessment of the Diploma Programme as a negative factor for the development of IM. On the contrary Teacher A said that:

> The foci of learning objectives in IB were cultural understanding and intercultural awareness ... which was the comparison between one's own culture and the target language's culture. I highly valued the learner profile and the notion of international mindedness ... but Chinese teachers are rather traditional. They normally just teach to the textbook ... but IB assessment forced teachers to go beyond their comfort zone. It meant that they needed to look for materials outside the textbook to meet the requirements prescribed in the assessment (01T17077090).

The ambiguity of the above views was attributed to different perceived challenges, suggested in Lai's study, in which the dilemma of 'helping students achieve a high score' and 'challenging students at the conceptual and higher-order thinking level' existed in the school community (Lai, Shum *et al* 2014).

Overall, the aforesaid differences in regard to the position of Language B in the IBDP programme design, the approach to teaching Mandarin B, and its pedagogical focus revealed different Chinese teachers' beliefs for enacting IM at a subject level. As Ancess (2000) argued, teacher's beliefs, their teaching approach and curriculum materials are interactive. So this study is also interested in seeing how these three dimensions might be interrelated, in other words, how respective respondents make sense of IM through developing or adapting teaching materials in line with the orientations of basic and deep understanding.

2. Materials adaptation and the enactment of international mindedness
Regarding the second research question, the interview data exhibits two different types of attitude towards textbook use and related strategies of materials adaptation. The respondents who tended to have basic understanding significantly relied on the textbook, whereas those who tended to have deep understanding adopted a textbook-free approach.

In the former textbook-based approach the strategies of material adaptation evolved around the textbook such as adding texts from other sources, skipping irrelevant topics, *etc.* ('Text' includes visual, audio stimuli and web-based materials.) The latter can be further understood as a dual-track material and textbook-free approach. A dual-track material approach describes the respondents who valued the use of authentic texts to operationalise the IB curriculum along with keeping a textbook as a tool to aid weaker students in learning Chinese.

A textbook-free approach describes the teachers who only focused on the use of authentic texts. In the enactment of IM, these two approaches shared a similar view that one textbook could neither meet IB learner's expectations nor fulfill the expected outcomes of the IB curriculum.

2.1. Findings
In regard to the notion of a textbook-based approach, there was a group of teachers who genuinely believed in the use of a textbook in learning Chinese. Teachers H and I claimed that units in the textbook they had chosen, *Qing Song Xue Zhong Wen,* had followed the concepts (topics) required in the Language B Guide. The textbook had collected texts from different media channels, so there was no need to do any adaptation but rather train your students through chapter by chapter (12T15/T16 Points 2 & 3). Teacher P iterated the same reason for using the same textbook but she would adapt the textbook through adding new, recent texts from media or changing the order of unit topics to coincide with relevant whole school events, assessment requirements, *etc.* (06T6086097, 06T6100113, 06T6190193).

Teachers B and D both emphasised that they also preferred to use a textbook because it could support both students and teachers, especially those who were inexperienced (07T12086093, 09T5103115). Nevertheless, Teacher B would adapt the textbook through adding new authentic texts to challenge those who had a more advanced Chinese proficiency level (07T12110120), whereas Teacher D would adapt the textbook through adding new texts or exercises in order to meet the requirements of Language B assessment (09T5084101).

She highlighted the importance of the Chinese linguistic system built into textbooks where the order of content (topics) and linguistic form should be appropriate for a foreign learner (09T5119123). She said:

> Basically we do not follow the [order of the] topics given by IB, but when you are learning the language, you must understand these topics, not only in verbal form, ...but also in written form... We do not want our nose to be held by IB, so we do not follow their line (09T5090093).

Another group of respondents strategically used the textbook as a curriculum in spite of existing drawbacks. Teacher E argued that the existing Chinese as a second language textbooks, in the absence of a variety of genre for different communicative purposes, were very much confined to the traditional way of textbook organisation in terms of vocabulary and grammar (10E2091103). He stated that no existing textbook was appropriate for the Mandarin B course, but his school still chose the textbook *Qing Song Xue Zhong Wen* because of the proximity of its topics to those prescribed in the subject guide (10E2036042, 10E2043049).

In short, we can say that those who were at the level of basic understanding tended to perceive the textbook as a curriculum and, in most cases, perhaps as the major curriculum resource to be followed by students and teachers. In response to the enactment of IM, the respondents stressed two strategies:

> selecting texts in which the topics matched those of the Language B Subject Guide and the content related to different regions of the world;

> adding guiding questions to texts to stimulate candidates' critical or creative thinking in their internal assessments.

In other words, as long as the topics of the textbook they had chosen fitted the topics prescribed in the Guide, only minimal adaptation would be necessary in the process of curriculum planning. The motivation of adapting materials was attributed to either the assessment requirements or the needs of some students who had a relatively advanced level in class.

This type of response suggested that the *cultural knowledge* and *linguistic skills of the target language* were regarded as the key concerns of the subject. According to the theory of language-based learning (Halliday 1993; Halliday 2004), the strand of *learning language* could be nicely used to describe the mindset of such teachers who tended to interpret Language B as a structural component of being internationally minded.

With regard to the notion of the textbook-free approach Teacher B, who adopted dual-track materials, said:

> I think every textbook has its advantage and disadvantage. [It is natural to see that] the design of a textbook may not match the IB curriculum, so teachers need to adapt it... [Using a textbook] is mainly due to the reason that [students feel it is] reliable (07T12097100).

Teacher N, who adopted a textbook-free approach, explained that it was important to have materials with up-to-date information in line with the development of the world as an internationally minded citizen. No textbook could meet such an expectation, so indigenous materials (authentic materials without editing) with a high quality of standard Mandarin should be carefully selected (02E3190199, 02E2207222). She doubted that any one textbook would be adequate to cover the Mandarin B syllabus:

> Have you used a set textbook which is particularly useful [in an IB context]? ... I really cannot tell. No! ...Topics [required by the curriculum] changed all the time... You would understand such change in the IB context ... could be understood as a short phrase 'keeping pace with time'... Following this central idea, there is no textbook [that would meet the IB expectation] (02E3181205).

Teacher K and Teacher L echoed this view that the teaching material of Mandarin B should be selected from a variety of sources, such as different textbooks and media according to the topics required in the Language B Subject Guide (01T8038047, 09T4060068). However, Teacher L tended to stress the quality of selected texts, *ie* whether the theme of the text could arouse students' interest and whether the language of the text was appropriately challenging (09T4060068, 09T4111116). Teacher K tended to focus on the way(s) of organising teaching materials in order to create a learning environment with different perspectives for students to express, justify or challenge their own ideas (01T8139160, 01T8246270).

In addition to text selection, some teachers highlighted the importance of topics, whereas others highlighted the function of teaching and learning tasks. Teacher M claimed that the topics required in the Language B Subject Guide had demonstrated the ethos of IB philosophy (10T9166175). Teacher J argued that teaching activities such as making use of student's background to create a learning environment with cultural differences was essential to demonstrate the attributes of the IB learner profile in addition to the selection of teaching material (01T7023033, 01T7083097).

In short, the aforesaid respondents did not limit the goal of learning a second language to a mastery of language skills but rather understood the subject as a means to achieve the development of international mindedness in the IB curriculum. Therefore, one textbook cannot be perceived as covering the syllabus but rather as one of a number of curriculum resources for students to learn to be internationally minded through language.

The way of language learning has been moved from the concept of learning language to the concept of learning through language, which is in line with the framework of a language-based learning theory (Halliday 2004) and the second strand of the language and learning continuum proposed in IB programmes (IB 2011b). Although not all teachers use the term, 'IM', it is evident that what they should learn in Mandarin B should not be limited to language skills and cultural knowledge about the target language only, but the knowledge and skills in support of 'being internationally minded', for instance, world knowledge and intercultural competence.

How the respondents adapted teaching and learning material for promoting IM in Mandarin B is another question. Their strategies articulated in the interviews could be studied in terms of three dimensions: the role of the teacher, the role of the learner and the role of the text.

2.1.1 The role of the teacher

Teacher N particularly stressed the role of the teacher in selecting appropriate materials that should contain a variety of standard vocabulary and text types. A variety of text types should be understood as representing different cultural contexts (02E3389404, 02E3404414, 02E3414422). Teacher E shared a similar understanding in regards to the importance of text type in selecting materials (10E20911103). Apart from text type, Teacher A also argued that teachers should pay attention to the ideological agenda of authentic materials. She said:

> We can find many teaching materials that are very Euro-centric or ego-centric, or Taiwan-centric. They are very narrow... I personally feel that we really need resources that would enable [students] to understand international mindedness, and then develop their own international mindedness (01T17219325).

In addition, Teachers J (01T5037046), K (01T8437445), L (09T4111116), M (10T9166175) and O (03T11215219) would also expect teachers to edit selected texts either to help student comprehension or for meeting the written standard of modern Chinese.

2.1.2 The role of the learner

Two different adaptation strategies were identified which showed different degrees of empowerment of the learners during the process of teaching materials development. Teachers E (10E2157166), J (01T7083097) and N (02E2481497) emphasised the richness of a learner's cultural background as a source of teaching support. Teacher N explained the importance of Language B learner's cultural background in relation to the realisation of IM when she said:

> Internationalisation ... means that you finally step across your own culture [to understand] other cultural knowledge, tradition and social customs, and then in the midst of understanding the culture of the target language, you continuously make comparisons and reflections on yours and see the difference... [If you do this], you will have been internationalised (02E3499506).

Teacher O even suggested that, as a process of learning, students should also participate in selecting the teaching materials they were interested in under teacher supervision (03T11195205).

2.1.3 The role of text

Two different adaptation strategies were also identified. The first was the interplay among selected texts and the second about the interplay between selected texts and student-centered pedagogy in teaching and learning Mandarin B.

Regarding the interplay among selected texts, Teacher K suggested making sense of three different texts with different perspectives from different sources under the *same* prescribed topic (01T8139160, 01T8246270) whereas Teachers J and O found that it was possible to start with a text and link it to other texts which displayed different concepts in relation to *different* prescribed topics in the Language B Guide (01T7112138, 03T11151176). The former strategy was convergent whereas the latter was divergent. Teacher N explained the divergent strategy in the following way:

> In those text(s) for the learner to read ... the vocabulary [and related concepts] could cover three or four prescribed topics, I am more willing to search for these kinds of texts ... [because they] could guide us to open our minds and easily make connections with other topics (02E3177180).

Regarding the interplay between selected texts and student-centered pedagogy, Teacher J focused on group-based activity in order to facilitate discussion and create differences of opinion prior to the formation of individual judgment (01T7207222) whereas Teacher N focused on individual reflection in order to critically compare the target language culture and the learner's culture. In addition, Teachers L and M both highlighted the importance of guiding questions given by teachers for students to think, discuss or independently learn (09T4125132, 10T9207221).

In short, this study suggested that both the appropriateness of language expression and the fulfillment of perceived goals were important in adapting materials. The former was concerned with the linguistic form of text, whereas the latter was concerned with the pedagogical issue of implementing curriculum as a reflection of IB philosophy. In the findings related to the latter, this study revealed several strategies which can be summarised as follows:

> To activate the interplay between students' own cultural resources and the target language texts in order to facilitate intercultural understanding.

> To empower students to be part of curriculum development in order to engage them as active learners in the process of intercultural understanding.

> To guide students with questions to activate their generic higher-order skills such as creative thinking, critical thinking, reflective thinking and the like.

To create an effect of dialogue among different texts with mutually-supported or opposite views from different perspectives.

Although assessment requirements, teacher capability and learner motivation contributed to the development of adaptation strategies, this study concluded that 'learner's involvement', 'openness through the use of texts' and '(re)-thinking an issue from a range of perspectives' were the core elements of these strategies.

Some devices were purposefully adopted in fulfillment of the perceived goal, whereas others may be implicitly in support of the goal. In order to effectively employ the strategies, Teacher N claimed that she always used a comparative approach to show opposite points of view in order to facilitate the understanding of cultural differences (02E3452464). Teacher C also took a similar approach to show different perspectives between local and global media in order to open more possibilities for learners and eventually develop a sense of international mindedness to a mature level (08T10388400).

No matter what strategies the respondents had mentioned, comparisons such as horizontal comparison between nations, vertical comparison between local and global, reflective comparison between self and others are perceived as effective instruments for learners to develop IM in Language B.

2.2. *Discussion*

In this study, three types of attitudes towards textbooks and two types of material adaptation approaches were identified. Those who had basic understanding of Mandarin B in relation to IM tended to adopt a textbook-based approach where the strategies of enacting IM would be limited mainly to the selection of topics and/or the design of text-related guiding questions for internal assessment. Those who had deep understanding tended to adopt a textbook-free approach whereby the strategies of enacting IM evolved around the empowerment of learners and the interplay between text(s) and/or student-centered pedagogy.

In terms of the respondents' attitudes towards textbook use, the findings suggested that there were three dimensions: a textbook-based approach, a dual-track material approach, and a textbook-free approach. Previous studies also shared a similar finding but the terms were slightly different (Nicol & Crespo 2006; Shawer 2010). As Shawer (2010) reviewed, different attitudes towards textbook were attributed to different curriculum approaches, *ie* curriculum fidelity, curriculum adaptation and curriculum enactment.

However, this study showed that there was no clear distinction between a dual-track material approach and a textbook-free approach in regard to the enactment of IM through the practice of material adaptation because the respondents did not perceive one textbook as an effective tool to achieve the goal of promoting IM. In this study, this was called a textbook-free approach in which authentic materials were highly valued.

The use of authentic materials and tasks was highlighted by respondents in this study because of its perceived function of maintaining the learner's motivation and achieving the goal of promoting IM. However, it should be noted that not all scholars or teachers agree about using authentic materials. Some researchers argued that authentic materials could cause many concerns for language learners (Ellis 1999; Day 2003). Other researchers also promoted authentic materials as meaningful resources to enhance a learner's motivation and competencies (Kuo 1993; Rilling & Dantas-Whitney 2009).

Having mentioned three types of attitudes towards textbook use, this study does not intend to take them as static descriptions to label an individual teacher's style but rather take them as conceptual descriptions of teachers' attitudes and behaviour in the community. As Brides & Mitchell (2002) suggested in their study, teachers may change from time to time and the transition may also go through the stages of 'saying goodbye', 'the neutral zone' and 'moving forward'.

Lam (2013) echoed this view, postulating the notions of textbook-bound and textbook-free as just two poles of a continuum to describe teacher behaviour when using materials for Mandarin B. In this study, the respondent Teachers K, M and O shared that they had begun by using a textbook and ended up teaching with no textbook after a few years of teaching experience.

For example, Teacher O said that she selected a textbook according to the prescribed topics of Language B, in addition to collecting texts from the web in the first year of her teaching, but she found the way she did this was very problematic. Thus, she decided to gradually use fewer teaching materials from the textbook but more texts from other sources on current issues in the second year of her teaching. In the third year she continued to cut down the use of the textbook and started to consider an approach of teaching a topic in collaboration with a couple of key concepts (03T11135142, 03T11143151, 03T11151176).

In terms of the respondents' teaching materials adaptation, this study revealed two types of strategies, textbook-based and textbook-free. The former strategy refers to the ways of adding or reordering texts or units in textbooks whereas the latter refers to the ways of adapting texts in a relatively sophisticated manner as a curriculum development device and/or a curriculum maker device (in response to student's needs) as suggested by Shawer (2010).

In this study, the respondents who took textbook-based strategies would focus on textbook evaluation through using the prescribed topics stated in the subject guide as selection criteria and tended to do minimal adaptation for the sake of assessment. On the contrary, those who took textbook-free strategies would focus on curriculum planning and curriculum design by using the topics prescribed in the guide as a framework for planning units at a macro level as well as emphasising learner's needs, selecting and organising pedagogical content and activities at a micro level.

This study revealed the strategies in relation to the enactment of IM using a textbook-free approach. These strategies could be understood as interplay among texts and the interplay between text and student-centered pedagogy. The first type of strategy allows teachers to add real choice, encourage higher-level cognitive skills and make the language input more engaging as suggested by Islam & Mares (2003). The second type of strategy allows teachers to increase the role of learners in the process of material adaptation for the sake of awareness development (Saraceni 2003).

In other words, this study showed how texts create dialogue for intercultural understanding and how learners are also cultural resources for teaching and learning, and suggested that both are vital in the enactment of IM. As Tomlinson (2003) argued, a text-driven approach of material development required teachers to be involved in text collection, text selection and text experience. Throughout this process, it is important for IB teachers as materials developers to make meaning of text(s) in the context of IB curriculum in which the notion of IM is promoted. It is also important for teachers to take advantage of having learners with multi-cultural backgrounds as a source of materials and/or as participants in material adaptation.

Finally, it is worth noting that teachers' pedagogical beliefs, educational experience, the IB curriculum expectations *etc* were perceived as challenges for teaching Mandarin in the IB context (Lai, Shum *et al*, 2014). However this study revealed that IB teachers who had different understandings of the curriculum tended to have different strategies to make sense of their teaching through materials adaptation.

One of the significant findings is that textbook-free strategies, unlike textbook-based strategies, were not limited to micro-level techniques such as adding, deleting/subtracting, simplifying, reordering or replacing for the sake of achieving perceived objectives, but rather referred to macro-level strategies such as (re)-contextualizing texts and learners in relation to intercultural understanding. Yet such strategies were criticised by some respondents, such as Teachers D and M, for not treating vocabulary and grammar in a systematic way.

The concept of sequencing and repetitiveness of characters, vocabulary and grammar is still perceived as a core pedagogical concern in the field of teaching and learning Chinese as a second language. Materials development, namely textbook development of Chinese as a second language, is largely informed by the pedagogical studies of Chinese grammar in relation to the field of Chinese applied linguistics and psycholinguistics (赵金铭 1996;施家炜 1998;杨寄洲 2000;吕文华 2002;Xing 2006;李泉 2006;刘珣 2012).

Therefore, how topic-based curriculum design and its corresponding strategies adopted by the respondents could address this concern while enacting IM in Language B is equally important along with the development of intercultural competencies.

Conclusion

The interview data of this study illustrated the interesting phenomenon of materials adaptation in IBDP Language B to develop IM. The study explored how respondents interpreted Language B in relation to IB philosophy, particularly to the notion of IM, and how they adapted curriculum materials in the subject. Table 1 below summarises the findings of interview data in terms of the 'understandings' and the practices of

Mandarin B teachers:

Understandings / Dimensions	Basic Understanding	Deep Understanding
Position of Language B in IBDP	Learning a second language as a structural component of being internationally minded	Learning a second language as a pedagogical tool to be internationally minded
Approach to teaching Language B	Learning language: Learning cultural knowledge and language skills of Mandarin	Learning through language: Learning higher-order thinking skills in global and cross-cultural contexts
Attitude towards textbooks	Textbook as curriculum: Textbook-based approach	Textbook as one of curriculum resources: Dual-track material approach or textbook-free approach
Teaching material adaptation	Textbook-based Strategies: Minimal adaptation through matching topics with the *Language B Guide* and adding texts for assessment	Textbook-free Strategies: Interplay among texts and interplay between texts and student-centered pedagogy

Table 1: Dimensions of 'understandings' of Mandarin B teachers.

All in all, the findings of this study showed that materials adaptation is closely associated with how teachers make sense of the curriculum they have taught. For those who perceived the textbook as curriculum, they tended to adopt textbook-based strategies in which matching topics with the Language B Guide and adding texts for assessment were used as manifestations of the ultimate goals of the IB course. In terms of curriculum understanding, they basically emphasised the notion of language acquisition for which the textbook provided a clear path. Learning a second language structurally contributed to the expected outcome of being internationally minded.

For those who perceived the textbook as one of a number of curriculum resources, they tended to adopt textbook-free strategies in which learners with different cultural backgrounds were utilised and authentic texts were collected to recreate meaning through juxtaposing articles from different perspectives, adding guiding questions, offering new contexts, *etc.* In terms of curriculum understanding, they emphasised the notion of learning through language and believed that the outcome of intercultural understanding could be achieved through purposefully adapting materials to respond to global and cross-cultural contexts in conjunction with student-centered pedagogy.

As a result, this study conceptualised the above two types of orientation and practice as basic understanding and deep understanding in line with the framework of teacher change proposed by Fullan (1991), later modified by Yin and Li (2008).

As discussed in previous sections, the researcher also argued that these two types of understandings and practices should be considered as a continuum of enacting IM in Language B rather than a dichotomy. It means that understanding of the culture of the target language only, could be emphasised prior to wider intercultural understanding, and communicative competence could be emphasised prior to intercultural competence.

If this was the case, it would be sensible for IBDP to remove the *ab initio* courses and provide beginners in Language B with six phases as in MYP Language B; the first phase assumes no prior knowledge of the language and students choose to enter at appropriate stages on the continuum according to their prior language knowledge. This restructuring should allow teachers to address the issue of new ethnocentrism (in Hall's words 2005) and the concern of sequencing and repetitiveness of Chinese characters, vocabulary and grammar.

Appendix 1: In-depth Interview Participants' Profiles

Stage	School	Teacher	Position	Experience	Code
1st	1	A	Head of Chinese[1]	3[2]	01T17
	2	B	Head of Chinese, Mandarin B (SL)[3] Teacher	1	07T12
	3	C	Head of Chinese, Mandarin B (HL) Teacher	5	08T10
	4	D	Head of Chinese, Mandarin B (SL) Teacher	2	09T5
	5	E	Head of Chinese, Mandarin B (HL/SL)[4], DP Workshop leader	11	10E2
	6	F	Head of Chinese, Mandarin B (HL) Teacher	3	11T13
	6	G	Mandarin B (HL) Teacher	6	11T14
	7	H	Mandarin B (SL) Teacher	5	12T15
	7	I	Head of Chinese, Mandarin B (SL) Teacher	5	12T16
2nd	1	J	Mandarin B (HL) Teacher	1	01T7
	1	K	Mandarin B (HL) Teacher	5	01T8
	4	L	Mandarin B (HL) Teacher	7	09T4
	5	M	Mandarin B (HL) Teacher	6	10T9
	8	N	Mandarin B (HL/SL) Teacher, DP Workshop Leader	13	02E3
	9	O	Mandarin B (HL) Teacher	2	03T11
	10	P	Mandarin B (SL) Teacher	5	06T6

1 Titles for people who lead Chinese curriculum are different, but all participants who lead the whole Chinese department are called Head of Chinese in this study.

2 The number in this column shows the number of years that teachers have taught in the IBDP Mandarin programme except Teacher A, who is mainly responsible for Chinese curriculum development. The number for Teacher A only shows the length of time leading the IBDP programme.

3 The subject with a specified level (HL or SL) indicates the current or the most recent level taught by teachers.

4 Teacher E was an IBDP Mandarin B teacher for more than ten years, but Teacher E was not teaching the subject in the academic year when the interview was conducted.

References

Allen, M. (2003). Frontier Crossings: Cultural Dissonance, Intercultural Learning and the Multicultural Personality. *Journal of Research in International Education* 2(1): 83-110.

Ancess, J. (2000). The Reciprocal Influence of Teacher Learning, Teaching Practice, School Restructuring, and Student Learning Outcomes. *Teachers College Record* 102(3): 590-619.

Bennett, M. (1986). A Developmental Approach to Training for intercultural Sensitivity. *International Journal of Intercultural Relations* 10(2): 179-196.

Bridges, W. and S. Mitchell (2002). Leading Transition: A New Model for Change. In F. Hesselbein and R. Johnston. (eds) *On Leading Change: A Leader to Leader Guide.* San Francisco, Jossey-Bass: 33-45.

Brown, M. W. (2009). The Teacher-Tool Relationship: Theorizing the Design and Use of Curriculum Materials. In J. T. Remillard, B. A. Herbel-Eisenmann and G. M. Lloyd. (eds) *Mathematics Teachers at Work: Connecting Curriculum Materials and Classroom Instruction.* New York, Routledge: 17-36.

Castro, P., U. Lundgren, *et al.* (2013). Conceptualizing and assessing International Mindedness: An exploratory study International Baccalaureate.

Cause, L. (2011). 'International mindedness': A field of struggle, confusion and hope. *Global Journal of Human Social Science* 11(7): 35-40.

CSMC (Centre for the Study of Mathematics Curriculum) (2012). Influences on the Enacted Curriculum. Retrieved from http://mathcurriculumcenter.org/research_framework.php. Viewed on September 6, 2014.

Day, R. (2003). Authenticity n the Design and Development of Materials. In W. A. Renandya (ed) *Methodology and Materials Design in Language Teaching: Current Perceptions and Practises and their Implications.* Singapore, RELC.

Doherty, C. and L. Mu (2011). Producing the intercultural citizen in the International Baccalaureate. In F. Dervin, A. Gagarda and A. Lavanchy. (eds) *Politics of Interculturality.* Newcastle upon Tyne, Cambridge Scholars Publishing: 165-188.

Ellis, R. (1999). Input Based Approaches to teaching grammar: A Review of Classroom Oriented Research. *Annual Review of Applied Linguistics*(19): 64-80.

Fryer, T. J. (2008). Stakeholder Experiences of a Dual-language School. Education. Leicester, University of Leicester. EDD.

Fullan, M. (1991). Curriculum Change. In A. Lewy. (ed) *The International Encyclopedia of Curriculum.* Oxford, New York, Pergamon Press: 279-280.

Gigliotti-Labay, J. (2010). *Fulfilling its Missions? The Promotion of International Mindedness in IB DP Programmes.* DEd dissertation, The College of Education, University of Houston.

Hall, G. (2005). *Literature in Language Education.* Basingstoke, UK, Palgrave MacMillan.

Halliday, M. A. K. (1993). Towards a Language-Based Theory of Learning. *Linguistics and Education* 5: 93-116.

Halliday, M. A. K. (2004). Three Aspects of Children's Language Development: Learning Language, Learning through Language, Learning about Language. In J. J. Webster, (ed) *The Language of Early Childhood: M. A. K. Halliday.* New York, Continuum: 308-326.

Hammer, M., M. Bennett, *et al.* (2003). Measuring Intercultural Sensitivity: The Intercultural Development Inventory. *International Journal of Intercultural Relations* 27(4): 421-443.

Harwood, R. and K. Bailey (2012). Defining and Evaluating International Mindedness in a School Context. *International Schools Journal* XXXI(2): 77-86.

Hayden, M. C., B. A. Rancic, *et al.* (2000). Being International: Student and Teacher Perceptions from International Schools. *Oxford Review of Education* 26(1): 107-123.

Hayden, M. C. and J. J. Thompson (1998). International Education: Perceptions of Teachers in International Schools. *International Review of Education* 44(5-6): 549-568.

Haywood, T. (2007). A Simple Typology of IM and Its Implications for Education. In M. Hayden, J. Levy and J. B. Thompson. (eds) *The SAGE Handbook of Research in International Education*. London, SAGE: pages 79-89.

Hersey, M. (2012). The Development of Global-mindedness: School Leadership Perspectives. *The College of Education*. Boca Raton, Florida Atlantic University. Doctor of Philosophy.

Hill, I. (2000). Internationally-minded Schools. *International Schools Journal* XX(1): 24-37.

Hill, I. (2007). International Education as Developed by the International Baccalaureate Organization. In M. Hayden, J. Levy and J. B. Thompson. (eds) *The SAGE Handbook of Research in International Education*. London, Sage: pages 25-37.

Hill, I. (2012). Evolution of Education for International Mindedness. *Journal of Research in International Education* 11(3): 245-261.

IB (2006). *IB Learner Profile*. Geneva, IB.

IB (2008). *Learner Profile Booklet*. Cardiff, IB.

IB (2011a). *Diploma Programme: Language B Guide (First Examinations 2013)*. Cardiff, IB.

IB (2011b). *Language and Learning in IB Programmes*. Cardiff, IB.

Inugai-Dixon, C. (2009). *One View of Language and Learning*. Reading, UK, NALDIC.

Inugai-Dixon, C. (2013). Multilingualism as a Fact, a Right and a Resource for Developing Interculural awareness and Honoring Diversity in International Baccalaureate Programmes. *ACLL Conference on Language Learning*. Osaka, Japan.

Islam, C. and C. Mares (2003). Adapting Classroom Materials. In B. Tomlinson. (ed) *Developing Materials for Language Teaching*. London, Continuum.

Kuo, C. H. (1993). Problematic Issues in ESP Materials Development. *English for Specific Purposes* (12): 171-181.

Lai, C., Shum, M. & Zhang, B. N. (2014). International mindedness in an Asian context: the case of the International Baccalaureate in Hong Kong. *Educational Research* 56(1):77-96.

Lam, T. F. (2013). The Use of Textbook in IBDP Language B Course from Chinese Teacher's Perpective. *First International Conference on Teaching Chinese a Foreign Language*, The University of Hong Kong.

Mesa, V. and B. Griffiths (2012). Textbook mediation of teaching: an example from tertiary mathematics instructors. *Education Studies in Mathematics* 79(1): 85-107.

Morais, D. and A. Ogden (2011). Initial Development and Validation of the Global Citizenship Scale. *Journal of Studies in International Education* 15(5): 445-466.

Nicol, C. C. and S. M. Crespo (2006). Learning to Teach with Mathematics Textbooks: How Preservice Teachers Interpret and Use Curriculum Materials. *Educational Studies in Mathematics* 62(3): 331-355.

Remillard, J. T. and M. B. Bryans (2004). Teachers' orientations toward mathematics curriculum materials: Implications for teacher learning. *Journal for Research in Mathematics Education* 35(5): 352-388.

Rilling, S. and M. Dantas-Whitney (2009). *Authenticity in the Language Classroom and Beyond: Adult Learners*. Alexandria, VA, TESOL.

Saraceni, C. (2003). Adapting Courses: A Critical View. In B. Tomlinson. (ed) *Developing Materials for Language Teaching*. London, Continuum.

Shawer, S. F. (2010). Classroom-level curriculum development: EFL teachers as curriculum-developers, curriculum-makers and curriculum-transmitters. *Teaching and Teacher Education*(26): 173-184.

Singh, M. and J. Qi (2013). *21st century International Mindedness: An Exploratory Study of its Conceptualization and Assessment*. South Penrith, University of Western Sydney.

Sylvester, R. (2007). Historical Resources for Research in International Education (1851-1950). In M. Hayden, J. Levy and J. B. Thompson. (eds) *The SAGE Handbook of Research in International Education*. London, Sage: 11-24.

Tomlinson, B. (2003). Developing Principled Frameworks for Materials Development. In B. Tomlinson. (ed) *Developing Materials for Language Teaching*. London, Continuum: pages 107-129.

Wilkinson, V. and M. Hayden (2010). The International Baccalaureate Diploma and Student Attitudes: An Exploratory Study. *Journal of Research in International Education* 9(1): 85-96.

Xing, J. Z. (2006). *Teaching and Learning Chinese as a Foreign Language - A Pedagogical Grammar*. Hong Kong, Hong Kong University Press.

刘珣 (2012). 对外汉语教材的发展与创新. 北京, 北京语言大学.

吕文华 (2002). 对外汉语教材语法项目排序的原则及策略. 世界汉语教学(4).

尹弘飙和李子建 (2008). 课程变革：理论与实践. 台北, 高等教育文化事业有限公司.

施家炜 (1998). 外国留学生22类现代汉语句式的习得顺序研究. 世界汉语教学 (4): 77-98.

李泉 (2006). 对外汉语教材研究. 北京, 商务印书馆.

杨寄洲 (2000). 对外汉语教学初级阶段语法项目的排序问题. 语言教学与研究(3).

赵贤洲 (1988). 建国以来对外汉语教材研究报告. 第二届国际汉语教学讨论会文选. 北京, 北京语言学院出版社.

赵金铭 (1996). 对外汉语语法教学的三个阶段及其教学主旨. 世界汉语教学(3).

韩萱 (2009). 全球视阈下的对外汉语教材评述. 云南师范大学学报7(4): 1-8.

Part three:

Innovative pedagogy in IB Chinese teaching

Chapter 8

Integrating IB philosophy and pedagogy into Chinese language teaching: what could educational technology bring to the dialogue?

Chun Lai

Abstract

The philosophical underpinning of IB centres on international mindedness, which reflects cosmopolitan values and global citizenship and embraces critical knowledge and skills for global interdependence. Integrating IB philosophy into Chinese language teaching demands breadth of curriculum coverage and experience, and student-centred progressive pedagogies that lend to the development of the related skills.

At the same time, Chinese language teachers are facing a delicate balancing issue. On the one hand, there are the curriculum demands for developing basic literacy skills, and providing a broad curriculum coverage and learning experience; on the other hand, teachers need to utilise the strengths of both traditional and progressive pedagogies.

In this chapter, we will discuss the potential of educational technology for facilitating the integration of IB philosophy and pedagogy into Chinese language teaching, and explore how educational technology could be used to resolve the curriculum and pedagogy dilemma. In addition, critical issues around the use of educational technology in teaching are discussed to maximise its potential. Technology never replaces the teacher. On the contrary, it means that the teacher must be able to skillfully manage the use of technology to enhance the educational design of lessons.

Introduction

The International Baccalaureate (IB) curriculum sets fostering international mindedness (IM) as its education mission and highlights the enhancement of intercultural understanding and respect through the development of the ten learner attributes listed in the IB learner profile. In its position paper, *What is an IB education?*, the IB stresses its 'commitment to creating a collaborative, global community united by a mission to make a better world' (IBO, 2013, p.7).

The IB's stance on IM reflects an emphasis on cosmopolitan values and global citizenship that involves the awareness of the interconnectedness and cultural diversity in the world, an open mindset and disposition towards the 'coexistence of cultures in the individual experience' and the competence to utilise such an awareness and mindset to move flexibly across different contexts and contribute to the betterment of the whole world (Cambridge

& Thompson, 2004; Doherty & Shield, 2012; Hannerz 1990, p.238). The IB's conceptualization of IM highlights being open to, respecting and accommodating differences, the interconnectedness and interdependency of global issues, and active local and global citizenry to create a better and peaceful world (Doherty & Mu, 2011; Singh & Jing, 2013).

Thus, IM depends on a whole set of understanding, skills, attitudes at the cognitive, affective and action dimensions (Cause, 2011; Hill, 2012). To develop IM, teachers need to engage students to explore various concepts that are critical to intercultural understanding and global development and to sharpen students' skills in reaching sophisticated understanding of those important concepts. The development of the sophisticated understanding fosters positive attitudes and humanitarian values and actions, which in turn enhances the depth of understanding (Harwood & Bailey, 2012; Hill, 2007, 2012).

In defining IB education, the IB highlights four characteristics: working within global contexts; exploring significant content; centering on learners; and developing effective approaches to teaching and learning (IBO, 2013, p.7). The first two define the nature and foci of its curriculum, and require subject matter to feature the global contexts of education and engage with a breadth of topics and experiences that are conceptual and connected so as to contribute to students' understanding, skills and attitudes that are essential to IM. The last two highlight that the pedagogical approaches to engage students with such a curriculum need to be student-centered and reflect constructivist approaches that support students' active inquiry, action and reflection (IBO, 2013).

IM, as the main philosophical underpinning of the IB curriculum, is expected to guide school operations and curriculum practices and become an integrative component of the curriculum (Cambridge, 2010; Gigliotti-Labay, 2010; Hill, 2012; IBO, 2008). Chinese language education, as a first language or as a second language, is one discipline in the IB curriculum framework and needs to serve this grand curriculum aim. Integrating IB philosophy into Chinese language teaching demands a broad curriculum coverage and experience, and student-centered progressive pedagogies that lend to the development of related knowledge, skills and attitudes.

However, Chinese language teachers have reported various challenges at the individual, curricular and contextual levels when integrating IB philosophy into Chinese language education (Lai, Shum & Zhang, 2014; Van Vooren *et al*, 2013). At the curricular level, Chinese language teachers report facing the challenges that additional language teachers normally encounter in transdisciplinary inquiry curriculum. These challenges include:

the gap between students' developing language proficiency and the level of cognitive demands in concept-based curriculum (Halbach, 2009; Ozer, 2010);

the tension between systematic learning of the subject content and the 'meaningful, applied learning situation in integrated contexts' (Venville *et al*, 2009, p.472);

the fight over the instructional time for inquiry and other progressive pedagogies and the instructional time for drills and practices that are needed for language skill development (Lai, Shum & Zhang, 2014; Loh, 2012; Van Vooren *et al*, 2013);

additional and differentiated support needed for inquiry-based learning due to varying student proficiency and readiness for inquiry (Lai, Shum & Zhang, 2014; Van Vooren *et al*, 2013); and

limited resources available to serve as appropriate materials for inquiry in a second language (Van Vooren *et al*, 2013).

In addition, Chinese language teachers are also facing some challenges unique to the Chinese language, namely the extra demand on instructional arrangement in teaching an orthographic language that does not have an easy mapping between its spoken and written form, and the stress such a demand puts on the heavily-packed curriculum (Lai, Shum & Zhang, 2014). Teachers also feel that progressive pedagogies normally take a long time and are not as efficient as traditional approaches that are featured by direct instruction and repeated practices.

In all, the challenges of integrating IB philosophy into Chinese language education at the curricular and pedagogical level lie in: 1) limited instructional time; 2) limited resources to support the use of progressive pedagogies; and 3) diversified support students need under various progressive pedagogies due to their developing cognitive and language abilities.

With its potential to extend learning beyond the classroom and create authentic, individualised learning experience, educational technology could help bridge the curricular and pedagogical demands of IB philosophy integration and the operation of Chinese language teaching. For one thing, educational technology enables and facilitates global interactions and progressive pedagogies that are needed for the realisation of the educational goal of the IB curriculum: it expands learners' experience beyond the confinement of the physical classrooms to create rich cross-cultural experiences and global engagement and actions that are critical to the development of IM; and it also affords authentic contexts, rich resources and individualised support for student-centered progressive pedagogies.

For another, educational technology could help to address the instructional time dilemma since it facilitates ubiquitous learning that extends learning beyond the classroom increasing the learning time, and supports individualised independent learning of some content that is best taught through direct instruction and repeated practices. Thus it frees up the in-class instructional hours for progressive pedagogies.

This chapter will discuss how and what technology could contribute to the integration of IB philosophy and pedagogy into Chinese language teaching. More importantly, critical issues around the use of educational technology in teaching will be discussed to maximise its potential for facilitating the integration of IB philosophy and pedagogy into Chinese language teaching.

Technology creates innovative and authentic learning experiences to support the integration

As argued in the previous section, the integration entails both the curricular and the pedagogical dimension. For the curricular arrangement dimension, intercultural education, global engagement and action are the foci. For the pedagogical dimension, student-centered progressive pedagogies and active inquiry are essential. This section will discuss how technology facilitates intercultural education and global engagement and supports the inquiry approach to learning, and more importantly, how to use technology effectively for such purposes.

Technology and intercultural education

Developing intercultural competency involves a relational, dialogic and reflective process that raises awareness of the role of culture in shaping students' interpretations of themselves and others and enables students with 'different ways of seeing' (DeCapua & Wintergerst, 2004, p.28). Intercultural competency is a multidimensional concept that entails knowledge, skill, attitude and behaviour domains (Perry & Southwell, 2011). Intercultural education consists of knowing (acquiring and updating one's knowledge about the cultures, people, worldviews, values and norms, *etc*); relating (the co-construction of identities and affective and social factors that affect intercultural engagement); encoding/decoding (verbal and nonverbal communication in culturally diverse communities); and transforming (constant assumption challenging, experience reflection and integration of new ways of understanding) (Chamberlin-Quinlisk, 2013).

Thus, lived experience and experiential learning that involves interaction with native speakers of the target culture are deemed more effective than learning that is confined in the classroom (Byram & Feng, 2004). This is where web-based technologies would play a critical role. First of all, digital media serves as an important source of intercultural information and provides intercultural exposure at a click's distance. More importantly, the information that the internet exposes to the students presents the dynamic, complex, ambiguous, heterogeneous and sometimes contentious nature of culture and authentic language use that are often deliberately avoided in textbooks for the sake of keeping things simple and straightforward.

Second, various technologies, such as blogs, wikis, online social networking tools, CMC, email, massively multiplayer online role playing games (MMORPG) and so on, have been used to create experiential learning experience (Elola & Oskoz, 2008; Lawrence, *et al*, 2009; Ware & Kramsch, 2005) and 'affinity spaces' (Gee & Hayes, 2011, p.35) that engage students with complex intercultural relationships that spur intercultural curiosity, the emotional investment and willingness to know and relate that are fundamental to intercultural understanding. Such 'lived' experience also affords the opportunities for identity (re)positioning and negotiation, exercising and sharpening encoding/decoding skills in a relatively non-threatening and stress-free environment where miscommunications incur limited real-life consequences.

The use of web resources to foster intercultural understanding is a necessity given the often distilled and oversimplified cultural and language content in most textbooks. Unfortunately, foreign language teachers also frown on the idea of using internet resources for intercultural education and feel that the textual descriptions of cultural conventions and customs are out of reach of their students who have limited linguistic resources in the target language.

However, textual information is only one of the resources available online, and the internet contains a large variety of audiovisual and pictorial cultural content that are wonderful materials for intercultural education. Sites like Flickr contain a rich collection of culture-loaded photos and descriptions that lend themselves well to vocabulary learning and in-depth discussions of cultural commonalities and variations (Brandt & Jenks, 2011). Engaging students to make YouTube videos themselves on cultural practices and artifacts can engage them in reflective practices on their culture and culturally-shaped selves (Brook, 2011).

Educators have been using digital technologies to enlarge the intercultural exposure and experience through enabling interactions with native speakers and people from the native culture and create tandem language and culture learning opportunities. Discussion forums and emails have been widely adopted. Furstenber and colleagues' (2001) seminal Cultura project is a classic example of using discussion forums for intercultural education.

In the project, tandem language classes where students were learning each other's languages were connected through discussion forums to write word associations of and define some culturally-loaded concepts such as friends, family, love, and so on, and discuss and elaborate on the cultural similarities and differences revealed from such practice. Students were also given make-up life scenarios to write up and discuss the cultural factors that shape their different reactions in those scenarios.

Recently, Web 2.0 technologies have also been used to engage students in collaborative projects and enhance their intercultural experience. For instance, Lee (2009) reported a project that involved using blogs and podcasting to engage the Spanish learners in the US and English learners in Spain. They undertook intercultural exchange activities, such as keeping blogs on teenagers' lives and podcasts on controversial topics in one's culture to elicit the partners' responses; they conducted ethnographic interviews with each other via podcast posts. The author found that such activities enhanced students' intercultural understanding.

Wang (2012) engaged his Taiwanese students with American students to work on collaborative projects to co-create products that reflected their understanding of a certain topic. Facebook was used as a platform to facilitate their discussion and collaboration. It was found that such collaborative projects via Facebook not only enhanced students' intercultural understanding but enabled students to continue their friendship beyond and after the class.

Furthermore, educational technologies have been used to create lived experience and contextualized cultural learning opportunities so as to promote intercultural understanding. Global Simulation is a pedagogical framework that has been adopted to foster intercultural competency. It involves creating a 'culturally grounded, fictitious scenario where students adopt specific character roles in the target culture' and take on the fictitious character's cultural identity to perform his/her social roles (Michelson & Dupuy, 2014, p.21). This pedagogical framework has been used to create lived experience with the help of web 2.0 technologies.

For instance, Mills (2011) implemented a Facebook project where the students played the role of residents living in a contemporary apartment building in Paris and opened Facebook pages, kept Facebook updates and interacted with each other in French in the identities of their adopted fictitious residents. Such a virtual simulation experience supports the knowing, relating, encoding/decoding and transforming that are key to intercultural education (Chamberlin-Quinlisk, 2013).

Virtual worlds and MMORPG have also been adopted to create such situated learning experience. It has been found that the virtual lived experience stimulates intercultural curiosity and intercultural sensitivity, supports identity refashioning, and even affects student's behaviours in real life (Bertuzzi & Zreik, 2011; Coffey *et al.*, 2014; Neville, 2012). Zheng and colleagues (2009) engaged students from US and China in co-questing in a virtual world, and found that their interactions around the cultural knowledge embedded in the quests fostered cultural awareness and sensitivity that went beyond the factual information level.

However, it has been reported again and again that immersing students in online intercultural communities and increasing their intercultural exposure do not necessarily bring about intercultural learning (Kramsch & Thorne, 2002; Lawrence *et al*, 2009; O'Dowd, 2007), and in some cases may reinforce cultural stereotypes and feelings of difference (Kern, 2000; Lawrence *et al*, 2009). When using internet materials as resources for intercultural education, educators are facing the challenges of judging the trustworthiness and the 'accentedness' of the information (Chamberlin-Quinlisk, 2013).

When creating online communities and immersing students in online interactions, different cultural expectations and norms for communication, social relations and communicative use of technology may incur misunderstanding among the students (Kramsch & Thorne, 2002; Lawrence, 2013; O'Dowd, 2007). Thus, pedagogical support mechanisms are critical to the effectiveness of technology-enhanced intercultural education.

Lawrence (2013) conceptualizes a pedagogical support model for intercultural learning that consists of three stages. The first is 'collaborative planning' whose purpose is to raise intercultural curiosity and sensitivity. At this stage, teachers may want to involve their students in conceptualising the topics, the cultural groups, the communication tools, and procedures of the projects, and to orient students to different cultural norms and expectations for online communication.

'Cultural general approaches' are recommended at this stage to guide students to understand how culture shapes one's interaction behaviours and expectations, engage them to explore the value of the differences that shape the communication patterns and cultural perspectives of their own culture and the target culture, and familiarise them with the online communication conventions and strategies to use to initiate and sustain online communication. The second stage is 'building identity investment' whose purpose is to enhance students' emotional and effort investment in the communication. At this stage, it is crucial to help build a good personal relationship between the students and their cross-cultural communication partners, highlighting common experience and negotiating common communication goals, norms and processes.

The third stage is 'actively intercultural work' where students work together with their teacher to apply cultural general learning principles to analyse the 'provocative points' and the 'failed communication' with the aim to develop a critical perspective towards one's own culturally-shaped behaviours and expectations and the multiple ways of interpretations of events/topics. In addition, Chamberlin-Quinlisk (2013) advocated for a critical stance towards the sources of the information when incorporating Internet materials into intercultural education. Teachers need to actively seek and build on the existence of alternative perspectives and, more importantly, help their students to develop such a stance towards internet sources so as to avoid stereotyping.

Technology and progressive pedagogies

Progressive pedagogies and educational models have been developed to address the deficiencies of traditional approaches that operate primarily on a transmission model. Progressive pedagogies highlight organising student-centered, inquiry-driven learning around issues of real-life significance that aim to develop conceptual understanding across disciplines (Cuban, 2001). Murray (2009) listed some progressive educational models including multiple intelligences, creativity, constructivism, meta-learning, adaptivity/individualization/differentiation, learning by doing, situated learning, community/service-based learning, life-long learning, participatory/action-based curriculum development and research, and so on. These progressive education models highlight three major principles:

> Education needs to be based on an understanding of students' capacities, interests and habits, namely, student-centered learning. Learning starts with students' interests and experiences, and teachers are to encourage and guide students to formulate significant questions relevant to their interests and experiences.

> Education is largely a social process and teachers are to create a community of learning where students could share their resources and expertise and work together towards social ends.

> Education is a reflective practice that plays out and supports the complex relationship between process and product (Sherman, 2009).

Thus in contrast to the primary focus on the content and product in traditional approaches, the progressive educational models are featured by a primary focus on the process and higher-order skills, such as thinking, reflective, collaboration and inquiry skills and so on. With its power to situate learning in real-life contexts and expand learning beyond the confinement of physical classroom, technology has a great role to play in creating the constructivist, situated, student-centered, real-life based and participatory learning experience that are advocated in progressive pedagogies. Payne (2009) argued that the advent of information technology accompanied the popularisation of constructivism, and 'may offer the only viable avenue to the implementation of constructivist and progressive educational principles' (p.xxi).

First, technology affords various human and non-human resources (*eg* the vast amount of authentic language and cultural resources, native speakers of the language, peer learners, language instructors, instructional programs, *etc*) at a click's distance to enable and support inquiry-based and discovery learning. Inquiry-based learning in language education could be both at the concept and intercultural level and at the language level, and there are technological resources that could support inquiry at these different levels.

At the concept and intercultural level, Webquest is a platform that is very handy to support structured scaffolded inquiry into web-based materials and facilitate constructivist problem solving around authentic problems (Halat, 2008; Zheng *et al*, 2008). Online inquiry-based learning could be easily constructed using online learning networks such as QuestGarden. com and Zunal.com. It has been argued that Webquest enables students to search for information in a structured efficient manner and supports the development of higher order thinking skills and collaboration skills (Chang *et al*, 2011; Torres, 2007). Foreign language educators have advocated the use of Webquest to engage students in active learning (Altstaedter & Jones, 2009; Sox & Rubinstein-Avila, 2009).

For instance, Falasca & Altstaedter (2011) engaged their intermediate-level Spanish learners with WebQuest activities to inquire about Chile, and found that students' intercultural competence increased as a result of the activities in that they started to adopt a more open and reflective view towards their own culture and that of Chile. Literature has also suggested that Webquest could enhance students' reading and writing proficiency as well as increasing their conceptual and intercultural understanding (Alshumaimeri *et al.*, 2012).

Hung (2015) used Webquest to create a structured flipped learning experience for the university English as a Foreign Language (EFL) students to understand digital storytelling and movie trailer creation. It was found that the flipped learning experience helped students attain better language learning outcomes and developed more active attitudes towards learning as compared with the students who only received in-class instruction.

Thus Webquest is an effective platform to engage students in inquiry-based learning of both concepts and language, using online textual, audio and visual materials. When using Webquest with learners of lower proficiency levels, training sessions are needed to build students' confidence and ability to interact with authentic materials, and extra scaffolds are needed to help make the online materials comprehensible to the students.

Teachers may consider providing students with technological tools (such as online annotation tools; the use of captions for video and audio materials; *etc*) that could help them make online materials comprehensible and teach them how to use these tools in more effective manners. As well as creating and supporting structured inquiry activities at the conceptual and cultural level, technology also provides support for data-driven inquiry activities around vocabulary, syntax and discourse learning.

One much advocated technological solution is concordancing, where students can search for a language item in the corpus and deduce how the language item works in the target language through analysing a large pool of examples of the language item in use. Boulton (2010) reviewed the past studies on concordancing and language learning, and concluded that concordancing could live up to the expectations of supporting inductive, inquiry-based learning of the language items for learners of all proficiency levels. Boulton further reminded teachers that training on how to pick up patterns of language use inductively prior to the concordancing activities might be needed to enhance students' likelihood of noticing and generating rules from the active inquiry learning process.

Second, technology provides important tools to create situational and experiential learning and mediates the co-construction of knowledge of the target language and culture. Technology's potential in creating situational and experiential learning with native speakers and peer learners through various social networking tools and virtual worlds has been elaborated on quite intensively in the previous section.

Such experiential learning enhances not only the development of intercultural competency but also language skill development. The situated learning experience could also be supported by mobile technologies which afford and enable personalised, situated and social learning anytime and anywhere (Burston, 2014; Stockwell & Hubbhard, 2013). Mobile devices allow learners to access, capture and deliver language content anytime anywhere, and thus afford learning in contexts and the continuity of learning across contexts (Jones *et al*, 2006). For instance, Wong and colleagues' (2010) Move, Idioms! project was an attempt to bridge learning inside and outside the classroom. This project combined mobile technologies together with other web 2.0 technologies to create social learning experience around contextualized language artefacts.

The Chinese students in that study were instructed to use iPhones to take photos of daily life events and artifacts in their immediate surroundings that illustrate the Chinese idioms they had been studying in class, and share their photos on the class wiki site to co-construct their understanding of the target idioms. Thus, the project makes use of mobile technologies' photo capture functions to create shared situated learning of language items. Furthermore, mobile technologies' context-sensitivity features have also been used to create timely support to students' language use. For instance, the Micromandarin project uses GPS to determine a user's location and then delivers vocabulary learning and practice materials that are relevant and needed to support the language use and communication at the location.

Wikis are another technological platform that have been widely adopted to create and support interactive, collaborative learning opportunities. Wikis have been applied and researched in L1 and L2 writing instruction, and are a typical example of how technology could support the co-creation of knowledge through collaborative learning. Research evidence has been accumulating in support of the efficacies of wiki-based collaborative projects for the co-construction of knowledge, facilitating deep learning and stimulating learner autonomy, creativity and critical thinking (Hodges, 2002; Lowry *et al*, 2004).

Wiki-based collaborative writing has been advocated as an important mechanism for individual writing development (Hodges, 2002), and students have been found to produce higher-quality writing products through group collaborative writing as compared to individual writing or pair writing (Dobao, 2012; Shehadeh, 2011).

More importantly, wiki-based collaborative writing has been found to benefit individual writing skill development (Chao & Lo, 2011; Kost, 2011; Li & Zhu, 2013). Commonly used educational wiki platforms include PBWikis and Wikispaces. However, at the same time, researchers have pointed out that collaboration does not naturally occur with the use of collaborative work platforms (Bradley *et al*, 2010; Limbu & Markauskaite, 2015). Students have also been found to focus primarily on meaning rather than on form, which largely constrains the potential of wiki-based collaborative projects for enhancing students' grasp of language forms (Kessler & Bikowski, 2010).

Thus, when incorporating collaborative projects in second language classrooms, teachers need to build in mechanisms and design tasks in ways that encourage and develop students' willingness and ability to collaborate and give students tips on how to expand opportunities for collaborative language learning. It is also advised to add some debriefing sessions upon the completion of the activities to direct students' attention to language forms.

Last but not the least, since student-centered learning is at the core of progressive pedagogies, how to structure and support the learning experiences around students' interests and needs is a thorny issue progressive pedagogies need to address. In most cases, it suggests the need for differentiated instruction and the support for individualized learning. Technology provides customised and individualised learning experience to support the differentiation of teaching and learning and makes available timely feedback to support the learning process.

Benjamin (2005) highlighted some features of technology that lend themselves well to differentiating instruction. These include:

the privacy technology affords that mitigate the potential damage to weaker students' self-esteem;

choices and varieties of learning activities technology could provide to accommodate different learning styles, interests and needs; and the collaborative and authentic learning activities that technology could support and the accompanying learning scaffolds from peers and from real life in such activities.

In addition, assistive technology greatly benefits students with learning disabilities. For instance, E-Readers with text to speech function help boost the confidence of learners with disabilities and facilitate their enjoyment of the texts that their peers are reading (Williamson-Henriques, 2013). Technology-based graphic organisers have positive effects on the reading comprehension skills of students with learning disabilities (Gifford, 2014). In terms of writing, MacArthur (2009) found that when word processing was combined with effective instruction in revision, it could enhance the learning of students with written language disabilities.

Thus technology could complement paper-based reading and writing tasks to provide motivating and meaningful learning activities for students with disabilities and support the smooth implementation of progressive pedagogies in the classroom.

The virtues of using technology in teaching and learning lie not only in creating learning experience that supports intercultural competency and progressive pedagogies, but also in meeting the fundamental education aims of the contemporary world. Warschauer and Matuchniak (2010) argue that information technology brings the 'fourth revolution in the means of production of knowledge' and transforms the 'industry' economy into 'information' economy. Hence IT redefines the essential skills needed to survive and prosper in contemporary society as higher order skills such as to evaluate and process information, complex problem solving and collaboration (Levy & Murnane, 2004).

Regular and flexible access to technological tools and the vast amount of information and innovative experience that comes along are regarded as fundamental to fostering these higher order skills (Warschauer & Matuchniak, 2010). Thus technology facilitates the integration of IB philosophy and pedagogy into teaching through creating optimal conditions that support the development of intercultural competency and the operationalisation of progressive pedagogies in class, and constructing favorable educational experiences that foster the attributes highlighted in the IB learner profile.

Technology addresses the instructional time dilemma

In addition to creating optimal educational conditions and experience to facilitate the integration of IB philosophy and pedagogy into Chinese language teaching, technology also has the potential to address the instructional time dilemma in the process of integration. Teachers often regard the tightly-packed language education curriculum and the need for systematic learning of the basics of the language as the biggest hurdle to the implementation of progressive pedagogies, which they believe to be more time-consuming and less efficient in covering the instructional contents as compared to traditional approaches.

Before we discuss the potential of technology in relieving the stress, we need to keep in mind that teaching demands a balance in both the curriculum content and pedagogy. Warschauer & Matuchniak (2010) highlight that quality educational experience needs to 'move away from a narrow focus on teaching the basics to a broader approach that emphasizes both basic and 21st century skills', which the scholars label as 'teaching the word and the world' (p.215). Furthermore, the advocates for progressive pedagogies in IB programs are in no way excluding traditional pedagogies since both pedagogical approaches have their virtues and purposes.

Murray (2009) proposes an integrative approach to teaching that incorporates progressive and traditional pedagogies. What matters more is teachers' precise understanding of the appropriate contexts for a range of methodologies and the relationships and synergies across them to maintain 'the right dynamic balance' (Murray, 2009, p.24). Thus integrating IB philosophy and progressive pedagogies should not be regarded as a luxurious add-on that may sacrifice the systematic learning of the basic skills, but rather should be taken as a core to IB teaching. In this section, we will discuss how technology could help teachers deal with the instructional time stress in striking the balance.

When discussing how to develop 21st century learning skills, Warschauer & Matuchniak (2010) point out that not only in-class use of technology to enrich learning experience is critical, but also out-of-school technology use is a fertile context for the development of 21st century skills. Thus they urge teachers to encourage students to use technology outside the classroom. Out-of-class learning needs to be promoted not only because of its potential in fostering 21st century skills but also because it serves as a great language learning context.

Out-of-class learning has been shown to be positively associated with language gains (Inozu *et al*, 2010; Larsson, 2012; Richards, 2009), and successful language learners have often been found to seek out and utilise various out-of-class opportunities for learning (Benson *et al*, 2003; Borrero & Yeh, 2010). Thus, to save instructional hours in class, teachers may think of how to use technology to enhance students' exposure to and use of the target language outside the classroom.

Encouraging and recommending self-directed use of technology for language learning outside the language classroom requires teachers to recommend useful resources and help students overcome the affective and metacognitive hurdles in out-of-class technology-facilitated learning (Lai, 2015). The affective and metacognitive hurdles that students might face include the lack of confidence and skills in interacting with authentic materials, especially for students of lower proficiency levels, and the lack of knowledge on how to use technological resources and tools effectively for language learning.

To help students overcome these two hurdles, teachers may want to bring authentic materials – textual, audio and visual – into the class and guide students to use various strategies to process them. Teachers can also showcase the use of different technological resources and tools and share cognitive and metacognitive tips on using them effectively for language learning. In addition, two general principles need to be followed when recommending out-of-class learning activities to the students.

First, sustainable out-of-class activities are most often friendship-driven and interest-driven (Warschauer & Matuchniak, 2010). Social networking sites, instant messaging, online communities around music and videos, games and internet interest groups such as Fan Fiction are good choices of technology in creating such activities in the target language. Second, diversity is critical to the quality of out-of-class learning, diversity in terms of balancing the learning experiences inside and outside the classroom and serving a multitude of language learning functions (Lai, Zhu & Gong, 2014). The selection of out-of-class activities needs to supply what's weak in their in-class instruction. If the in-class instruction is mainly form-focused activities, then out-of-class learning needs to incorporate a lot of meaning-focused activities. Furthermore, the out-of-class activities one engages in need to serve different language learning purposes and functions.

Another venue to address the instructional hour dilemma is to use technology to bridge students' in-class and out-of-class learning experience so that learning could be free from the time constraints of the in-class instruction. Mobile technologies have been advocated as a suitable tool to create such seamless learning experience. The Move, Idioms! project (Wong *et al*, 2010) introduced in the previous section is a typical example of using technology to create seamless learning that extends beyond the in-class instruction.

The LOCH project (Ogata *et al*, 2008) is another example of using mobile devices to create seamless learning. In this project, students used their Personal Digital Assistant (PDA) to record their interactions with native speakers in different real-life contexts, and then they bring their recorded interactions into the class to discuss, under the guidance of the teacher, the problems they had encountered during the interactions, the strategies they used, and specific language use they had picked up during the interactions.

So and colleagues' (2009) Chinatown Learning Trail project is another example of using mobile devices to bridge in-class and out-of-class learning in the context of foreign language education. In class, the teacher guided the students to generate some questions about the Chinatown district and do some initial research with books, web, stories *etc* to formulate initial responses to the questions. Then the students went on a field trip to Chinatown using Google Maps to mark and share the location of landmarks they visited and jotted down notes on their observations and opinions.

After they returned to the classroom, they were guided to revisit their understanding of, and responses to, the questions they put down initially. Thus using the photo-capturing and location sensitivity functions of mobile technologies to create out-of-class learning experience that connects with in-class learning not only adds authenticity to learning but also lowers the burden of learning in in-class instruction.

The flipped classroom is another technological option that saves instructional time in class. The flipped classroom basically inverts what students do inside and outside class. In traditional models, teachers are busy instructing the basics with limited time left for knowledge application through projects or discussion, and then outside the class, the students are left alone to tackle the challenges of applying what they've learned in class to solve problems. In the flipped model, students study the tutorials (such as the teacher-recorded lecture of the fundamentals, video tutorials, resources on the content area) and engage in online discussions on the questions arising from studying the tutorials outside the classroom as homework to get ready for the class. Then they come to the class to engage in various kinds of hands-on knowledge application activities under the guidance of the teacher to deepen their understanding, thus turning the class into a more active learning context (Egbert *et al*, 2014; Keengwe *et al*, 2014).

This approach not only enables active learning but also lends a greater likelihood of individual support in class (Houston & Lin, 2012). Egbert and colleagues (2014) described a seven-unit flipped Chinese language learning design. In the flipped classroom, students completed most of the direct instruction of the Chinese course, such as vocabulary, writing, speaking and listening, outside the classroom through studying audio-visual and textual materials prior to coming to the class. In the class, the instructor led them in review, discussion and communication around the unit theme and provided individualised support to students in need.

Researchers found that the seven-week study helped students grasp basic, classroom-oriented conversations in the target language. Although the flipped learning concept was proposed to create more active learning, it could be a viable approach to address the instructional hour dilemma as well. It basically calls for a critical evaluation and utilisation of the strength of technology and teachers in language learning. If technology could teach the basics of the language well, then let technology handle it and free the class instructional hours for higher-order tasks guided by the teachers, such as spontaneous communication, complex problem solving, collaborative learning, *etc*. In this way, the precious instructional hour in class would be freed up for more meaningful learning activities and progressive education that lend well to the development of students' 21st century learning skills and the attributes that are highlighted in the IB learner profile.

Conclusion

In this chapter, we discussed the various potentials of technology in supporting the integration of IB philosophical underpinnings and pedagogies into Chinese language education. We highlighted that technology could compensate for the physical, time, and human and non-human resource constraints of in-class instruction to create the optimal educational experience and conditions for the development of intercultural understanding. Technology also supports the implementation of progressive pedagogies that are critical to the development of 21st century skills and the IB learner attributes.

With such a rosy picture, a note of caution is needed. Technology is never the panacea for education; nor is it in the case of integrating IB philosophy and pedagogy into Chinese language teaching. What matters most is the instructional and pedagogical design. It is not technology use in class that makes your teaching progressive; rather it is there to create the conditions and facilitate the implementation of your progressive pedagogical design.

Furthermore technology is a double-edged sword. The integration of technology into the classroom involves issues that may hinder its effectiveness and even the flow of the class instruction. These issues include classroom management; predominant focus on meaning with a corresponding loss of focus on language forms; students' lack of the necessary technical and cognitive skills to benefit from the technology-enhanced environment; and so on. Thus the decision to integrate technology needs to be carefully evaluated. Teachers need to avoid using technology for technology's sake, but rather use it only when the instructional purpose cannot be achieved or cannot be achieved effectively and efficiently without its use.

Teachers also need to consider carefully what technological activities to encourage and structure outside the classroom and what to use inside it. The overall principles of technology use in class are to use technological resources and activities to facilitate progressive pedagogies as espoused by the IB, and to use technological resources in ways to create opportunities and incentives for students' self-directed technology use outside the classroom.

Furthermore, when engaging students with technology-enhanced language learning activities, pre-task, during-task and post-task models are needed. The pre-task phase needs to focus on preparing students with the necessary technical, cultural, language background information, training in the communication and language learning strategies to use during the task, and familiarising students with the genre and the discourse features of a given technological activity.

The during-task phase would be where students use technologies to engage in active learning with teacher guidance. The post-task phase would be a debriefing session where students' product and process data are analysed for language and cultural learning opportunities, and challenges and 'failed communication' encountered during the task are discussed to enhance intercultural understanding and 21st century skill development.

References

Alshumaimeri, Y. A., Almasri, M. M. (2012). The effects of using Webquests on reading comprehension performance of Saudi EFL students. *TOJET: The Turkish Online Journal of Educational Technology*, 11(4), 295-306.

Altstaedter, L.L., & Jones, B. (2009). Motivating students' foreign language and culture acquisition through web-based inquiry. *Foreign Language Annals*, 42(4), 640-657.

Benjamin, A. (2005). *Differentiated instruction using technology: A guide for middle and high school teachers*. Larchmont, NY: Eye on Education.

Benson, P., Chik, A., & Lim, H. Y. (2003). Becoming autonomous in an Asian context: Autonomy as a sociocultural process. In D. Palfreyman & R. C. Smith (Eds.), *Learner autonomy across cultures: Language education perspectives (pp.23–40)*. Basingstoke, England: Palgrave Macmillan.

Bertuzzi, J. P. & Zreik, K. (2011). *Mixed reality games – Augmented cultural heritage*. Retrieved online June 13, 2013 from http://cumincades.scix.net/data/works/att/sigradi2011_083.content.pdf.

Borrero, N., & Yeh, C. J. (2010). Ecological English language learning among ethnic minority youth. *Educational Researchers*, 39, 571–581. doi:10.3102/0013189X10389810

Boulton, A. (2010). Learning outcomes from corpus consultation. In M. Moreno Ja_en, F. Serrano, Valverde & M. Calzada P_erez (Eds). *Exploring New Paths in Language Pedagogy: Lexis and Corpus-Based Language Teaching (pp.1-22).* London: Equinox.

Bradley, L., Linstrom, B., & Rystedt, H. (2010). Rationalities of collaboration for language learning on a wiki. *ReCALL, 22(2),* 247–265.

Brandt, A. & Jenks, C. (2011). 'Is it okay to eat a dog in Korea ... like China?' Assumptions of national food-eating practices in intercultural interaction. *Language and Intercultural Communication 11*(1), 41–58.

Brook, J. (2011). The affordances of YouTube for language learning and teaching. *Hawaii Pacific University TESOL Working Paper Series* 9(1, 2), 37–56.

Burston, J. (2014). MALL: The pedagogical challenges. *Computer Assisted Language learning,* 27(4), 344-357.

Byram, M. & Feng, A. (2004). Culture and language learning: Teaching, research and scholarship. *Language Teaching,* 37(3), 149-168.

Cambridge, J.C. (2010). The International Baccalaureate Diploma Programme and the construction of pedagogical identity: A preliminary study. *Journal of Research in International Education 9(3),* 199–213.

Cambridge, J. C. & Thompson, J. J. (2004). Internationalism and globalization as contexts for international education. *Compare 34 (2),*161–175.

Cause, L. (2011). International-mindedness: A field of struggle, confusion and hope. *Global Journal of Human Social Science 11(7),* 35–40.

Chamberlin-Quinlisk, C. (2013). Media, technology and intercultural education. *Intercultural Education, 24(4),* 297-302.

DeCapua, A., & Wintergerst, A. C. (2004). *Crossing Cultures in the Language Classroom.* Ann Arbor, MI: Michigan University Press.

Chang, C. S., Chen, T. S. & Hsu, W. H. (2011). The study on integrating Webquest with mobile learning for environmental education. *Computers & Education, 57(1),* 1228-1239.

Chao, Y. C. & Lo, H. C. (2011). Students' perceptions of wiki-based collaborative writing for learners of English as a foreign language. *Interactive Learning Environments, 19(4),* 395-411.

Coffey, A. J., Kamhawi, R. Fishwick, P. & Henderson, J. (2013). New media environments' comparative effects upon intercultural sensitivity: A five- dimensional analysis. *International Journal of Intercultural Relations, 37(5),* 605- 627.

Cuban, L. (2001). Encouraging progressive pedagogy. In L. A. Steen (Ed.) *Mathematics and democracy: The case for quantitative literacy (pp.87-91).* Princeton, NJ: National Council on Education and the Disciplines.

Dobao, A. F. (2012). Collaborative writing tasks in the L2 classroom: Comparing group, pair and individual work. *Journal of Second Language Writing, 21(1),* 40- 58.

Doherty, C. & Shield, P. (2012). Teachers' work in curriculum markets: Conditions of design and relations between the IB Diploma and the local curriculum. *Curriculum Inquiry 42(3),* 414–441.

Doherty, C. & Mu, L. (2011). Producing the intercultural citizen in the International Baccalaureate. F. Dervin, A. Gajardo and A. Lavanchy (Eds.). *Politics of Interculturality (pp.165–188).* Newcastle upon Tyne: Cambridge Scholars Publishing.

Egbert, J., Herman, D. & Chang, A (2014). To flip or not to flip? That's not the question: Exploring flipped instruction in technology supported language learning environments. *International Journal of Computer-Assisted Language Learning and Teaching, 4(2),* 1-10.

Elola, I. & Oskoz, A. (2008). Blogging: Fostering intercultural competence development in foreign language and study abroad contexts. *Foreign Language Annals, 41(3),* 454-477.

Falasca, M. & Altstaedter, L. L. (2011). Using webquests to develop intercultural competence in the foreign language classroom. *NECTFL Review, 67,* 15-30.

Furstenberg, G., Levet S., English, K., & Maillet, K. (2001). Giving a virtual voice to the silent language of culture: The Cultura Project. *Language Learning & Technology 5(1),* 55–102.

Gee, J. P.., & Hayes, E. R. (2011). *Language and learning in the digital age.* New York: Routledge.

Gifford, M. (2014). *The effects of technology-based graphic organizers to teach reading comprehension skills of students with learning disabilities.* Unpublished Master's Thesis. Rowan University.

Gigliotti-Labay, J. (2010). *Fulfilling its missions? The promotion of IM in IB DP programmes.* EdD dissertation. The College of Education, University of Houston, Houston, TX.

Halat, E. (2008). A good teaching technique: WebQuests. *The Cleaning House, 81(3),* 109-111.

Halbach, A. (2009). The primary school teacher and the challenges of bilingual education. In E. Dafouz & M. Guerrini (Eds). *CLIL across educational levels.* Madrid: Santillana/ Richmond Publishing, 19-26.

Hannerz, U. (1990). Cosmopolitans and locals in world culture. In M. Featherstone (Ed.). *Global culture: Nationalism, globalization and modernity (pp.237–251).* London: Sage.

Harwood, R. & Bailey, K. (2012). Defining and evaluating international- mindedness in a school context. *International School Journal XXXI (2),* 77–86.

Hill, I. (2007). International education as developed by the International Baccalaureate. In J. Thompson, M. Hayden & J. Levy (Eds.). *The Sage handbook of research in international education (pp.25–37).* London: Sage.

Hill, I. (2012). Evolution of education for IM. *Journal of Research in International Education, 11,* 245–261.

Hodges, C. G. (2002). Learning through collaborative writing. *Reading Literacy and Language, 36,* 4-10.

Houston, M. & Lin, L. (2012). Humanizing the classroom by flipping the homework versus lecture equation. In P. Resta (Ed.). *Proceedings of society for information technology & teacher education international conference (pp.1177– 1182).* Austin, TX: AACE.

Hung, H. T. (2015). Flipping the classroom for English language learners to foster active learning. *Computer Assisted Language Learning, 28(1),* 81-96.

IB (2008). *The diploma programme: A basis for practice.* Cardiff: International Baccalaureate.

IB (2013). *What is an IB education.* Geneva, Switzerland: the International Baccalaureate.

Inozu, J., Sahinkarakas, S., & Yumru, H. (2010). The nature of language learning experiences beyond the classroom and its learning outcomes. *US-China Foreign Language, 8,* 14–21.

Jones, A., Issroff., K, Scanlon, E, Clough, G and McAndrew, P (2006) Using mobile devices for learning in Informal Settings: Is it Motivating? *Paper to be presented at IADIS International conference Mobile Learning.* July 14-16, Dublin.

Keengwe, J., Onchwari, G., & Oigara, J. N. (2014). *Promoting active learning through the flipped classroom model.* Hershey, PA: IGI Global.

Kessler, G. & Bikowski, D. (2010). Developing collaborative autonomous learning abilities in computer mediated language learning: Attention to meaning among students in wiki space. *Computer Assisted Language Learning, 23(1),* 41-58.

Kern, R. (2000). *Literacy and Language Teaching.* Oxford: Oxford University Press.

Kost, C. (2011). Investigating writing strategies and revision behavior in collaborative wiki projects. *CALICO Journal, 28(3),* 606-620.

Kramsch, C. & Thorne, S. (2002). Foreign Language Learning as Global Communicative Practice. In D. Block & D. Cameron (Eds.) *Language Learning and Teaching in the Age of Globalization (pp.83–100).* London: Routledge.

Lai, C. (2015). Modeling teacher's influence on learners' self-directed use of technology for language learning outside the classroom. *Computers & Education, 82,* 74-83.

Lai, C., Shum, M. S. K. & Zhang, B. N. (2014). IM in an Asian context: The case of the International Baccalaureate in Hong Kong. *Educational Research, 56(1),* 77- 96.

Lai, C., Zhu, W. M. & Gong, G. (2014). Understanding the quality of out-of-class English learning. *TESOL Quarterly.* Advance Online Publication. doi:10.1002/tesq.171

Larsson, B. (2012). *English out-of-school activities: A way of integrating outwards?* Unpublished Master's Thesis. Gävle, Sweden: University of Gävle.

Lawrence, G. (2013). A working model for intercultural learning and engagement in collaborative online language learning environments. *Intercultural Education, 24(4),* 303-314.

Lawrence, G., Young, C., Owen, H. & Compton, C. (2009). Using Wikis for Collaborative Writing and Intercultural Learning. In M. Dantas-Whitney & S. Rilling (Eds.) *Authenticity in the Adult Language Classroom (pp.199–212).* Alexandria, VA: TESOL

Lee, L. (2009). Promoting intercultural exchange with blogs and podcasting: A study of Spanish-American tellcollaboration. *Computer Assisted Language Learning, 22(5),* 425-443.

Levy, F. & Murnane, R. J. (2004). Education and the changing job market. *Educational Leadership, 62(2),* 80-84.

Li, M., & Zhu, W. (2013). Patterns of computer-mediated interaction in small writing groups using wikis. *Computer Assisted Language Learning, 26(1),* 61-82.

Limbu, L., & Markauskaite, L. (2015). How do learners experience joint writing: University students' conceptions of online collaborative writing tasks and environments. *Computers & Education, 82,* 393-408.

Loh, C.E. (2012). Global and national imaginings: Deparochialising the IBDP English A1 curriculum. *Changing English: Studies in Culture and Education 19(2),* 221–235.

Lowry P.B, Curtis A. & Lowry M.R. (2004). Building a taxonomy and nomenclature of collaborative writing to improve interdisciplinary research and practice. *Journal of Business Communication, 41,* 66-99.

MacArthur, C. A. (2009). Reflections on research on writing and technology for struggling writers. *Learning Disabilities Research & Practice, 24(2),* 93-103.

Michelson, K. & Dupuy, B. (2014). Multi-storied lives: Global simulation as an approach to developing mutltiliteracies in an Intermediate French course. *L2 Journal, 6,* 21-49.

Mills, N. A. (2011). Situated learning through social networking communities: The development of joint enterprise, mutual engagement, and a shared repertoire. *CALICO Journal, 28*(2), 345-368.

Murray, T. (2009). What is the integral in integral education? From progressive pedagogy to integral pedagogy. *Integral Review, 5(1)*, 1-38.

Neville, D. O. (2012). *The story in the mind: Using 3D games for second language and culture development*. Retrieved on 23 June, 2015 from http://s3.amazonaws.com/academia.edu. documents/30385939/dgbl_narrative_02.pdf?AWSAccessKeyId=AKIAIR6FSIMDFXPEE RSA&Expires=1371610138&Signature=8jhLJDOGl2xm9JeD%2BKN7hcUl4eI%3D&resp onse-content-disposition=inline.

O'Dowd, R. (2007). *Online Intercultural Exchange: an Introduction for Foreign Language Teachers*. Clevedon: Multilingual Matters.

Ogata, H., Gan, L. H., Cheng, J. Y., Uceda, T., Oishi, Y., Yano, Y. (2008). LOCH: Supporting mobile language learning outside classrooms. *International Journal of Mobile Learning and Organisation, 2(3)*, 271-282.

Ozer, O. (2010). *A case study of transdisciplinary approach of integrated curriculum: Perspectives of early childhood teachers*. Unpublished Master's Thesis. Turkey: Middle East Technical University.

Payne, C.R. (2009). *Information technology and constructivism in higher education: Progressive learning frameworks*. Hersey, PA: IGI Global.

Perry, L. B. & Southwell, L. (2011). Developing intercultural understanding and skills: Models and approaches. *Intercultural Education, 22(6)*, 453-466.

Richards, J. C. (2009, April). *The changing face of TESOL*. Plenary Speech at TESOL Convention and Exhibit, Denver, Colorado, United States. Retrieved on 20 June, 2015 from http://www.professorjackrichards.com/wp-content/uploads/chang-ing-face-of- TESOL.pdf

Shehadeh, A. (2011). Effects and student perceptions of collaborative writing in L2. *Journal of Second Language Writing, 20(4)*, 286-305.

Sherman, S. C. (2009). Haven't we seen this before: Sustaining a vision in teacher education for progressive teaching practice. *Teacher Education Quarterly, 36(4)*, 41-60.

Singh, M. & Jing, Q. (2013). *21st century IM: An exploratory study of its conceptualisation and assessment*. Cardiff: International Baccalaureate.

So, H. J., Seow, P. & Looi, C. K. (2009). Location matters: Leveraging knowledge building with mobile devices and web 2.0 technology. *Interactive Learning Environments, 17(4)*, 367-382.

Sox, A., & Rubinstein-Avila, E. (2009). WebQuests for English-language learners: Essential elements for design. *Journal of Adolescent and Adult Literacy, 53(1)*, 38- 48.

Stockwell, G. & Hubbard, P. (2013). *Some emerging principles for mobile-assisted language learning*. Monterey, CA: The International Research Foundation for English Language Education.

Torres, I. P. (2007). *WebQuest: a collaborative strategy to teach content and language*. University of Granada.

Van Vooren, C., Lai, C., Ledger, S., Villaverde, A. B. ,& Steffen, V. (2013). *Additional language teaching and learning in International Baccalaureate Primary Years Programme schools*. Cardiff: International Baccalaureate.

Venville, G, Rennie, L, & Wallace, J. (2009). *Disciplinary versus integrated curriculum*. Institute of Advanced Studies, University of Western Australia, 10. Retrieved on 16 May, 2015 from http://www.ias.uwa.edu.au/new-critic/ten/venville

Wang, C. M. (2012). Using Facebook for cross-cultural collaboration: The experience of students from Taiwan. *Educational Media International, 49(1),* 63- 76.

Ware, P. D., & Kramsch, C. (2005). Toward an intercultural stance: Teaching German and English through telecollaboration. *Modern Language Journal, 89(2),* 190-205.

Warschauer, M. & Matuchniak, T. (2010). New technology and digital worlds: Analyzing evidence for equity in access, use and outcomes. *Review of Research in Education, 34(1),* 179- 225.

Williamson-Henriques,K. M. (2013). *Secondary Teachers' Perceptions of Assistive Technology Use for Students with Learning Disabilities.* Unpublished Doctoral Dissertation. The University of North Carolina at Greensboro.

Wong, L. H., Chin, C.-K., Tan, C.-L., & Liu, M. (2010). Students' personal and social meaning making in a Chinese idiom mobile learning environment. *Educational Technology & Society, 13*(4), 15–26.

Zheng, D., Young, M. F., Wagner, M., & Brewer, R. A. (2009). Negotiation for action: English language learning in game-based virtual worlds. *The Modern Language Journal, 93(4),* 489–511.

Zheng, R., Perez, J., Williamson, J. & Flygare, J. (2008). Webquests as perceived by teachers: Implications for online teaching and learning. *Journal of Computer Assisted Learning, 24(4),* 295-304.

Chapter 9

The road to successful Chinese language learning: effective strategies for teaching and learning Chinese characters

Elizabeth Ka-yee Loh, Martin Ting-fung Mak
& Loretta Chung-wing Tam

Abstract

This chapter explores how the Integrative Perceptual Approach (IPA) for teaching Chinese characters (Tse, Marton, Ki & Loh, 2007) may help develop Chinese as a Second Language (CSL) learners' orthographic sensitivity and elevate their literacy level in accordance with International Baccalaureate (IB) philosophy and pedagogy. With special reference to an exemplary case of an IB Chinese Language B classroom in Hong Kong, the authors seek to examine the underlying causes of learning difficulties amongst CSL learners, and illustrate a number of effective and interesting strategies as well as best practices for applying the IPA for teaching Chinese characters.

Strategies complementary to the existing IB Chinese Language B curriculum, particularly the use of authentic materials in meaningful contexts and teaching characters in relational clusters, enable CSL learners to discern the variants and invariants amongst related characters and to develop key aspects of the Chinese language. These learners' orthographic sensitivity to written Chinese and intercultural communication skills are thus sharpened during the aforementioned learning process, whereby their personal growth is cultivated and enriched in line with the IB Learner Profile (IBLP).

Introduction

Chinese is an ideographic language with a huge number of characters. Readers need to learn word by word in order to pick up the meaning and the pronunciation of each character. As a result, the learning outcome is disappointing and the sustainability is low in comparison with most other languages. Many people (especially those learning Chinese as a second language) come to a conclusion that learning Chinese language is too difficult for them, while gradually losing their interest or even giving up.

The ability to recognise Chinese characters is fundamental to Chinese language learning. In order to learn the characters effectively, students should master two critical features: components and the spatial structures. There are about 540 foundational components. These constitute characters that fit into a square space in a text, and can be further classified into 15 spatial structures (Huang, 2003; Ki et al., 2003; Tse, 2000). The 77 commonly used components constitute approximately 1500 characters

(Tse, 2006; Tse *et al.*, 2008). Students who are aware of components and structures can gain implicit knowledge from the multilevel representation of characters (Shu *et al.*, 2000).

The IPA for teaching Chinese characters (Tse, Marton, Ki & Loh, 2007), based on the phenomenographic approach (Marton & Booth, 1997) to learning, has proven to be an effective strategy to develop students' awareness of components and structures, and to increase their literacy level (*eg* Lee *et al.*, 2011; Loh *et al.*, 2013; Tse & Loh, 2014; Tse, Loh, Lam, Cheung & Zha, 2007; Tse *et al.*, 2012). By using meaningful contexts and the students' own language as the basic teaching materials, structural features, written forms and pronunciations are taught systematically and simultaneously. Students learn characters in relational clusters, discern the similarities and variations among these related characters, and the teacher highlights and emphasises the crucial aspects of Chinese characters and words.

The International Baccalaureate (IB) suggests that the IB Language B course should be taught in line with the ten attributes of an IB Learner (IB, 2013) as well as the pedagogical principles that underpin the IB programmes, namely the promotion of critical- and creative-thinking skills, and learning how to learn.

The organisation also strongly encourages teachers to design their own course, and to teach it in a way that takes into consideration specific needs and interests of students (IB, 2011). The IPA, which proposes customised use of authentic teaching materials in meaningful contexts for enhanced, active learning of Chinese characters, aligns well with both the IB Learner Profile and the Language B syllabus in terms of objectives and pedagogy.

This chapter introduces a number of effective strategies for teaching Chinese characters to which this IPA is applied, and illustrate how these complementary ways can enhance Chinese as a Second Language (CSL) students' reading ability, while achieving both the teaching and learning objectives of the existing IB Chinese Language B curriculum with special reference to a best practice case study.

The challenge of teaching and learning in culturally and academically mixed CSL classrooms

Teaching and learning CSL has, in recent decades, emerged as a discipline in its own right while attracting much scholarly attention. With the sharp increase of non-native learners around the world, pedagogies and curricula are undergoing vigorous improvisation to address the pressing issue of catering for the diverse needs of its learners.

CSL learners, regardless of their ethnicity, gender, and age, are prone to various learning difficulties in acquiring the language through their course of learning. Nevertheless, adolescent CSL learners in Chinese-dominated communities might share certain traits and challenges. The first issue is the enormous disparity between their first language (L1) and their target language, *eg* alphasyllabary language users might find it hard to make sense of Chinese characters' structures and stroke sequences.

The second issue lies in the cultural differences among people of varied ethnic origins regarding literacy practice and education. While ethnically

Chinese children born and raised in Chinese-dominated communities are no strangers to dictation and rote learning, both of which remain popular Chinese language teaching strategies, their non-Chinese counterparts (particularly those from countries outside east Asia) often find it less easy to spend time to learn the characters and passages by heart.

Teaching and learning CSL in multicultural classrooms raises further concerns in terms of facilitation and evaluation of learning effectiveness. With rapid globalisation and high mobility of the international labour force, students from different ethnic, linguistic, and cultural backgrounds are at times made to study CSL in the same settings. Although they are often assigned to different streams or 'pathways' according to their Chinese proficiency at the time of enrolment, teachers are often burdened with the need to address their diverse concerns, as well as the varied expectations from the parents. Assurance of learning effectiveness has thus become an immense challenge, while evaluation of learning effectiveness turns into a highly sophisticated process of adjusting the assessment tools and criteria in order to strike a balance between measurements of different parameters, such as performance and competence.

In the following sections, we look into the exemplary case of Hong Kong which features culturally and academically diverse CSL classrooms, and address the aforementioned issues from both theoretical and practical perspectives. A number of effective strategies developed on the basis of the IPA for teaching Chinese characters (Tse, Marton, Ki & Loh, 2007) are explored through an example of implementation at an international school in the territory where the International Baccalaureate (IB) is adopted. While character recognition and writing are the focus, other aspects of CSL learning are given attention throughout the implementation.

Theoretical basis

Previous studies in Chinese language education, second language acquisition, sociolinguistics and literacy studies have addressed a key concern in the discipline of CSL, *ie* factors leading to the major obstacles to CSL teaching and learning. Orthographic knowledge is often considered as one of the most challenging aspects of the Chinese language, particularly among CSL learners with alphabetic L1s. As a predominantly ideographic language with a monosyllabic orthographic system (DeFrancis, 1989), Chinese can be classified into two major types of characters: single characters (独体字, which are not able to be divided into distinct components); and compound characters (合体字, which can be further divided into multiple, reusable components).

Components are the smallest structural units of both the traditional and simplified Chinese orthographic scripts, which carry information about meaning and pronunciation and are made up of strokes, the smallest building blocks of written Chinese. Thus far, 540 foundational components and 15 spatial structures have been identified in the simplified Chinese script (Huang, 2003; Ki *et al.*, 2003; Tse, 2000).

Possession of orthographic knowledge is a prerequisite for acquisition of morphological and grammatical awareness in relation to print input, as characters are the basic units of fabrication for morphological constructions from words through to sentential levels (Norman, 1988). Components, spatial structures and characters are to be learned by heart, and such memorisation is not so different from the acquisition of English spelling rules in which specific clusters, sounds, and meanings are related to each other.

To achieve basic functional literacy in modern Chinese, one has to know at least 500 Chinese characters (Chen, 1999). However CSL learners, especially those with alphabetic L1s, experience varied levels of difficulty in mastering the compositional rules (*eg* positional constraints) of the Chinese language due to the enormous disparity between Chinese and their native language. Such students generally lack awareness of components, structures, and compositional constraints as mentioned in Shu *et al* (2000), the latter of which is crucial to the acquisition of orthographic knowledge from multilevel representation of characters. Orthographic sensitivity, that being said, is essential to Chinese character learning (Leong *et al*, 2011).

Krashen's (1982) Theory of Second Language Acquisition (SLA) adopts a psycholinguistic approach to second language (L2) learning, and offers clues to enhance CSL learners' awareness of Chinese orthographic structure. The scholar argues for the importance of acquisition over learning (Acquisition-learning Hypothesis), and the use of authentic, comprehensible input with slight scaffolding on the 'i+1' level (the Input Hypothesis) for effective learning.

He also states that L2 learners should be situated in social interactions for optimal motivation and learning results, whereby anxiety is minimized to avoid mental blocks (the Affective Filter). Firth and Wagner (1997) later called for enhanced awareness of the contextual and interactional dimensions of language use, as well as an increased participant-relevant sensitivity towards fundamental concepts (Firth & Wagner, 1997; 2007), which are valuable additions to the field of SLA.

Many L2 learners, including CSL learners in Chinese-dominated communities, are nonetheless deprived of sufficient opportunities to use their target language in their daily life. The reasons are many, among them that they are either too shy to speak up (Norton, 2013); or have little exposure to their host society (Kwan, 2012; Lam *et al.*, 2014) as they tend to communicate with their family and friends in their own L1 or English, the latter of which is being used as an international or 'high' (H) language (Ferguson, 1959). In the case of CSL learners, one's writing proficiency would be even more at risk than speaking, as it generally takes more time for them to learn the characters than simple conversations.

Acquisition of the lexicon and automatisation of orthographic decoding are both prerequisites for being a good reader (Leong *et al*, 2011); they can provide solutions to reading and writing difficulties. Traditional methods of Chinese language teaching (such as dictation and rote learning) are largely based on memorisation, which in no way addresses the lack of orthographic sensitivity among lower proficiency level CSL learners, as well as the cultural and academic diversity in CSL classrooms. Involving such students in social interactions for the purpose of language learning requires meticulous planning and effective strategies.

The IPA for teaching Chinese characters (Tse, Marton, Ki & Loh, 2007) is an innovative method based on variation theory (Bowden & Marton, 1998; Marton & Booth, 1997). It follows a phenomenographic tradition which is concerned with how people perceive and conceptualise the world (Marton, 1986). The method considers the different ways in which people experience the same phenomenon. Learning is a function of discernment. It involves discerning the variant and invariant parts of the learning objects, and then generalising the experience into other learning situations.

Understanding subject matter (or 'object of learning' in the words of the aforementioned phenomenographers) generally goes from whole to part, as one tends to experience a certain situation as a whole before rendering the perspective on its component parts (Lo, 2012; Marton & Booth, 1997) and *vice versa*. That said, effective learning is only possible with discernment of the object of learning from its context, and to make discernment possible one has to be exposed to, and experience, variations of the subject matter purposefully and systematically (Bowden & Marton, 1998).

In the same vein, this IPA for teaching Chinese characters based on variation theory places much emphasis on learning through discernment of parts (*eg* components of Chinese characters) in relation to wholes (*eg* Chinese characters) and *vice versa*, while experiencing variations of the object. Learners are guided to systematically and purposefully discern structural features of related characters in clusters to enhance their awareness; at the same time other key aspects of Chinese characters and words are emphasised. The following table illustrates nine major principles (see Table 1) derived from the IPA with reference to the application of variation theory (Tse, Marton, Ki & Loh, 2007, pp.393-394):

Principle	Application of Variation Theory
1. Every text/rhyming text should be selected with clear character learning objectives in mind.	Each text should focus on specific structural features of characters or words for different goals of discernment, *ie* which characters or components to learn to write/to read. Example: Course text with a focus on characters constituted by the "木" ("wood") component.
2. The instructional process typically goes from whole to parts, *ie* (a) from text to words to characters and (b) from characters to component parts. In turn, how the component parts constitute the whole character, the characters to words and to the whole text, should also be discerned by the learners.	In accordance with the natural sequence of learning (from whole to parts and parts to whole). Examples: 1. From whole to part: "森林里有很多树木" (there are lots of trees in the forest) →"森林" (forest)→"森"(forest) = "木"(wood) + "林"(woods); "林"(woods) = "木"(wood) + "木"(wood)→"木"(wood) (sentence→phrase→word→character→component) 2. From part to whole: "木" (wood)→"木"(wood) + "木"(wood) = "林"(woods) and "木"(wood) + "林"(woods) = "森"(forest)→"森林"(forest)→ "森林里有很多树木"(there are lots of trees in the forest) (component→character→word→phrase→sentence).

3. Structural awareness is brought about through learning characters in related clusters (with the same components and/or structural features).	Characters are categorised according to their component parts, meaning or sound to form clusters. Teachers can make use of the invariant (similarities) and the variant (differences) parts for guiding students to discern the critical features of the clusters in a systematic and purposeful manner. Examples: Categorised in the form of word clusters: "森" (forest), "林" (woods), "杷" (loquat), "椅" (chair), "桌" (table) (all of the above variants carry the component and meaning of the invariant "木") 森 (forest) = 木 (wood)+ 木 (wood)+ 木 (wood) 林 (woods) = 木 (wood) + 木 (wood) 杷 (loquat) = 木 (wood) + 巴 (sticky) 椅 (chair) = 木 (wood + 奇 (unusual) 桌 (table) = 占 (tall and erect) +木 (wood) Categorised according to the phonetic features: 杷 (loquat; /pá/) = 木 (wood) + 巴 (/bā/) 吧 (modal particle; /ba/) = 口 (mouth) +巴 (/bā/) 把 (grip; /bǎ/) = 手 (hand) + 巴 (/bā/) 爸 (father; /bà/) = 父 (father) +巴 (/bā/) (all of the above carry the invariant "巴"(sticky; /ba/), which is a phonetic component paired up with the variants "木"(wood), "口" (mouth), "手"(hand), "父"(father) which represent the meanings, to form new characters)
4. Learners are led actively to discern such structural features, e.g. the relationship between the form (形符/意符), pronunciation (声符) and meaning (意义) of the characters.	Learning through discernment: the relationship between the form, pronunciation and meaning of the characters is brought to their awareness. This integrates 'the way of seeing' (ie perception of meaning and structures of the language) into "the process of doing" (ie using the language, including reading and writing) (Tse, Marton, Ki & Loh, 2007, p.384). Example: Discernment of meaning and pronunciation - Learners are taught to decode "把"(grip) by breaking it down into "手" (hand, the semantic component) and "巴" (/bā/, the phonetic component).
5. Learners are encouraged to make connections between target characters and texts to their previous knowledge and life experience.	One of the most effective ways of learning character is based on the children's (a) life experience and (b) their spoken language. The learners have the intention and the message to be shared with others. What they do not know is the Chinese characters and the pronunciation in Chinese. Examples: Learners are encouraged to connect the newly-acquired components and vocabulary to their daily life, such as relating words with the "木" (wood) component to home furniture (such as "床"[bed]), "柜" [wardrobe]) and fruits (such as"柚子" [pomelo], "柠檬" [lemon]).

6. Learners' mental lexicons related to the key message of the selected text/ rhyming text are retrieved, for the expansion of literacy level.	This is one of the most effective ways to expand the learners' literacy level, as the learning content is words in the learners' minds, and given that the capacity of short-term memory is limited among human beings (ie only 5-9 items among adults, or on average 7) (Miller, 1956). Adoption of semantic network as a basic unit for memorization has an advantage of multiplying the learners' Chinese vocabulary and reducing the rate of forgetting, as groups or clusters of words from students' own mental lexicons are to be learned by heart. Example: Chinese words under a certain category are retrieved from the learners' memory. The category "水果", for instance, may include multiple hyponyms such as "橙子" (orange), "柠檬" (lemon), "柚子" (pomelo) and "梨" (pear). Learners are then encouraged to write them down in the form of a mind map reflecting the semantic network.
7. Character analysis and composition games can be used to consolidate structural awareness about components and the composition of characters.	Composition games and creative dictation drawing on the students' mental lexicon serves as a good alternative to traditional dictation and vocabulary exercises, such as a component (eg "木" [wood])-based list of characters/words one can remember from her/his past experience. It serves well as a task for reinforcing Principles 3 and 6 above. Card games[5] also enhance learners' understanding of part-whole and whole-part relationships at character, phrasal and sentential levels (see Figure 1).
8. Character learning must be anchored in text and a context meaningful to the learner.	Learning of characters, as well as the fusion of the character shape with meaning and sound, are to be based on the children's (a) life experience and (b) spoken language.
9. Common rhyming texts well known by children are good choices of passages to be used in early stages of learning.	One of the problems that the learners encounter is the sustainability of what they have learnt. Using rhyming texts strengthens the learners' sustainability (Barber, 1980). Learning language through music is an effective approach whereby learners' memories are stimulated by the melody in relation to rhyming texts, words, characters and components; this in turn consolidates knowledge through practice. Furthermore, characters in popular rhyming texts (eg Pop song lyrics like Jay Chou's "青花瓷" ('Blue and White Porcelain', 2007) are possibly categorised according to invariants (similarities) and variants (differences) in the visual aspects of their component parts, allowing students to be exposed to different variations while being guided to discern their object of learning in context. Example: Students may learn about sounds and components from traditional ballads and nursery rhymes, such as "外婆桥" ("Grandma's Lullaby"). It includes a number of rhyming characters (like "摇" (shake), "谣" (song) and "桥" (bridge) sharing the same Mandarin rime /iao/, as well as characters sharing the same component (like "拉" [pull] and "摇" [shake] sharing the "手" [hand] component)

Table 1. Nine principles of the Integrative Perceptual Approach for teaching Chinese characters as related to variation theory.

5 Students use various component cards to constitute Chinese characters (from part to whole); the newly formed Chinese characters can be 'broken' into different components (from whole to part).

Figure 1. Sample of card games for Chinese character learning – characters with the commonly-used component '木'.

In the next section, a sample CSL module for secondary students designed in accordance with the above principles is given to illustrate the use of various effective strategies to which the IPA for teaching Chinese characters is applied in line with the IB Learner Profile (IBLP).

Sample teaching design

The following is a CSL module that took place in a Grade 9 classroom with 24 students at an international school in Hong Kong adopting a GCSE curriculum intended to pave the way for their subsequent IB studies in Years 12 and 13. Mandarin and Simplified Chinese characters are the medium of instruction in Chinese language lessons.

The class was ethnically diverse, and most of the students were native English speakers who started learning Chinese since Grade 1. A couple of students were able to speak some Cantonese but did not have matching proficiency levels of reading and writing, while the others conversed mainly in English with very limited Chinese proficiency. The text (Appendix I) is entitled '我有了自己的房间' ('I Got My Own Bedroom') (Ma & Li, 2006).

1. Preparation: the day before the lesson
Objectives: Enhancing students' observational and self-learning abilities.

Operational procedure:
> Students took photos of the most interesting electric appliances, furniture and ornaments in their bedrooms for class activities.

2. Implementation of Module
Session 1 (60 minutes)
Objectives:
Cultivating students' listening and speaking abilities while enhancing their orthographic knowledge.

181

Theoretical basis:
> The communicative approach, social interactions, mental lexicon, reading aloud.

Teaching materials/tools:
> Chalkboard writing (mental lexicon, including characters, phrases, and *pinyin*), photos prepared by students, Worksheet #1 (for students to copy down their favorite mental lexicon, English glosses, drawings and *pinyin*).

Operational procedures:

Step	Rationale	Relevance to IBLP
i. Teacher read aloud the first and second paragraphs.		
ii. Teacher raised questions on the mental lexicon related to "我自己的房间".	Retrieval of mental lexicon related to the students' own life experience, with clear character learning objects, in order to make the learning content more interesting while reducing the affective filter	Equipping students to be *reflective* learners, by offering them an opportunity to assess and understand their strengths and limitations
iii. Students were divided into groups (three to four students per group). Teacher asked them to interview their own group members on the most interesting electrical appliances, furniture or ornaments. The interviewees were to show photos of what they described as the most interesting pieces that they photographed the day before. iv. Interviewers wrote down the responses of the interviewees (including the Chinese characters [by themselves, if possible; or with the support of their groupmates/teachers], English glosses, drawings and pinyin [not the major learning objectives, for the support of students' pronunciation only] (see Figure 2). It was expected that they could pronounce the characters even without reading the pinyin.	Communicative language teaching (CLT) adopted to enhance student motivation, so as to effectively expand literacy level Giving students an opportunity to practise writing the words they already knew from oral interactions, so that they can learn both the spoken and written forms at the same time.	Equipping students to be *caring communicators* through peer collaborative learning; guiding them to work effectively and willingly with others and to express themselves confidently and creatively; guiding them to show respect towards the needs and feelings of others. Equipping students to be *inquirers* and *thinkers*, by offering them an opportunity to conduct inquiry and actively enjoy learning, while applying their thinking skills confidently and creatively.

v. Students reported their findings in Chinese.	Giving students an opportunity to learn from others' experience; in-class peer evaluation for enhancing learning ability	Equipping students to be *inquirers* and *thinkers*, by offering them an opportunity to conduct inquiry and actively enjoy learning, while applying their thinking skills confidently and creatively Equipping students to be *open-minded risk-takers*, so that they would be willing to approach uncertainty with courage and to grow from the experience.
vi. Teacher wrote the mental lexicon on the whiteboard (see Figure 3). Students chose those they found interesting and wrote them down on their worksheet.	Increasing students' literacy level via the task of note-taking.	Equipping students to be *open-minded risk-takers*, so that they would be willing to approach uncertainty with courage while growing from the experience.
vii. Teacher read aloud the third paragraph, asked students to identify characters from the text which they have just learnt, and then explained the difficult words and phrases in the text.	Catering for the huge differences amongst students within each IB Chinese Language B pathway. Giving students an opportunity to identify the mental lexicon present in the set text.	
viii. All students read the text aloud together.		

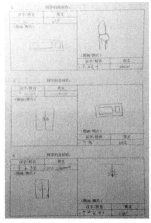

Figure 2. Sample of students' work – interviews with group members.

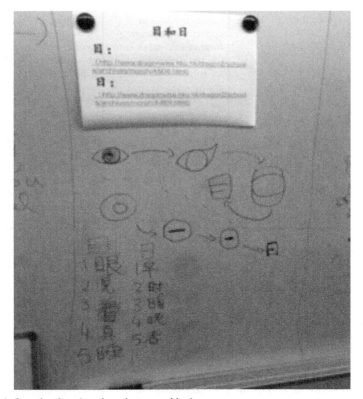

Figure 3. Sample of students' work – mental lexicon.

Session 2 – A and B (120 minutes)
Objectives:
   Enhancing students' orthographic knowledge; 木 (being one of
   the 77 most commonly used components featured in the samples
   shown, is marked by its nature as a single component with high
   word-formation potential), is the character learning objective of
   the text.

Theoretical basis:
   Component learning, character learning with fun.

Teaching materials/tools:
   [A]'快速学汉字—部件识字游戏'(*Component Learning Game*
   by S K Tse, Simplified Chinese Version), Worksheet #2 (for
   students to copy down their favorite mental lexicon, English
   glosses, drawings and *pinyin*; better still for word formation and
   sentence making as well); [B] Specifically-designed double-layer
   flashcards (text on the outside and corresponding visual on the
   inside).

Operational procedures:

Step	Rationale	Relevance to IBLP
i. Recap on mental lexicon and key component to be learnt "木".	• Targeting the '木' component for forming new characters.	• Equipping students to be reflective, encouraging them to give thoughtful consideration to their own learning and experience; Inquirers: learning independently and with others.
ii. Students were asked to provide characters and phrases related to home furnishings with the component '木' (wood), as well as other words from their mental lexicon containing the component '木'. Eg 床(bed), 衣柜 (wardrobe), 桌子(table), 椅子(chair).	• Recalling students' memory (whole to part).	
iii. Students were divided into groups and asked to form characters (in the text, on the blackboard, as well as what they had learnt) with the component '木' with the game cards. They were required to write down their answers on the worksheet before reporting to the class (see Figures 4 and 5). The group with the most correct answers would be the winner. iv. Teacher emphasized the component '木' (word cluster) which appears in most of the characters which the students mentioned or formed (ie the whole). Teacher also explained that this is all wooden furniture. Some of the characters are with the left-right structure (eg 柜[wardrobe]), some with the top-middle-bottom structure (eg 桌[table]), and some with the inner-outer structure (eg 床[bed]) (ie the part). This is to strengthen students' awareness of common components and their basic structural features.	• Arousing awareness of the '木' component, and the structure of characters carrying the '木' component 2 Encouraging the students to "reuse" the component to form characters with '木'(or '木'-related) connotations. • Peer collaborative learning and evaluation in writing, speaking, and listening 4 Enabling discernment and arousing awareness of the variant and the invariant parts of Chinese characters.	• Equipping students to be risk-takers and communicators through peer collaborative learning; guiding them to work effectively and willingly with others and to express themselves confidently and creatively. • Equipping students to be knowledgeable thinkers, by offering them an opportunity to exercise initiative in applying thinking skills critically and creatively while acquiring in-depth knowledge.

v. Classification game (point scoring) Teacher provided a set of 24 double-layer flashcards (e.g. furniture, ornaments, electrical appliances). vi. Students were asked to make extra flashcards with their own photos. This is to strengthen students' sustainability of what they have learnt in class. vii. Teacher distributed flashcards (students were not allowed to get what they made on their own).	• Giving students an opportunity to practice identifying form, meaning and sound in one go • Helping them to discern components and structures at the same time (from part to whole for consolidating students' knowledge). • Sociocultural learning approach: linking language learning to students' own life experience while reducing the affective filter.	• Equipping students to be risk-takers and communicators through peer collaborative learning; guiding them to work effectively and willingly with others and to express themselves confidently and creatively; encouraging them to be brave and articulate in defending their beliefs. • Equipping students to be principled and balanced, by giving them an opportunity to act with integrity and honesty with a strong sense of fairness, justice and respect while taking responsibility for their own actions; informing them of the importance of intellectual, physical and emotional balance.
viii. Students were divided into groups and categorised the cards on hand. ix. Students would score 2 points for right answers based on text/pronunciation hints. x. Students would score 1 point for right answers based on the visuals. xi. Students would score 3 points for writing characters with the component '木' correctly, to encourage them to re-use and to consolidate what they have learnt in class. xii. Students were asked to grade the performance of the other groups. This provides opportunity to read and use the target language.	• Strengthening students' semantic network and classification of Chinese words (*eg* furniture, electrical appliances), which are two areas CSL learners are particularly weak in.	
xiii. Teacher provided another set of 15 double-layer flashcards.		

xiv. Students were divided into groups. They were asked to put individual flashcards under different categories, eg Flashcards '床' ('bed') and '衣柜' ('wardrobe') were supposed to go under the same category '臥室' ('Bedroom'). This is to consolidate students' knowledge of various types of room decoration. xv. The group completing the game the earliest would score 5 points, the second scoring 4, the third scoring 3, and so on. xvi. Students would score 2 points for right answers based on text/pronunciation hints. xvii. Students would score 1 point for right answers for referring to the visuals.	• Use of characters in a peer collaborative setting. • Task-based learning.	
xviii. Students were asked to report in both verbal and written forms. They were also required to grade the performance of the other groups. This provides opportunity to read and use the target language.	• Enhancing students' listening and reading.	

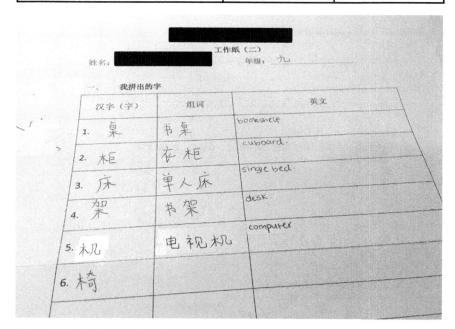

Figure 4. Sample of students' work – Chinese characters with the component '木'.

Figure 5. Class activity – flashcard grouping game (with time limit).

Session 3 (60 minutes)
Objectives:
    Enhancing students' writing ability.

Theoretical basis:
    Chinese grammar (sentence structures).

Teaching materials/tools:
    Worksheet #3 (for the sentence making tasks).

Operational procedures:

Step	Rationale	Relevance to IBLP
i. Teacher explained the sentence structures, including: 1. ⋯⋯，因为⋯⋯ ('..., because') 2. 不但⋯⋯，而且⋯⋯ ('Not only... but also...') 3. ⋯⋯，但是⋯⋯ ('..., but...') 4. ⋯⋯，要不然⋯⋯ ('..., or else...').	• Learning Chinese grammar.	• Equipping students to be reflective, so that they would give thoughtful consideration to their own learning and experience. • Equipping students to be knowledgeable and reflective thinkers, encouraging them to exercise initiative in acquiring in-depth knowledge for developing understanding across a broad range of disciplines including Chinese Language.
ii. Students drew lots and made sentences (writing). iii. Peer evaluation among students. iv. Teacher concluded on the students' peer evaluation task.	• Use of target components and characters to write sentences.	

Session 4 (6 minutes)

Step	Rationale	Relevance to IBLP
Teacher concluded on the knowledge covered in this module.		
i. Homework assignment: students were asked to decorate a room for different clients, by using the furniture, electric appliances, or ornaments they had learnt in the class.	• Task-based learning as a needs analysis for the imaginary clients.	• Equipping students to be *reflective thinkers* giving thoughtful consideration to learning which is relevant to their daily lives. • Equipping students to be *caring* and *open-minded*, so that they would be able to show empathy and respect towards the needs and feelings of others, while being open to the perspectives, values and traditions of other individuals and communities.
ii. They were asked to explain in Chinese (verbally and in written form) the setting of the room, how the setting would fit the needs of the client assigned to each group.	• Giving students an opportunity to use the language in both verbal and written forms, as well as enhancing students' reading and listening.	
iii. They were also encouraged to use the sentence patterns they had learnt in Lesson 3 to explain their designs.	• Giving students an opportunity to learn from others' experience; in-class peer evaluation for enhancing learning ability.	

Discussion of the teaching design: some best practices

The module featured in the previous section offers an illustration of how the IPA for teaching Chinese characters can be effectively applied via various effective strategies in a secondary CSL classroom. In the following, a number of best practices as outlined in the module are discussed with reference to the nine principles of the IPA.

Learning characters in a meaningful context

Being the core of the nine major principles behind the IPA for teaching Chinese characters, character learning in a context meaningful to the learner is of utmost importance to facilitate acquisition. Not only does this strategy motivate students with familiar concepts and visuals but it also situates the students in a learning context to which they can relate.

Throughout the module, both the use of mental lexicon and authentic materials alongside the course text helped to facilitate students' learning of Chinese characters through their personal experience as non-zero beginners. Access to the students' Chinese mental lexicon, a second language in this case, helped them relate the sounds (speaking and listening) to the characters (character recognition) through bridging mental lexicon tasks (writing and reading) while effectively expanding their literacy level.

While the use of mental lexicon helped students to decipher form, sound and meaning, the use of authentic materials alongside the course text under teachers' guidance, such as making flashcards with the students' own mental lexicons, would further reinforce students' memory while addressing the role of their past experience in their acquisition of new Chinese vocabulary and knowledge building.

Given the fact that the photos were taken by themselves in their own homes, the flashcards were based on what they or their family possess and use in reality. Students would find it much easier to recall the relationships between the new characters and vocabulary they learnt and what exists in a real, daily setting, that would in turn enrich their mental lexicon. Students are thus more likely to use the vocabulary they have learnt in future, real-life language contexts, which in turn helps to consolidate their knowledge and enables more practical, functional and meaningful learning.

From whole to parts and from parts to whole

The instructional process of whole to parts, as suggested in variation theory as a universal tendency, was adhered to throughout the lesson, including both sessions 1 (relating pronunciation to characters through the reading aloud activity) and 2 (relating concepts to individual characters, words, and phrases through the mental lexicon activities). Throughout the module, characters were introduced to the students with the sequence of phrase → word → character → component, enabling them to discern the boundaries among the aforementioned levels of written Chinese.

On both the character and phrasal levels, the classroom activities were centered on invariants (*eg* the component '木', and the spatial concept/ entity '卧室') as well as the variants (*eg* other components constituting characters carrying '木', and other spatial concepts/entities like '客厅'), whereby language awareness was enhanced in parallel with acquisition of vocabulary and sentence structures. Session 2A is an example of class activity aligning with the 'From the whole to parts' strategy, whereby a flashcard game requiring students to form characters using the component '木' was facilitated.

The teacher played a key role in guiding students through the process of discernment of the aforementioned invariants and variants to enhance students' structural awareness via visualisation, as well as to expand their vocabulary with lexical input from both the teacher and their peers. Students were able to learn about the etymology of individual components and their alternative forms (变形部件), which would be useful for reinforcing their memory and reducing errors in their written production.

Language input of this activity into the class was accessed again in the form of a mental lexicon in session 2B, whereby students were encouraged to recognise, classify and write down characters with the component '木' (wood) to score points. This, nevertheless, is featured by an additional strategy 'From parts to whole', which leads students to repeatedly discern the invariants and variants while applying such language knowledge (including orthographic and morphological knowledge) in their writing. The entire session 2 thus integrates 'the way of seeing' (*ie* perception of meaning and structures of the language) into 'the process of doing' as emphasized in the IPA for teaching Chinese characters (Tse, Marton, Ki & Loh, 2007, p.384).

Opportunities for peer collaborative learning

During class activities involving access to students' mental lexicon and use of authentic materials, students were also placed in actual social interactions through which they were able to communicate in the target language through verbal and written means with their peers. Interactive tasks, including games, were planned for the entire module in which different aspects of language use (*ie* speaking, listening, reading, and writing) were covered.

Session 1 of the module featured in the sample teaching design shows a good example of how speaking and listening can be incorporated into a writing task, in which students were asked to interview their fellow group members regarding their own bedroom settings while putting down the responses in writing.

Such peer collaboration not only provided an opportunity for language practice through real-life conversations, but also facilitated social interaction offering comprehensible input and building students' intercultural communicative competence (Duff, 2010) in line with IB philosophy and pedagogy as expressed in the IB Learner Profile (International Baccalaureate, 2013).

While discernment is meant to be experienced by learners rather than being told by others, such interactive tasks allowed students to explore variations of Chinese characters first-hand with their peers, which should engender structural features of the target language (Marton & Booth, 1997; Tse, Marton, Ki & Loh, 2010) and enhance their motivation for learning Chinese as a second language.

This also aligns with Krashen (1982), Firth & Wagner (1997; 2007), as well as principles 1 and 6 of the IPA for teaching Chinese characters, while encouraging peer collaborative learning (Wentzel *et al*, 2002) and enhances acquisition of extended knowledge in a context the students can personally relate to. Experiential learning is an important plank of IB pedagogy.

Conclusion

In regard to the current challenges in CSL teaching and learning, particularly the awareness of components and compositional rules among lower Chinese proficiency level adolescent CSL learners, a number of effective teaching strategies have been introduced in this chapter to illustrate how the IPA can be applied. As an approach based on theories of SLA and phenomenography, the IPA aligns with IB philosophy and pedagogy while providing complementary ways that help achieve both the teaching and learning objectives of the current IB Chinese Language B curriculum.

The IPA is, in many ways, a proven solution to students' difficulty in Chinese character learning among alphasyllabary language-speaking students in local schools in Hong Kong (Loh, under review). Designed in accordance with the learning sequence for Chinese language, *ie* listening → speaking → character learning (orthographic knowledge, morphological knowledge) → reading (morphological knowledge, syntactic rules, semantic rules) → writing (joint/independent rewriting and writing), it provides a complementary perspective on curriculum development for the academically and culturally diverse IB CSL classroom, which will hopefully, in the long run, help the learners attain higher Chinese proficiency levels in joyful and creative ways.

Acknowledgement

The research team would like to thank the participating school and students for their support of this joint research project. Special thanks also go to Mr. Andy Jiawei Zhao for his assistance in preparing the teaching materials/ tools and data input.

References

Barber, E. (1980). Language acquisition and applied linguistics. *ADFL Bulletin, 12*, 26-32.

Bowden, J., & Marton, F. (1998) *The university of learning: Beyond quality and competence in higher education.* London: Kogan Page.

Chen, P. (1999). *Modern Chinese and sociolinguistics.* Cambridge: Cambridge University Press.

DeFrancis, J. (1989). *Visible speech: The diverse oneness of writing systems.* Honolulu: University of Hawaii Press.

Duff, P. A. (2010). Language socialization. In S. McKay & N. H. Hornberger (Eds.), *Sociolinguistics and language education.* Clevedon, UK: Multilingual Matters, 427-455.

Ferguson, C. A. (1959). Diglossia. *Word*, 15, 325-340.

Firth, A., & Wagner, J. (1997). On discourse, communication, and (some) fundamental concepts in SLA research. *The Modern Language Journal*, 81(3), 285-300.

Firth, A., & Wagner, J. (2007). Second/Foreign language learning as a social accomplishment: Elaborations on a reconceptualized SLA. *The Modern Language Journal*, 91(S1), 800-819.

Huang, R. (2003). *Theories and practice of teaching of Chinese characters* (in Chinese). Taipei: Lexis.

International Baccalaureate (2011). *Language B guide.* Cardiff: International Baccalaureate.

International Baccalaureate (2013). *IB learner profile.* Cardiff: International Baccalaureate. Retrieved on March 31, 2015 from the World Wide Web: http://www.ibo.org/globalassets/digital-tookit/flyers-and-artworks/learner-profile-en.pdf

Ki, W.W., Lam, H.C., Chung, A.L.S., Tse, S.K., Ko, P. Y., & Lau, C.C. *et al.* (2003). Structural awareness, variation theory & ICT support. *L1 Educational Studies in Language & Literature*, 3, 53-78.

Krashen, S. D. (1982). *Principles and practice of second language acquisition.* Oxford: Pergamon.

Kwan, C. Y. (2012). 中文作为第二语言：教学误区与对应教学策略 [Chinese as a second language: misconceptions in teaching and homologous teaching strategies]. *Newsletter of Chinese Language*, 91(2), 61-82.

Lam, J.W.Y., Cheung, W.M., & Hui, S. Y. (2014). 飞越困难，一起成功：教授非华语学生中文的良方 [Overcoming difficulties for mutual success: good practices for teaching Chinese to Non-Chinese speaking students]. Hong Kong: CACLER, Faculty of Education, The University of Hong Kong.

Leong, C. K., Tse, S.K., Loh, E.K.Y., & Ki, W.W. (2011). Orthographic knowledge important in comprehending elementary Chinese text by users of alphasyllabaries. *Reading Psychology* 32(3), 237-271.

Lee, M.T.N., Tse, S.K. & Loh, E.K.Y. (2011). The impact of the integrative perceptual approach on the teaching of Chinese characters in a HK kindergarten. *Early Child Development & Care*, 181(5), 665-679.

Lo, M. L. (2012). *Variation Theory and the improvement of teaching and learning.* Gothenburg: University of Gothenburg.

Loh, E.K.Y., Tse, S.K., & Tsui, S.K. (2013). A study of the effectiveness of a school-based Chinese character curriculum for non-Chinese speaking kindergarteners: Hong Kong experience (in Chinese). *Journal of Han Character & Han Writing Education*, 30, 277-323.

Loh, E.K.Y. (under review). Using drama in education to enhance Chinese language proficiency of non-Chinese speaking secondary school students. Manuscript submitted for publication.

Ma, Y., & Li, X. (2006). *Chinese Made Easy Textbook, Level 3 (Simplified Characters).* Hong Kong: Joint Publishing.

Marton, F. (1986). Phenomenography – a research approach to investigating different understandings of reality. *Journal of Thought*, 21(3), 28-49.

Marton, F., & Booth, S. (1997). *Learning and awareness.* Mahwah, NJ: Lawrence Erlbaum.

Miller, G. (1956). The magical number seven, plus or minus two: Some limits on our capacity for processing information. *The Psychological Review*, 63, 81-97.

Norman, J. (1988). *Chinese.* Cambridge: Cambridge University Press.

Norton, J.E. (2013). Performing identities in speaking tests: Co-construction revisited. *Language Assessment Quarterly* 10 (3): 309-330.

Shu, H., Anderson, R.C., & Wu, N. (2000). Phonetic awareness: Knowledge of orthography-phonology relationships in the character acquisition of Chinese children. *Journal of Educational Psychology*, 92, 56-62.

Tse, S.K. (2000). *Pleasurable learning of Chinese characters* (in Chinese). HK: EDB.

Tse, S.K. (2006) 综合高效识字法 [Integrative Perceptual Approach to learning Chinese characters]. In Chinese Character Culture and Education Research Center of The Chinese Society Of Education (Ed.) 识字教育科学化方法选粹[Selected papers on the science of Chinese character teaching and learning] (in Chinese). Beijing: China Light Industry Press.

Tse, S.K., Cheung, W. Y. C., Loh, E.K.Y., & Lui, W. L. (2008). *Chinese language education for students with special needs* (in Chinese). Hong Kong: Hong Kong University Press.

Tse, S.K., Li C.L.J., & Loh E.K.Y. (2012). Teaching Chinese reading in a differentiated approach: Case study in a secondary school. In S.K. Tse, W.W. Ki, & M.S.K. Shum (Eds.), *The Chinese language learning and teaching of non-Chinese speaking: Curriculum, teaching materials, teaching strategies and assessment* (in Chinese). Hong Kong: Hong Kong University Press, 47-55.

Tse, S.K., & Loh, E.K.Y. (2014). 怎样教非华语幼儿学习中文 [Effective teaching and learning of Chinese for non-Chinese speaking preschoolers]. Beijing: Beijing Normal University Publishing Group.

Tse, S.K., Marton, F., Ki, W.W., & Loh, E.K.Y. (2007). An integrative perceptual approach for teaching Chinese characters. *Instructional Science*, 35(5), 375-406.

Tse S.K., Marton, F., Ki, W. W., & Loh E.K.Y. (2010). Learning characters. In F.

Wentzel, K.R., & Watkins, D. E. (2002). Peer relationships and collaborative learning as contexts for academic enablers. *Social Psychology*, 31(3), 366-377.

Chapter 10

The effectiveness of 'Reading to Learn' pedagogy in teaching China poverty issues in the IBDP second language Chinese classroom

Mark Shiu-kee Shum, Kwok-ling Lau & Dan Shi

Abstract

This paper examines the effectiveness of 'Reading to Learn, Learning to Write, R2L' pedagogy (Rose & Martin, 2012) in the International Baccalaureate Diploma Programme (IBDP) Chinese second language classrooms in an international school in Hong Kong. The R2L pedagogy was applied to teach non-Chinese speaking students to read and write texts on China poverty issues in explanation genre in five lessons. During the teaching cycle, the teacher adopted the procedures from preparing for reading, detailed reading, joint re-writing, to joint construction in order to provide sufficient scaffolding for students before they wrote their individual compositions.

This paper chose student writings which represent low, medium and high achievers respectively. Their pre-test and post-test writings were analysed using Reading to Learn assessment criteria. Classroom discourse analysis (Christie, 2002) and Systemic Functional Linguistics (SFL) (Halliday, 1994) were used for student text analysis. In addition, semi-structured interviews were conducted to elicit student opinions about this pedagogy.

A preliminary observation of the pre-test and post-test writings suggested that, after the teaching, students could write the causes of, and possible solutions for, poverty issues in China following the explanation genre schematic structure illustrated in the reading texts of poverty in China. The interview data indicated that the pedagogy was generally well received by the students. It is hoped that the findings will help improve the teaching of Chinese as a second language in IB curriculum development and teacher training in language education.

Key words: Reading to Learn, non-Chinese speaking students, Chinese as a second language, text analysis, International Baccalaureate Diploma Programme.

Introduction

The International Baccalaureate (IB) advocates the development of international mindedness as the main concept in all IB programmes. To achieve the IB's mission and cultivate global citizenship, the goals of the Diploma Programme encourage students to ask challenging questions, to learn how to learn, to develop a strong sense of their own identity and culture, and to develop the ability to communicate with, and understand, people from other countries and cultures.

Students are required to take six subjects in the Diploma Programme. In language curriculum development, educators are cultivating students' acquisition of the knowledge, comprehension, application, analysis, synthesis and evaluation skills of Bloom's Taxonomy. Moreover, students are developing critical thinking, research skills, problem solving skills, and literature appreciation.

In order to help students learn more effectively in IBDP Chinese, the Reading to Learn, Learning to Write R2L pedagogy (Rose & Martin, 2012) was used to teach non-Chinese speaking students to read and write texts on poverty issues in China in explanation genre in five lessons in the IBDP Chinese second language classroom in a Hong Kong international school.

Reading to Learn (R2L) pedagogy

Genre-based literacy pedagogy is an interactive and scaffolding language teaching methodology which is crucial for, and widely emphasised by, Hallidayan educational linguistics, in what has become known as the Sydney School (Martin, 2000; Christie, 2002; Rose, 2011a, 2011b; Rose & Martin, 2012, Shum, 2010, 2013). The Sydney School stresses the social functions of language. In terms of language education, the aim of language teaching is to assist students with the ability to complete literacy tasks in school and in society. As the genres involved in these literacy tasks are of great importance, it is essential to teach the students to master them in order to acquire the ability required for academic success.

The R2L pedagogy is further developed as a genre-based methodology with its focus on the design of classroom interaction and the model of reading (Rose & Martin 2012: 133-134). The approach aims at scaffolding student literacy using high quality, age-appropriate and daily life functional texts. It redesigns classroom teaching patterns to integrate reading with writing to enable success for all learners (Acevedo, 2010). It emphasises the design of teaching activities that first adequately provide all students with the skills needed for the learning tasks, then works on the tasks, and finally elaborates on this as the preparation for the next more challenging tasks. The concept of this 'prepare – task – elaborate' cycle is actualised by nine sets of learning activities at three levels of scaffolding support (Rose & Martin 2012: 147, 308-309):

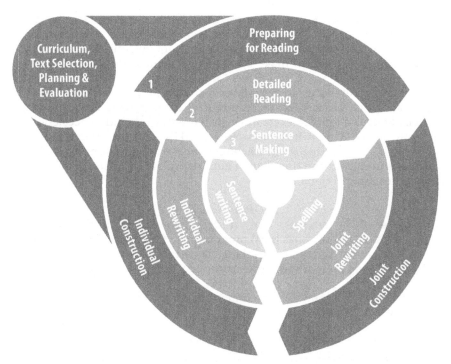

Figure 1: The three levels of strategies in Reading to Learn, Learning to Write pedagogy (Rose and Martin, 2012, p.147).

Level 1	Preparing for reading	Joint construction	Individual construction
Level 2	Detailed reading	Joint rewriting	Individual rewriting
Level 3	Sentence making	Spelling	Sentence writing

At Level 1, the teacher prepares students with a brief outline of key elements of a genre specific text with the text being read aloud. Then the teacher guides the whole class to construct a new but less detailed text together on the board, following the model of the text. After that students are asked to write their own text with reference to the model text and the text jointly constructed by the whole class (Rose & Martin 2012: 71-72, 169). The aim of Level 2 is to 'enable all students to read a text with thorough comprehension, and to apply its language patterns in their own writing' (Rose & Martin 2012: 147).

At this level the teacher guides students to read a short paragraph sentence-by-sentence, and asks them to identify and highlight the keywords with explanations from the teacher. After that the teacher guides the whole class to rewrite a paragraph using the same sophisticated language pattern, and then students are asked to write their own paragraph with reference to the model text and the paragraph rewritten by the whole class (Rose & Martin 2012). The foundation language skills such as spelling and writing are incorporated at Level 3.

Selected sentences from the text are used for this level of exercise. The teacher guides students to sequence the words for sentence making, and words are further cut into their letter patterns for spelling practice. After that students are asked to make up their own sentences (Rose & Martin 2012). All strategies in different levels are closely inter-related, as the task and elaboration of one strategy is the preparation for the next one.

This approach has proved to be powerful in narrowing down the gap between high and low achievers in English classrooms, and in accelerating the growth rate of the whole class (Rose, 2011b). Yet the effectiveness of adopting this R2L pedagogy in teaching Chinese to non-Chinese speaking students is unknown and this chapter aims to explore this issue in the IBDP Chinese teaching context.

IBDP curriculum

Hill (2014: 177) stresses that students should have international perspectives on global issues in IB programmes. The pedagogy emphasises critical and interdisciplinary thinking, constructivism, lifelong learning skills, developing human spirit and attitudes of compassion and respect for human kind.

Walker (2005: 1) summarises six important characteristics of international education as follows:

Communication: knowing how to access information.

Negotiation: the skills of persuading people to compromise or change their minds.

Political awareness: understanding why nations have particular priorities.

Cultural understanding: recognizing that different groups have different mindsets.

Global issues: studying issues and their impact across nations.

Criteria for truth: the way we judge what is right or wrong.

These components are emphasised in the IBDP Curriculum across different subjects.

Hill (2012: 254) accentuates the aim of UNESCO's declaration in 1974 that 'international education' is teaching about peace, democracy, and human rights. Education should promote international mindedness and intercultural understanding by means of developing students' critical thinking, language skills, and civilizations.

The aims of the IB Diploma Programme (IB 2013:2) are to develop international mindedness and intercultural understanding through acquiring knowledge, skills and attitudes. The study of other languages is one important way of achieving this. Chinese B is one of the World

Languages in the Diploma Programme. The IBDP Language B Guide (IB 2013: 9) indicates that the aims of group 2 are to cultivate students' ability in language skills, social interaction and intercultural understanding at both higher level (HL) and standard level (SL). Students choose one or the other level. The main focus of the course is on language development in terms of receptive reading and listening skills, and productive and interactive written and oral skills.

The differences between B Higher and B Standard levels are reflected in the objectives and the assessment criteria. Students are expected to write more in-depth in Language B at the Higher level. At both Higher and Standard levels, a successful second language student should not only learn and assimilate basic language structures but should also be able to apply the language in a range of situations and purposes.

According to the IBDP Language B Guide (IB 2013:13), the Language B syllabus includes three parts: The Core: Social Relationships, Communication and Media and Global issues' and five options: health, customs and traditions, leisure, cultural diversity, science and technology. At both Higher and Standard levels, students have to study two works of literature.

Aim of the study and research questions

The aim of this study is to examine the effectiveness of Reading to Learn, Learning to Write, R2L pedagogy in an IBDP Chinese second language learning situation. The research questions are listed in Table 1 as follows:

Research questions	Methodology
1. Does R2L pedagogy help to improve students' writing performance of explanation genre concerned with China poverty issues in an IBDP L2 Chinese classroom in Hong Kong?	Text analysis of students' pre- and post-tests: Schematic structure and process types.
2. What are students' perceptions of their learning experience with R2L pedagogy?	Semi-structured interview with students.

Table 1: Research questions and methodology.

Methodology

The R2L pedagogy is applied over five lessons to teach non-Chinese speaking students to read and write texts on Chinese poverty issues in explanation genre. The teacher collected the writings from students representing low, medium and high achievers respectively. Their pre-test and post-test writings were analysed using R2L writing assessment criteria. It is hypothesised that after R2L teaching, students could write about the causes and possible solutions concerning China's poverty issues with marked improvements of explanation genre in terms of schematic structure and skills of expression.

Arrangements of the R2L teaching and learning cycle

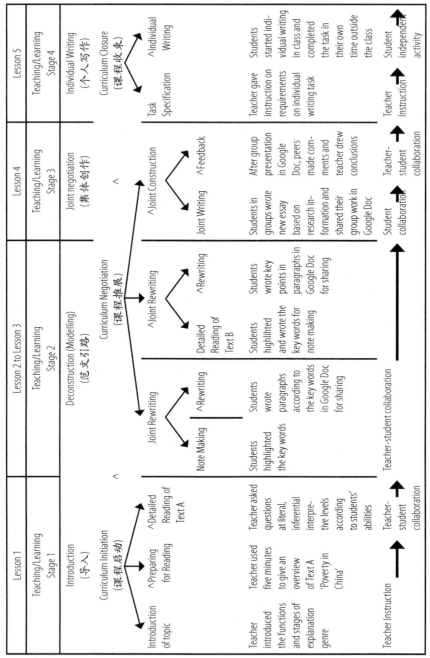

Notational conventions (after Eggins, 1994:40) '^' describes a fixed sequence of elements of schematic structure, i.e. X ^ Y = Stage X precedes Stage Y.

Figure 2 Curriculum Macrogenre of Teaching Explanation Genre in IBDP Chinese Class (after Christie, 2002:116; Shum, 2006: 13)

Object of learning: China poverty issues in explanation genre

This study focused on teaching explanation genre. Explanation texts are factual genres used across the curriculum. The social purpose of explanation genre is to provide logical, time-related information to explain phenomena or events happening in our world.

Students learn the explanation genre to explain the reasons or actions that address or contribute to a particular phenomenon or outcome. Stages of the explanation genre are Phenomenon / Explanation1 ^ Explanation 2 ^ Explanation 3 ^ Explanation... ^ Conclusion. To give an example of the explanation genre, the following is a text the teacher used in this R2L lesson.

Stages of explanation genre

Topic: The methods used by the Chinese government to control income discrepancy. (中国政府控制收入差距的方法).

Phenomenon: The problems of the income discrepancy (提出中国居民收入差距大的问题) – the government applied the following effective policies to promote productivity and consumption in remote areas in China. (政府采用以下有效的政策,可提升非沿海地区 (落后地区) 的生产力和消费力)。

Explanation 1: The Chinese government creates the fair income tax policy. (首先,政府逐步制定公平的税收政策。)

Explanation 2: The government accelerates economic development in poor areas. (其次,中央政府加速发展低收入地区。)

Explanation 3: The government improves social security. (再次,政府改善社会保障制度。)

Explanation 4: The government encourages consumption and production. (最后,政府鼓励国产中档消费品的生产和消费是另一个有效的方法。)

Conclusion: The government uses a variety of policies to improve the income discrepancy problem in China. (总结, 政府运用多种方法改善收入差距的问题。)

The teaching and learning cycle

In this study, a pre-test was conducted before the teaching and learning cycle, the purpose of which was to examine students' prior knowledge of explanation genre in terms of context, discourse, grammar and graphic features. In order to explore how the teacher conducted Chinese teaching in R2L pedagogy, the study adopted the model of Curriculum Macrogenre (Christie, 2002: 116; Shum, 2006: 13) to describe the teaching and learning cycle of China's poverty issues in explanation genre. The Curriculum Macrogenre of teaching explanation genre in an IBDP Chinese Class is shown in figure 2 above and further discussed below.

Curriculum initiation took place in Lesson 1; this is the introduction stage, the first of three stages. In the introduction of topic stage, the teacher introduced the social functions and schematic structure of explanation genre. In the preparing for reading stage, the teacher used five minutes to give an overview of Text A 'poverty in China'. In the detailed reading of text A stage, the teacher led the class to read text A 'The methods used by the Chinese government to control income discrepancy' (中国政府控制收入差距的方法) and asked questions at three levels of difficulty, namely literal, inferential and interpretive according to students' abilities. She ensured all students could answer the questions and praised the students to give them a sense of achievement.

Curriculum negotiation took place from lessons two to four, divided into the stages of de-construction in lessons two to three and joint negotiation in lesson four. In the de-construction stage, in lesson 2, the teacher first asked students to take notes by highlighting the key words of text A 'Poverty in China', and then to re-write the text in paragraphs according to the key words for sharing in Google Doc. In lesson three, the teacher provided students with text B 'Two Exemptions and One Subsidy Policy – the way the Chinese Government tackled poverty problems' and conducted detailed reading.

Teachers continued to use questioning skills to help students grasp the main ideas of the text and highlighted the key words and sentence structures. They wrote down key points in Google Doc for sharing. Rose & Martin (2012) indicate that the teacher should guide students to learn by scaffolding interactions during the teaching and learning cycle.

In the joint construction in lesson four, after the teacher set the writing target, students were separated into groups to collaborate on writing a new essay and shared their work in Google Doc with the whole class. They discussed issues concerning the methods used by the Chinese government to solve the income discrepancy between city and rural areas (中国政府如何解决城乡收入差距的方法?).

Students were not only using key words, phrases, and sentence structures in texts A and B which they came across in lessons one, two and three; they were also encouraged to conduct web-based research on new information such as education and medical policies, and to seek support from non government organisations such as UNICEF and OXFAM to explore possible solutions for income discrepancy between city and rural areas. Students were asked to share their group work in Google Doc. After group presentations in Google Doc, their peers were encouraged to make comments and the teacher drew conclusions on students' achievements. Students were asked to prepare for individual writing in the next lesson.

Curriculum closure took place in lesson five. At this individual writing stage, the teacher first gave instruction on the requirements for the individual writing task. Then the students started individual writing in class and completed the task in their own time outside the class.

Points to note during teaching and learning

At the beginning of the lesson, students struggled in reading and writing. R2L can help students to learn more effectively. The teacher has to prepare the lessons very well and provide sufficient scaffolding for the students by preparing for detailed reading of selected essays using the schematic structure of the explanation genre. The teacher modified the teaching strategies based on the students' prior knowledge and abilities. As the teacher reckoned that her Year 12 Chinese B Standard level students had adequate knowledge in completing the writing task, she chose not to conduct level 3 intensive strategies such as spelling, sentence making and sentence writing.

It is very important that all the students participate in learning. Rose & Martin (2012) stress that detailed planning of learning interaction ensures that all students are continually successful at all points of the lessons, so that the teacher's affirmation, evenly distributed to all students, is absolutely significant. It can promote students' motivation as successful learners and build confidence through answering the literal questions (meaning accessible within the sentence), inferential questions (meaning recoverable across the text) and interpretive questions (meaning it is beyond the text, in the reader's experience or knowledge of the topic) with scaffolding inquiry-based learning.

The classroom learning atmosphere was open and positive with mutual respect. Rose& Martin (2012:320) indicate that 'peer scaffolding' can empower students to take more initiative and learn more effectively. The teacher asked students to give comments on the group work which can help them appreciate different points of view and learn to work effectively together through group discussion.

In joint re-writing, the teacher encouraged students to express their opinions and make judgments in the discussion. The teacher was open-minded and she affirmed the students in the discussion in order to encourage and help them to broaden international mindedness. Students were encouraged to conduct research to develop their inquiry skills focused on multiple perspectives. For example, students could explore China's poverty problems and give suggested solutions from economic, societal, and educational perspectives.

Although students wrote only one paragraph during joint re-writing in the group discussions, it was very useful for them to develop their literacy, research and critical thinking skills in independent writing in Year 12. Students could write their essay individually based on their own interests in Year 13, for example, how do the Chinese improve medical problems in poverty areas? '中国如何改善贫穷农村的医疗问题？How do the Chinese solve the educational and medical problems in poverty areas? 中国如何解决贫困山区儿童的教育和医疗保健问题？'

Results and discussion

Assessing students' writing performance

In order to examine the effectiveness of using R2L pedagogy, writings from students representing low, medium and high achievers, with the assumed names of Leo, May, and Howard, respectively, were collected and analysed by using R2L assessment criteria (Scale from 0-3 with 14 items of evaluation) and Systemic Functional Grammar (Halliday, 1994). Due to the word limitation, the data shown below are the English translation of students' writings. The Chinese sample text of explanation writing by lower achievers can be found in the Appendix.

Schematic structure	Text
Phenomenon	**How the Chinese government controls income discrepancy** *The issue we will discuss today* is *the poverty issue in China. We will explore the poverty issue from the perspectives of the economy, society, and education. We propose below plausible solutions and suggestions.* **(Relational processes)**
Explanation 1	*China has many tax reforms to* reduce *poverty. The tax policy the government has gradually set is fair. In the past, the government* implemented *tax incentives to* attract *foreign capital, so that some citizens on the east coast became rich first.* **(Material Processes)**
Explanation 2	Developing *income sources for farmers* **(Material Processes)**
Elaboration	*China's income has a gap.* **As** *the government* focused *on developing the coastal areas, farmers in rural areas thus* suffered *the pain of poverty.* **(Material Processes)**

Table 2: Pre-test by Low Achiever (Leo).

Schematic structure	Text
Phenomenon	**How can China solve the Education and Health Care Problems of Children in the Poor Mountainous Areas?** *Dear UNICEF officer,* *How are you? I* am *a secondary school student. I have read your organization's introduction on the condition of the poor mountainous areas in China. I would like to explore the education issues of children living in the poor mountainous areas. Male and female are unequally treated. There is a significant decrease in the education of girls in the mountainous areas compared with boys. The United Nations points out that female participation in the workforce* (is) *67.4% and 79.7% for males,* showing *gender inequality. The major problem of poverty* is *in the poor mountainous areas, where many females do housework, take care of children, and are involved in agriculture.* **Thus**, *due to poverty, females in the poor mountainous areas lack basic education and health care.* **(Relational Processes)**
Explanation 1	*In education, the UN* advocates *gender equality, and* develops *education and a sustainable plan of births. To provide the necessary resources for vulnerable children, the Chinese government and the United Nations* build *more schools in the mountainous areas, so that boys and girls can* receive *equal education.* **(Material Processes)**

Explanation 2	To improve the health of children in the mountainous areas, by building health care centers and hospitals, employing learned inhabitants of the mountainous areas. **For example**, establishing a cooperative health care system in the rural areas and medical expense subsidies from 70 – 80% for patients with children living in the mountainous areas; this would produce an increase in health care and the number of people seeking medical attention. **In addition**, I have to guarantee that UNICEF and the Chinese government continue to fund the poor rural areas with a view to increasing education and work opportunities, and finally gender equality. **(Material Processes)**
Conclusion	**To conclude**, I hope the Chinese government and UNICEF will help to alleviate the problems faced by the children living in the poor mountainous areas. *And* that they will alleviate gender inequality, build more schools and increase health care. **(Mental processes and material processes)** *Yours faithfully,* *Da Wei*

Table 3: Post-test by Low Achiever (Leo).

Tables 2 and 3 show the writing performance of one of the low achievers in the pre- and post-tests explaining how to deal with the poverty issue in China. From the perspective of the construction of the schematic structure, the stage of Phenomenon was identified by the student in the pre-test pointing out the issue of poverty in China, which is followed by further consecutive explanations. However, the explanation was formed mainly with incomplete sentences and isolated meaning groups, without any phases existing in each stage. The incompletion of meanings due to a lack of lexico-grammatical resources makes the field, tenor, and mode weak to the readers, as indicated in Table 8 below by R2L assessment criteria.

In contrast, great progress was shown in the student's post-test. Not only have the stages in the schematic structure been systematically constructed with the identification of issue, the proposal of explanation, and conclusion, but also the phases have been well elaborated to support the thematic points proposed in the stage of Explanation from the two aspects of education and medical services.

As shown in Table 3, the function of each stage is reflected by different language forms and features. Relational processes were mostly used to identify the phenomenon to be explained in the text, while at the stage of explanation, material processes were frequently applied to denote the actions that were suggested to solve the poverty issue in China. In the concluding section, the mental process 'hope' was used to supplement the recommended actions with personal ideology in order to strengthen the modal stance of the author in suggesting solutions for poverty problems in China.

Schematic structure	Text
Phenomenon	**How could China solve the poverty problem?** *Poverty* is *a major problem in the 21st century in China. A survey by UNICEF found that poor citizens in general used not more than USD2 daily only.* ***Thus*** *in these few years, China has been exploring ways to solve the poverty problem. Poverty problem in China* includes *economy, education, and society.* **(Relational processes)**
Explanation 1	*Firstly, a few years ago, China* reduced *tax in the coastal cities to* encourage *their career and economic development. This policy* caused *a decrease in the income of farmers and the rural areas,* retarding *their economic development and* widening *their income gap.* ***If*** *China would like to* reduce *this gap, they should* reduce *tax in the rural areas or help them to* improve *productivity.* **(Material processes)**

Table 4: Pre-test by Medium Achiever (May).

Schematic structure	Text
Phenomenon	**How could China alleviate health care problems in poor rural areas?** *In the rural areas of China, poverty and health care* is *a very big problem.* ***Yet****, these two problems stand shoulder to shoulder. In poor rural areas, the villagers' way of living* is *very backward. They do not have appropriate medical protection,* **yet** *they do not have enough money to get doctor's help as well.* **As a result when** *they* are *ill not only* are *they unable to plant agriculture,* **but** *they could not find medical help as well.* **(Relational)**
Explanation 1	**Firstly,** *rural areas* are *relatively far-off from cities* **(Relational process)***. To them, many items needed in the daily lives are relatively difficult to* acquire. *Under such circumstances, farmers already have to* spend *a large sum of money to* pay *for electricity or other daily necessities.* **In the end,** *they would not* have *money to send their children to school.* **When** *their children have no education, no one in the rural areas would have any medical experience.* **(Material & Relational)**
Explanation 2	*Secondly, in cities, health care* is *also a business* **(Relational process)***.* **Thus** *doctors also have to* sell *medical products according to the shopping malls in cities. This will* cause *poor rural areas not to have enough money to* buy *medical support. Because of this, not only do poor rural areas not* have *enough money to* consult *doctors now,* **but** *they also* have *difficulties in* buying *medical equipment.* **(Material & Relational)**
Conclusion	**In conclusion, if** *poor rural areas continue to be without people's attention, their way of living would continue to* decrease. *There are many methods to* alleviate *poverty in the rural areas of China. One of the methods is to* provide *primary health care to the rural areas. It is with primary health care, that the rural areas could* improve *their lives. To* alleviate *poverty in the Chinese rural areas, we have to* give *people more attention first, and to* understand *their difficulties.* **And then** provide *them with the needed assistance.* **(Material processes)**

Table 5: Post-test by Medium Achiever (May).

Tables 4 and 5 show the learning outcome of the representative of the medium achiever by means of a comparison between the pre-test and the post-test before and after R2L teaching practices. Before intervention in the pre-test, it can be seen that the student was able to identify the phenomenon of income disparity as the major problem in China. However, unlike the low achiever completing the pre-test with incomplete sentences, the medium achiever worked on the pre-test with incomplete stages of explanation and no existence of conclusion. The incompleteness of staging and phases not only makes the field and the tenor of the text fragmentary but also weakens the purpose of the explanation writing as assessed in Table 8.

After the pedagogic intervention, the student's learning outcome was well reflected in the post-test. Having pointed out the issues of poverty and medical services as the main problems in the rural parts of China, this student provided two levels of explanations with key points listed as topic sentences to facilitate the identification of the phenomenon. However, the topic sentences are considered as being relatively off the topic of the text with respect to how to improve the poverty and medical services in the rural parts of China.

These two levels of explanation focused only on the 'what' element of the fact that rural parts are far from urban areas and medical service is a kind of commercial business in urban areas (also reflected in the language feature of the use of relational processes). Rather the explanation should have accentuated the 'how' element of offering suggestions concerned with the solution of the poverty problems and insufficient medical services to meet the requirements of the topic. The solution was not mentioned until the last stage of Conclusion, constructed with material processes for proposed actions as recommended solutions.

Schematic structure	Text
Phenomenon	**Methods of the Chinese government for solving poverty problems** *Income gap* is *a big problem with Chinese residents. In recent years, the large income gap among Chinese residents* is *a government concern.* **(Relational Processes)**
Explanation 1	**Firstly,** *since 1995, the tax revenue of our country has* increased *by 20% on average for 12 consecutive years; tax revenue has great impact on the income of the Chinese. The Chinese government* implements *tax policy, in order to* solve *the income gap problem. The current tax policy is fair,* attracting *foreign companies to China. The government has* reduced *taxation in the poverty-stricken parts of China. Farmers* belong *to the low-income group. In order to* increase *farmers' income, the government should* reduce *farmers' tax liability.* **For example,** *by* waiving *most of the taxes on special agricultural products and on animal husbandry, in order to* improve *farmers' living conditions.* **(Material Processes)**

Table 6: Pre-test by High Achiever (Howard).

Schematic structure	Text
Phenomenon	**How does the Chinese government solve the poverty issue?** *The issue we will discuss today is the poverty issue in China. For the Chinese government and the eyes of the world, China still has many poverty problems, and faces great challenges. China has a population of 1.3 billion, which is the largest population in the world. About 50 percent of the population lives in rural areas, these people have a lower education level, and lower income. Many of the rural areas in China are remote, undeveloped and lacking in resources, and people live in poverty. Yet, in a few years the national government has many solutions to these problems.* **(Relational processes)**
Explanation 1	**Firstly,** *the government tried to control the population of China. In recent years, China's economy develops continuously, the government strongly advocates birth planning, population in China is controlled,* **thus** *more people obtain the chance to receive education,* **and** *people could find a job more easily and improve their lives. In 2005, the poverty-stricken population of China has decreased from 835 hundred million to 207.7 hundred million.* **(Material processes)**
Explanation 2	**Secondly,** *the Chinese government has implemented tax policy until it cancels the income gap. Since 1995, the tax revenue of our country has increased 20% in average for 12 consecutive years; tax revenue has great impact on the income of the Chinese. The Chinese government implements tax policy, in order to solve the income gap problem. The current tax policy is fair. It attracts foreign companies to China. The government has reduced taxation in the poverty-stricken parts of China.* **(Material Processes)**
Further Elaboration	**Thus,** *to decrease the income gap between the coastal areas and the less economically developed areas, the government should remove as much as possible tax incentives in the coastal areas, and aid the economic development of the backward areas. Money is all the problem of the world, it will establish the key to greed and desire. A world without money would be a safer place. Farmers belong to the low-income group. In order to increase farmers' income, the government should reduce farmers' tax liability. For example, by waiving most of the taxes on special agricultural products and on animal husbandry, in order to improve farmers' living conditions.* **(Material and relational processes)**
Conclusion	**To conclude,** *the Chinese government has implemented many more benefits to improve the poverty situation in China and it is very successful. According to "The Economic Times" the poverty level in China has decreased 71% in 30 years.* **(Material and relational processes)**

Table 7: Post-test by High Achiever (Howard).

Tables 6 and 7 show the performance of one of the high achievers in both the pre-test and post-test before and after learning via R2L pedagogy. The writing performance in the pre-test is quite similar to that of the medium achiever in terms of the incomplete construction of the staging in explaining the problem of the income differences in China. Although the author only completed a small proportion of the text, what has been completed was better composed than the medium achiever with regard to the lexis and grammar used in the text for mode construction (see table 8).

Relational processes were deployed to identify the phenomenon, which is followed by the frequent use of material processes in the next session to construct the staging of explanation. After the intervention, the post-test not only featured all the good points shown in the pre-test, but also sparkled with the improvement of the weak points detected in the pre-test. Its completeness with clear-cut schematic structure and diversified lexico-grammatical choices makes the composition well explained and elaborately detailed.

At the first stage of phenomenon, the author pointed out both the issue to be explained and its background information, which help the readers gain a deeper understanding of the problem to be solved. Then solutions are provided in the second stage of explanation with a transitional sentence at the end of the first stage: 'However, the government has many solutions towards these problems during these several years'. Signaled by this transitional sentence, the exact actions and moves offered by the Chinese government were unveiled and listed in the topic sentences as a series of explanations in the second stage, with each of the stages being elaborated in phases by means of supporting examples and rationales.

The text concludes with the releasing of the positive results after having undertaken all these aforementioned actions introduced in the second stage. The function of each stage is featured by the distinctive language forms, with the use of relational processes to identify the 'what' element of the issue in the first stage as well as to distribute the attribute of being successful after carrying out all the actions in the last concluding stage. The material processes were mainly deployed to tease out the steps proposed by the Chinese government, matching the topic of 'how' to solve the poverty problem in China.

Items	Details	Low		Medium		High	
		Pre	Post	Pre	Post	Pre	Post
CONTEXT							
Purpose	How appropriate and well-developed is the genre for the writing purpose?	1	3	1	2	1	3
Staging	Does it go through appropriate stages, and how well is each stage developed?	1	3	1	2	1	3
Phases	Phases are the steps that a text goes through (within each stage). How well organised is the sequence of phases in the text?	0	3	1	1	1	2
Field	How well does the writer understand and explain the field in factual texts?	1	3	1	2	1	3
Tenor	How well does the writer objectively inform the reader in factual texts?	1	3	1	2	1	3
Mode	How highly written is the language for the school stage? Is it too spoken?	1	2	1	2	2	3
Context Total Marks		5/18	17/18	6/18	11/18	7/18	7/18

DISCOURSE							
Lexis	Lexis is the word choices that writers use to build the field of a text. How well is lexis used to construct the field?	1	2	1	2	1	2
Appraisal	Appraisal is the word choices that writers use to evaluate. They include feelings, judgements of people, and appreciations of things.	1	2	1	2	1	2
Conjunction	Conjunction is the logical relations between sentences, and within sentences. Is there a clear logical relation between all sentences?	1	2	1	2	1	2
Reference	Reference is the words that are used to keep track of people and things through a text. Is it clear who or what is referred to in each sentence?	1	1	1	2	1	2
Discourse Total Marks		4/12	7/12	4/12	8/12	4/12	8/12
GRAMMAR							
Grammar	Accuracy and variety of grammatical conventions of written Chinese	1	2	1	2	2	3
Grammar Total Marks		1/3	2/3	1/3	2/3	2/3	3/3
GRAPHICAL FEATURES							
Spelling	How accurately spelt are core words (frequent) and non-core words (less-frequent)?	2	2	2	2	2	2
Punctuation	How appropriately and accurately is punctuation used?	1	2	2	2	2	2
Presentation	Are paragraphs used? How legible is the writing? Is the layout clear?	1	2	1	3	1	3
Graphic Features Total Marks		4/9	6/9	5/9	7/9	5/9	7/9
Total Marks		14/42	32/42	16/42	28/42	18/42	35/42

Table 8: Assessing the performance of the low, medium and high achievers. (Rose & Martin, 2012)

Thus, derived from the text analysis via systemic functional grammar (Halliday, 1994), it has been found that students at the three different levels of achievement have made great progress after the teacher's pedagogic intervention. The three cases investigated show that R2L pedagogy has proved effective in helping NCS students' learning of contextual ideas, schematic structure and language features that are a necessity in explanation writing.

Evaluated via R2L assessment criteria, the analysis further illustrates that both the low and high achievers have made more improvement than students at the medium level. Their improvements would not have taken place without the teacher's strategic pedagogic support and scaffolding. The teacher designed the teaching and learning cycles according to the difficulties and obstacles faced by students in the pre-test.

Students' learning experience with R2L pedagogy

In addition to the assessment of students' writing performance, students' learning experience with R2L pedagogy was derived from semi-structured interviews with students after teaching intervention. From students' perspectives, R2L pedagogy helps them realise effective writing and enables them to transfer the writing skills grasped from one context to another.

Realising effective writing

Hanna: Definitely. We know more deeply what's going on, not just only some basic points, I think we can write better. I mean writing essay or the end test.

Jitin: I think it's good to read first and write, so if you understand the topic, then you can write about it. I think, we can understand the words and then write. And it is useful.

Tristan: Just like writing about cause and effect. It just makes explaining your ideas easier. And you can use the way of writing [the stage of writing]. It's just really structured and easy to understand.

From the semi-structured interviews with students representative of the low, medium, and high levels of achievement, it was found R2L pedagogy was useful and effective in helping them with genre writing, especially the genre of explanation as introduced in the current study. As suggested by the students, the integration of reading and writing has become the key to success. R2L pedagogy featuring an interlocking teaching style accentuates the incarnation of teaching cycles involved with reading and writing as well as spoken and written language, signifying the end of the previous teaching step is the start of the next step.

Reading prior to writing has equipped students with the contextual knowledge and language repertoire needed for writing. In the course of preparing for reading, students were fully prepared before the teacher posed questions and started teaching activities. Meanwhile, questions were asked according to students' ability in order to show their unique talent. During detailed reading, students were kept informed of the background information about the issue, the schematic structure of the target text, and the lexicogrammatical resources involved for meaning construction.

With all these genre-based contextual and linguistic preparations from the teachers' explicit guidance through interaction, students were endowed with the idea to write about, the appropriate language to express the idea, and the structure to outline the idea. Before working on their own in independent writing, more scaffolding was offered to facilitate students in joint construction. In this way, the students tend to become confident in genre writing, having both ideas for sharing and language for expressing those ideas.

Cultivating transferable writing skills

Conor: Yes, it should help a lot, the keywords are really helpful to transfer the idea from different issues about the world and maybe just adding a bit more keywords about different situations; but overall it's helpful.

Jitin: Yes, whatever we learnt from the group essay, we tried to take ideas and from the article we try to take ideas and paraphrase again and make an essay about poverty.

Tristan: I followed the same structure, selected the three subjects, for example energy, the waste of it, listed the problems and just came up with the solutions.

R2L pedagogy not only helps to realise effective writing, but also enables the acquired writing skills to be transferred to another context, as perceived by the students in the semi-structured interviews. Once they have acquired a good command of the ideas, the structure, and the key expressions of one particular phenomenon in one context, students are capable of transferring what they have learnt to another issue to be explained in another context.

The keywords linked to the issue and the schematic structure of the genre writing learnt from one text can be applied to the composition of another. Students are then able to write the variants of explanation genre: starting with the phenomenon, followed by key points of reasons behind the phenomenon, and ending with suggested solutions. Consequently, in the current study, through teacher's scaffolding, students are able to produce causes and recommend solutions with regard to the poverty issue in China.

Along with the explanation and understanding of the global issues of environment, energy, or poverty, *etc*, international mindedness is developed by applying acquired experiential knowledge and language skills to everyday contexts. Through responding to global/social issues, students are guided to show empathy and concerns towards global phenomena and the happenings around the world. Accordingly, students' higher-order thinking ability, critical thinking, research skills, and problem solving skills have, to a large extent, been cultivated.

Conclusion

The teaching practices have made the most of the R2L pedagogy, providing sufficient scaffolding and explicit guidance for non-Chinese speaking students prior to their independent writing. The model of knowledge about language and pedagogy supports all students to do high-level tasks by means of guidance through interaction (Rose & Martin, 2012). Distinct from the traditional way of teaching, students are fully scaffolded and prepared by the teacher's step-by-step detailed progression before being challenged by the questions to be posed and the classroom activities to be conducted.

Questions with different levels of difficulty are asked according to students' varying abilities. Affirmation and encouragement are strongly advocated to stimulate student motivation. During the pedagogical processes, text field and students' own life experiences tend to be well combined and developed with an emphasis on the integration of reading and writing. The objective is to render the skills learnt transferable into the context of their daily lives, which, in turn, develops students' international mindedness and global citizenship.

According to the text analysis and assessment of students' pre- and post-tests, the R2L pedagogy has proved effective in helping students grasp the content knowledge of the issue, the schematic structure of explanation genre, and the lexico-grammatical resources necessary for producing explanation writing with possible causes and solutions for the poverty issue in China.

We also found that, among all the participants at the three different levels of achievement, the students at the high and low levels made greater progress than the medium achievers. The R2L pedagogy includes every student equally in learning and successfully reinforces students' confidence by enhancing their literacy skills and developing international mindedness and global citizenship.

Student perceptions widely reflected that R2L pedagogy can not only help realise effective genre writing but also facilitates transferring the acquired writing skills to everyday contexts of genre writing and transdisciplinary teaching and learning across the curriculum. Hopefully, the study can facilitate the development of teaching Chinese as a second language in IB programmes and provide pedagogical references for teacher training in Chinese language education.

References

Acevedo, C. (2010). *Will the implementation of Reading to Learn in Stockholm schools accelerate literacy learning for disadvantaged students and close the achievement gap?* A Report on School-based Action Research, Multilingual Research Institute. Stockholm: Education Administration.

Cambridge J. and Thompson J. (2004). Internationalism and globalization as contexts for international education. *Compare* 34 (2) 161-175.

Christie, F. (2002). *Classroom Discourse Analysis: A Functional Perspective.* London: Continuum.

Halliday, M. A. K. (1994). *An Introduction to Functional Grammar.* London: Arnold.

Hill, I. (2012). Evolution of education for International Mindedness. *Journal of Research in International Education.* 11 (3) 245-261.

Hill, I. (2014). Internationally minded schools as cultural artefacts: Implications for school leadership. *Journal of Research in International Education,* 13 (3) 175-189.

IB (2013). IBDP Language B Guide: First Examination 2015, Cardiff, Wales: UK.

Martin, J.R. (2000). Grammar meets genre – reflections on the 'Sydney School'. Arts: *The Journal of the Sydney University Arts Association,* 22, 47–95.

Rose, D. (2011a). Genre in the Sydney School. In J Gee & M Handford (eds) *The Routledge Handbook of Discourse Analysis.* London: Routledge, 209-225.

Rose, D. (2011b). *Reading to Learn: Accelerating learning and closing the gap.* Teacher training books and DVD. Sydney: Reading to Learn www.readingtolearn.com.au retrieved on 23 April 2015.

Rose, D. & Martin, J. R. (2012). *Leaning to Write, Reading to Learn: Genre, Knowledge and Pedagogy in the* Sydney School. Sheffield: Equinox.

Shum, M. S. K. (2006). Teaching Chinese report writing: Melbourne and Hong Kong-Implications for Global Curriculum Sharing. In M. S. K. Shum, *et al.* (eds.), *Teaching writing in Chinese speaking areas.* New York: Springer. (p7-27)

Shum, M. S. K. (2010). *The Functions of Language and the Teaching of Chinese: Application of Systemic Functional Linguistics to Chinese Language Teaching.* Hong Kong: Hong Kong University Press.

Shum, M. S. K. (2013).The Effect of R2L Strategies in enhancing Chinese reading and writing skills of South Asian Ethnic Minority Students. *Toward Cross Cultural Learners of Chinese Teaching and Learning: Challenge and Breakthrough.* 30 Nov-1 Dec 2012, University of Hong Kong.

Walker, G. (2005). What have I learned about international education? *Biennial Conference of IB Nordic Schools.* Stockholm: 9 September 2005. (p.1- 8)

Appendix: sample texts of explanation genre writing of the lower achiever (Leo)

Pre-test Writing	Post-test Writing
中国政府解决城乡收入差距的方法 　　今天我们要讨论的问题是中国的贫穷问题。 我们会从经济、社会，教育，探讨贫穷问题，我们提出以下可行的解决方法和建议。 　　中国有很多税制改革 的减少贫穷. 这无暇，税收政策政府逐步制定的公平. 以前，政府实施税收优惠政策为例吸引外资，让东部沿海地区. 一部分的人民先富裕起来. 　　为农民开拓收入来源 　　中国有差距的收入. 在农村地区的农夫因为政府集中发展沿海地区，所以他们受贫穷的苦.	中国如何解决贫困山区儿童的教育和医疗保健问题? 尊敬的联合国儿童基金会主任： 　　您好，我是一个中学生。看过 贵会介绍中国贫困山区的情况，我要探讨贫困山区儿童的教育问题; 男女不平等，山区的女童比男童接受教育显著降低，联合国的指出妇女参与在劳动力在67.4%和79.7%，显示性别不平等。贫穷的主要问题在贫困山区, 很多女性工作在家作品家务，照顾儿女和农业，因此女性在贫困山区因为贫穷，缺乏接受基础教育、 医疗保健。 在教育上，联合国提倡性别平等，发展教育和可持续生计。要帮助中国儿童帮助弱势的儿童提供必要的资源; 中国政府和联合国在山区建设更多学校，让男童和女童可以接受平等教育。 　　在医疗上，改善贫困山区儿童的健康, 过建设保健中心和医院, 采用博学山区居民. 例如, 在农村合作医疗制度，医疗费用补贴由70-80%为病人在山区儿童，增加让更多人接受卫生保健，求关注。而且, 我要保证联合国儿童基金会和中国政府继续基金农村贫困地区继续增加教育和工作机会, 最终性别平等。 　　总的来说，我希望你，希望中国政府和联合国儿童基金会，帮助减少贫困山区儿童的问题在。并减少性别不平等，增建学校和增加医疗卫生保健。 　　敬祝 安好 　　　　　　　　　　　　　大为 　　　　　　　二零一四年十一月十五日

CPSIA information can be obtained at www.ICGtesting.com
Printed in the USA
BVOW11s2055180116

433357BV00005B/55/P